Globalisation, Comparative Education and Policy Research

Volume 48

The *Globalisation, Comparative Education and Policy Research* book series aims to meet the research needs of all those interested in in-depth developments in comparative education research. The series provides a global overview of developments and changes in policy and comparative education research during the last decade. Presenting up-to-date scholarly research on global trends, it is an easily accessible, practical yet scholarly source of information for researchers, policy makers and practitioners. It seeks to address the nexus between comparative education, policy, and forces of globalisation, and provides perspectives from all the major disciplines and all the world regions. The series offers possible strategies for the effective and pragmatic policy planning and implementation at local, regional and national levels.

The book series complements the *International Handbook of Globalisation and Education Policy Research.* The volumes focus on comparative education themes and case studies in much greater scope and depth than is possible in the Handbook.

The series includes volumes on both empirical and qualitative studies of policy initiatives and developments in comparative education research in elementary, secondary and post-compulsory sectors. Case studies may include changes and education reforms around the world, curriculum reforms, trends in evaluation and assessment, decentralisation and privatisation in education, technical and vocational education, early childhood education, excellence and quality in education. Above all, the series offers the latest findings on critical issues in comparative education and policy directions, such as:

- developing new internal strategies (more comprehensive, flexible and innovative modes of learning) that take into account the changing and expanding learner needs;
- overcoming 'unacceptable' socio-economic educational disparities and inequalities;
- improving educational quality;
- harmonizing education and culture;
- international co-operation in education and policy directions in each country.

Joseph Zajda

Engagement, Motivation, and Students' Achievement

Springer

Joseph Zajda
Faculty of Education and the Arts
Australian Catholic University
East Melbourne, VIC, Australia

ISSN 2543-0564 ISSN 2543-0572 (electronic)
Globalisation, Comparative Education and Policy Research
ISBN 978-3-031-61612-9 ISBN 978-3-031-61613-6 (eBook)
https://doi.org/10.1007/978-3-031-61613-6

This Springer imprint is published by the registered company Springer Nature Switzerland AG
The registered company address is: Gewerbestrasse 11, 6330 Cham, Switzerland

*To Rea, Nikolai, Belinda, Sophie, Imogen,
Paulina, Jan, Dorothy, and Jim*

Foreword

Engagement, Motivation, and Students' Achievement is book 48 in the 48-volume book series *Globalisation, Comparative Education and Policy Research*. The book analyses major discourses of the use of engagement and motivation in schools globally. The current culture of performing schools, affected by forces of globalisation and the ubiquitous global academic achievement, as defined by PISA indicators (OECD), must embrace academic performance standards. The book focuses on the overall impact of engagement on teachers, students' motivation, students' well-being, and standards. It examines the role of engagement and motivation impacting on teachers and students in the classroom and the overall impact of models of inclusive classroom to improve their performance in the classroom. The book analyses such topics as cultural identities and engagement, students' personalities and their impact on learning, the role of intelligence in learning, social learning, engagement in collaborative groups, and teachers' role in promoting engagement in the classroom.

The book contributes in a very scholarly way, to a more holistic understanding of the nexus between globalisation, engagement, motivation, and students' achievement. The chapters offer a timely analysis of current education and policy reforms affecting schools. The book provides innovative ideas concerning the future directions of the use of engagement, motivation, and students' achievement both locally and globally.

Joseph Zajda, Ph.D., FACE
Faculty of Education and Arts
Australian Catholic University
East Melbourne, VIC, Australia

Preface

Engagement, Motivation, and Students' Achievement is book 48 in the 48-volume book series *Globalisation, Comparative Education and Policy Research*. The book analyses discourses of the use of engagement and motivation theories in schools globally to improve academic achievement. It focuses on the overall impact of engagement and motivation theories on teachers, students' engagement, well-being, academic excellence, standards, equity, and global competitiveness. It examines the role of engagement and motivation theories impacting on teachers and students in the classroom and the overall impact of cognitive, social cognitive, affective, and psycho-motor domains, used to engage and motivate students to improve their performance in the classroom. The book contributes towards a better understanding of the nexus between globalisation, dominant models of engagement, motivation, students' engaging learning environments, and their academic achievement.

Joseph Zajda, Ph.D., FACE
Faculty of Education and Arts
Australian Catholic University
East Melbourne, VIC, Australia

Editorial by the Series Editor

Engagement, Motivation, and Students' Achievement is book 48 in the 48-volume book series *Globalisation, Comparative Education and Policy Research.*

At the level of critical discourse analysis, we need to consider dominant ideologies and practices defining power, domination, and their overall impact on the nature of engagement and motivation in schools, both locally and globally. As such, the book offers a synthesis of current research findings on globalisation and motivation in schools. It is suggested that there is an urgent need to continue to analyse critically the new challenges confronting the nexus between engagement, motivation, and schooling.

The book analyses major discourses of the use of engagement and motivation in schools globally. In the current culture of performing schools, affected by forces of globalisation, and the ubiquitous global academic achievement, as defined by PISA indicators (OECD), schools must embrace academic performance standards. The book focuses on the overall impact of engagement on teachers, students' motivation, students' well-being, and standards. It examines the role and levels of engagement and motivation in the classroom.

The book analyses such topics as cultural identities and engagement, students' personalities and their impact on learning, the role of intelligence in learning, social learning, engagement in collaborative groups, and teachers' role in promoting engagement in the classroom. This book critiques dominant discourses and debates pertaining to globalisation and motivation in schools. Drawing on diverse paradigms, ranging from critical theory to globalisation, the book, by focusing on globalisation and motivation in schools, critically examines recent research dealing with this topic.

The book contributes in a very scholarly way, to a more holistic understanding of the nexus between globalisation, engagement, motivation, and students' achievement. The chapters offer a timely analysis of current education and policy reforms affecting the nature of engagement and motivation in schools. The book provides innovative ideas concerning the future directions of the use of engagement, motivation, and students' achievement, both locally and globally.

We thank the anonymous international reviewers who have reviewed and assessed the proposal for the continuation of the series (volumes 37–48) and other anonymous reviewers, who reviewed the chapters in the final manuscript.

I want to express my deep gratitude to Suzanne Majhanovich (Western University, Ontario), Pamela Hallam (Brigham Young University), Yvonne Vissing (Salem State University), John Whitehouse (The University of Melbourne), Sev Ozdowski (University of Western Sydney), and Vince Wright (Education consultant, Taupo, New Zealand) for their insightful and constructive comments. I am also grateful to the anonymous international reviewers who reviewed the chapters in the final manuscript.

Contents

About the Series Editor

Joseph Zajda, BA (Hons), MA, M.Ed., Ph.D., FACE co-ordinates and teaches in graduate courses: M.Teach. courses: (EDES591, EDHI299&599, and EDSS600) in the Faculty of Education and Arts at the Australian Catholic University (Melbourne Campus). He specialises in globalisation and education policy reforms, social justice, history education, human rights education, and values education. He has written and edited 52 books and over 150 book chapters and articles in the areas of globalisation and education policy, higher education, history textbooks, and curriculum reforms. Recent publications include Zajda, J. (2023), *Globalisation and Inclusive Schooling: Engaging Motivational Environments*, Springer; Zajda, J. (2023), *Discourses of Globalisation, Cultural Diversity and Values Education*, Springer; Zajda, J. (2022), *Discourses of Globalisation, and the Politics of History School Textbook*, Springer; Zajda, J. (2022), *Globalisation and Education Reforms: Overcoming Discrimination*, Springer; Zajda, J. (2021), *Globalisation and Education Reforms: Creating Effective Learning Environments*, Springer; Zajda, J. & Majhanovich, S. (2022), *Race, Ethnicity and Gender in Education: Emerging Paradigms*, Springer; Zajda, J. & Vissing, Y. (2022), *Discourses of Globalisation, Ideology, and Human Rights*, Springer; Zajda, J. (Ed). (2021), *3rd International Handbook of Globalisation, Education and Policy Research*, Springer; Zajda, J. (2021), *Globalisation and Education Reforms: Creating Effective Learning*, Dordrecht: Springer; Zajda, J. & Majhanovich, S. (Eds.) (2021), *Globalisation, Cultural Identity and Nation-Building: The Changing paradigms*, Springer; Zajda, J. (Ed). (2020), *Globalisation, Ideology and Education Reforms: Emerging paradigms*, Springer; Zajda, J. (Ed). (2020), Human Rights Education Globally, Dordrecht: Springer; Zajda, J (Ed.). (2020), *Globalisation, Ideology and Neo-Liberal Higher Education Reform*, Dordrecht: Springer; Zajda, J. & Rust, V. (2020), *Globalisation and Comparative Education*, Dordrecht: Springer; Zajda, J. & Majhanovich, S. (Eds.) (2020), *Globalisation, Cultural Identity and Nation-Building: The changing Paradigms*, Dordrecht: Springer; Zajda, J. (2019) (Ed.), *Globalisation, Ideology and Politics of Education Reforms*, Dordrecht: Springer; Zajda, J. (2018), *Globalisation and Education Reforms: Paradigms and Ideologies*, Dordrecht: Springer; Zajda, J.

(2017), *Globalisation and National Identity in History Textbooks: The Russian Federation*, Dordrecht: Springer; Zajda, Tsyrlina-Spady & Lovorn (2017) (Eds.), *Globalisation and Historiography of National Leaders: Symbolic Representations in School Textbooks*, Dordrecht: Springer; Zajda & Ozdowski (2017). (Eds.), *Globalisation and Human Rights Education*, Dordrecht: Springer; Zajda & Rust (Eds.) (2016), *Globalisation and Higher Education Reforms*, Dordrecht: Springer; editor and author of the *Second International Handbook on Globalisation Education and Policy Research*, Springer, 2015; Zajda, J. (2014), The Russian Revolution. In G. Ritzer & J. M. Ryan (Eds.), *The Wiley-Blackwell Encyclopedia of Globalization Online*, Zajda, J. (2014); Zajda, J. (2014), Ideology. In D. Phillips (Ed.), *Encyclopedia of Educational Theory and Philosophy*, Thousand Oaks: Sage; Zajda, J. (2014), Values Education. In D. Phillips (Ed.), *Encyclopedia of Educational Theory and Philosophy*, Thousand Oaks: Sage; Zajda, J. (2014), Values Education. In D. Phillips (Ed.), *Encyclopedia of Educational Theory and Philosophy*, Thousand Oaks: Sage; and Zajda, J (2008), *Schooling the New Russians*, Melbourne: James Nicholas Publishers.

He is the editor of the **forty-eight-book** series Globalisation and Comparative Education (Springer, 2013&2025). He edits the following journals below:

http://www.jamesnicholaspublishers.com.au/journals/ct/; Editor, *Curriculum and Teaching*, volume 39, 2024.
http://www.jamesnicholaspublishers.com.au/journals/es/; Editor, *Education and Society*, volume 42, 2024.
http://www.jamesnicholaspublishers.com.au/journals/wse/; Editor, *World Studies in Education*, volume 24, 2024.

His works are found in 605 publications in 4 languages and some 12,103 university library holdings globally.

He is the recipient of the 2012 Excellence in Research Award, the Faculty of Education, the Australian Catholic University. The award recognises the high quality of research activities and particularly celebrates sustained research that has had a substantive impact nationally and internationally. He was also a recipient of the Australian Awards for University Teaching in 2011 (Citation for Outstanding Contributions to Student Learning, for an innovative, influential, and sustained contribution to teacher education through scholarship and publication). He received the Vice Chancellor's Excellence in Teaching Award at the Australian Catholic University (Melbourne Campus). He was awarded an ARC Discovery Grant (with Monash University) for 2011–2015 for a comparative analysis of history national curriculum implementation in Russia and Australia ($315,000). He was elected as the fellow of the Australian College of Educators (June 2013).

He completed (with Prof. Fred Dervin, University of Helsinki) the UNESCO report: *Governance in education: Diversity and effectiveness, BRICS countries*, Paris: UNESCO (2024).

Chapter 1
Engagement, Motivation, and Students' Achievement

1.1 The Role of Engagement and Motivation in Schools

This above all: To thine own self, be true.
Shakespeare

In my new book, *Engagement, motivation, and students' achievement* (2024), which adds to my previous books Globalisation*, and dominant models of motivational theories in education* (2023a), and *Globalisation and inclusive schooling: Engaging motivational environments* (2023b), I wish to focus more on major factors contributing to students' engagement in educational settings, models of inclusive schooling that promote quality engagement, cultural identities and their impact on engagement in the classroom, the role of intelligence and its influence on students' academic achievement, and the significance of social learning in students' engagement.

I would like to suggest that we are both environmentally and genetically programmed to act on the world, to do things and flourish. It is similar to the idea advanced by Noam Chomsky, a linguist, who believed that one's ability to learn language is dictated by genetically encoded universal grammar, and that 'universal grammar is wired into children's brains' (Chomsky, 1957). Similarly, motivation is wired into our brains, and compels us to do things, that results in rewarding outcomes.

There is a consensus among researchers that motivation is the most significant construct defining the nature of human beings, their continuing survival, and subsequent necessary for planned behaviour and actions, to achieve designated goals. Motivation comes from the Latin word *movere*, meaning 'to move'. In plain language, motivation is what gets you going, keeps you going, and determines where you're trying to go. Motivation is also influenced by one's will to learn (Stuart, 2023).

There is no doubt that motivation affects all of us, in different ways, and at different times. Individuals, due to their genetic and environmental factors, are programmed to act, and to achieve their needs, wants, and desires. The continuing survival of

J. Zajda, *Engagement, Motivation, and Students' Achievement*, Globalisation, Comparative Education and Policy Research 48,
https://doi.org/10.1007/978-3-031-61613-6_1

humanity over the last hundred thousand years was the result of this inner drive, designed to act and satisfy basic survival needs. This idea of satisfying basic needs was later developed and popularised by Maslow's (1962) influential book *Toward a psychology of being*. To be motivated, or to do something, requires an effort and choice. The aphorism 'To be or not to be', is the opening sentence of a monologue by Prince Hamlet in the 'nunnery scene', in *Hamlet*, Act 3, William Shakespeare's play. Shakespeare's play offers a choice for individuals: to do or not to do. Similarly, in the Terminator's movie, in one the most famous catchphrases, we are given the choice: 'Come with me if you want to live' (*The Terminator*, movie 1984). The line was first delivered in the 1984 movie *The Terminator*, when Kyle Reese, played by Michael Biehn, destroys cyborg from the future, the T-800, performed by Schwarzenegger, and saves Sarah Connor, played by Linda Hamilton (see Zajda, 2023a).

Motivation in the classroom can be defined as an internal process in the mind that energises, directs, and maintains students' behaviour, to successfully perform designated activity, and tasks. Motivation has been described as 'an internal process that initiates and sustains behaviour' (Schunk et al., 2014). Robert Slavin (2022) has defined motivation as 'an internal process that activates, guides and maintains behaviour over time'. Similarly, Woolfolk & Margetts (2022) defined motivation as 'an internal state that arouses, directs, and maintains behaviour' (Woolfolk & Margetts, 2022). Motivation results in the selection, persistence, intensity, and continuation of behavior.

When students choose specific learning activities, and performance goals, and put in a certain amount of effort and time to achieve these goals, they are, by definition, motivated. As noted in the OECD (2023) in 'Student engagement and motivation', policy document, 'It takes engagement and motivation to learn', and that 'students' engagement with school', play a key role in their learning, and ability to master content knowledge in key learning areas:

> ...students' engagement with school and their willingness to do what it takes to reach their goals not only play a central role in shaping students' ability to master academic subjects, they are also valuable attributes that will enable students to lead full lives, meeting challenges and making the most of available opportunities along the way. In other words, much more is required of students – and adults – than just cognitive proficiency. Students need to be engaged, motivated, willing to learn new things and feel they can succeed; without those dispositions, they will be unable to translate their raw potential into high-level skills, no matter how intelligent and gifted they are.... (OECD, 2023)

The concept of motivation, as I argued in my book, *Globalisation, and dominant models of motivational theories in education* (2023a) is significant in 'every sphere of life, and organizational culture, affecting individuals, in performing their specified tasks'(p. 2). As motivation is one of the most studied psychological constructs in educational psychology (Koenka, 2020), we tend to use it constantly in our everyday language. Sport coaches use it all the time, to get the best performance for their teams and participating individuals. There is a global consensus that motivation plays a 'key role in the teaching and learning environment. Both teachers and students use relevant motivation theories and strategies to improve the nature of learning and academic achievement' (Zajda, 2023a, p. 2). Students, who are motivated, are 'much more likely to achieve their potential and find success' (Hawthorne, 2021). Similarly, Andrea Cox (2022) believes that motivation plays a 'key role in education' (Cox, 2022). More importantly, motivation also results in 'more positive behaviour' and promotes students' 'greater sense of well-being' (Hawthorne, 2021). In short, motivation in the classroom results in students' greater engagement, positive behaviour, well-being, and improved academic achievement, which are discussed in this book later. Therefore, teachers need to be conscious of providing effective pedagogical strategies that can be used to meet the motivational needs and desires of each one of their students.

1.1.1 The Role of Self-concept in Students' Learning

There exists a positive relationship between student's self-concept, engagement, and motivation. Students' need to feel good about themselves and believe in their abilities to perform classroom activities. The student's self-concept is one of the most important factors affecting engagement and motivation. The self-concept is informed by one's perception, or an idea, or an image one has, because of how one's sees or understand something. The Latin *cogito, ergo sum,* usually translated into English as 'I think, therefore I am', is the first principle of René Descartes's philosophy, reflecting perception, thinking, and acquiring knowledge. The French mathematician and philosopher René Descartes in his book *Discourse on Method* (1637) considered it to be the first step in demonstrating the attainability of certain knowledge.

One's self-concept can be defined as the mental image we have of ourselves. It is influenced by many factors, including our identity, environment, and interaction with various individuals, regarded as significant others, consisting of our parents, the family, teachers, and peers. The self-concept is also related to self-esteem and self-efficacy. Self-esteem can be defined as how we value and perceive ourselves. I suggested in my book, that self-efficacy, as a construct, was developed by Bandura to 'explain the role it played in his theory of social learning' (Zajda, 2023a, p. 44). Self-efficacy can be defined as individuals' belief in their ability to perform a behaviour, to achieve specific performance attainments (Bandura, 1997). Self-efficacy demonstrates one's confidence in the ability to exert control over one's own motivation, behaviour, and social environment.

Bandura (1997) proposed four sources of self-efficacy:

- mastery experiences,
- vicarious experiences,
- verbal persuasion, and
- physiological and affective states

These are used by individuals, to 'judge their capableness, strength, and vulnerability to dysfunction' (Bandura, 1997, p. 78). According to Artino (2012), of the four sources of self-efficacy, *enactive mastery experiences* proved to be the 'most influential source of efficacy information because they provide the most direct, authentic evidence that an individual can gather the personal resources necessary to succeed' (Artino, 2012).

In short, self-efficacy, as an individual's belief in being able to complete designated activities successfully, is determined by 'cognitive, social, emotional, and behavioural factors. (Zajda, 2023a, p. 44).

Earlier, Mann (2004) had already analysed the nexus between self-efficacy, self-esteem, and mental health outcomes. He discovered that self-efficacy was positively correlated with self-esteem, and concurred with Bandura (1997), who affirmed that 'the levels of self-esteem and self-confidence can influence self-efficacy' (Bandura, p. 365), and showed a direct link between self-esteem, happiness, and mental wellbeing.

1.2 Extrinsic and Intrinsic Motivation

Educational psychology distinguishes between two types of motivation: extrinsic and intrinsic motivation. Extrinsic motivation occurs when the learner does something to earn external reward. For instance, the student engages in an activity (does homework), to earn a reward and receive praise.

Extrinsic motivation is widespread, but there are at least three limitations:

- Behaviour may be temporary and as soon as the reward is given, the student may revert to old behaviour.
- Students may develop a materialistic attitude toward learning (e.g. if I complete this assignment what will I get?)
- Giving extrinsic rewards may lessen intrinsic motivation they may have for a certain activity.

Initially, tangible rewards can be effective to motivate students to perform. For example, children have toys bought for them at an early age. Teachers should avoid indiscriminate use of extrinsic rewards for influencing classroom behaviour, especially when task seems naturally enjoyable. Some individuals believe that certain students are unmotivated. While people are entitled to their beliefs, these beliefs, or opinions, should not be treated as scientific facts.

Unlike extrinsic motivation, intrinsic motivation occurs when the learner does something to experience internally felt satisfying results. For example, a student may wish to study a subject, or a topic, or acquire a skill, or play a musical instrument, like piano, because it produces internally felt positive consequences, such as feeling good, becoming more knowledgeable, independent, and competent. The best learners tend to be self-motivated and employ intrinsic motivation skills.

1.3 Motivation Interventions in the Classroom to Improve Engagement and Learning

Classroom interventions can be defined as 'a short-term focused teaching program with objectives aimed at students, or small groups of students with specific needs' (Wellpoint Care Network (2023). Some teachers use interventions in their classroom to motive students and to improve learning and academic achievement. In the classroom, teaching interventions are often used, as a pedagogy, to enhance engagement, motivation, and performance. It represents a value-added learning and teaching. The most popular types of interventions in the classroom include:

- one to one teaching, or tutoring,
- collaborative group teaching,
- peer tutoring, and
- feedback.

Using our knowledge and perspectives of motivation in the classroom, we can also refer to the 7 most used intervention strategies:

- Behavioural interventions
- Cognitive interventions
- Social, emotional and wellbeing intervention
- Metacognition
- Self-regulation
- Cooperative and collaborative groups interventions
- The use of homework to improve meaningful learning and retention. (Adapted from https://www.highspeedtraining.co.uk/hub/effective-interventions-in-education/).

1.3.1 Behavioural Interventions in the Classroom to Improve Learning and Performance

In examining dominant models of motivation, I would like to start with analysing behavioural theory of learning, the basis of behavioural interventions, which uses operant conditioning, to activate behaviour modification. One of the advantages of the use of behavioural theory in the classroom, is its focus on measuring standards of performance for each lesson and providing relevant strategies for teachers to develop effective classroom control and management techniques.

According to behaviourist perspective, learning is prompted by a series of external factors and takes place, when measurable, observable, and permanent changes in particular behaviour occurs. Students tend to respond to learning new tasks, by changing, or repeating behaviour, based on the external reward and reinforcement they receive. Such major psychologists as Pavlov, Watson, Skinner, and Thorndike have done considerable research into behavioural views of learning. Skinner, based on his research, suggested that *immediate* rewards and reinforcement were important and controlling factors in the operant conditioning (behaviourism) model of motivation (Skinner, 1953).

According to Skinner and other behavioural psychologists, behavioural learning theories focus on explanations of the type of learning that emphasise only visible behaviour and *observable* changes in behaviour. They also focus on the ways in which 'pleasurable and unpleasant consequences of behaviour change individuals' behaviour over time' (Slavin, 2022). For most behaviourists, *reinforcement* is a necessary condition for learning. For them, it is reinforcement that causes the S-B-R model to form. In contrast, cognitive psychologists believe that learning occurs independently of reinforcement.

Overall, behavioural theory of motivation follows the following steps:

- follows operant conditioning and behaviour modification procedures
- addresses specific objectives and learning outcomes (standards) in lesson plans
- uses lesson plans for teaching
- evaluates success and failure
- determines what and how much must be taught
- assesses students each lesson, by means of measurement of knowledge and skills
- treats learning as an event, rather than a process.
- focuses on developing mastery of knowledge.

The advantages of behavioural theory of motivation include its use of operant conditioning to improve students' behaviour and enhance standards of performance. In behavioural theory of motivation, *standards* are defined in all lesson planning. In addition, behavioural theory of motivation is very effective in the use of behaviour modification strategies in the classroom, to promote desirable behaviour, and relevant techniques for effective classroom control and management.

1.3.2 Cognitive Interventions in the Classroom to Improve Learning and Performance

Cognitive interventions in the classroom are based on cognitive model of learning. Cognitive explanations of motivation are grounded on the belief that **mental** processes control one's attitudes, behaviour, learning and knowledge acquisition. Consequently, cognitive theories focus on the way people acquire, process, and retain information and interpret meaning of specific situations. Cognitive theories of motivation explain the nexus between cognitive processes, meaningful learning, and achievement. Cognitive explanations of motivation also refer to why and how students think about the kind of knowledge acquired in the classroom, which ultimately influences their subsequent engagements, motivation, learning and behaviour. Cognitive theories of motivation assume that students need to be alert, engaged, and active in the classroom, and need to be involved in the meaning-making process, when confronted with new concepts and ideas.

The six major types of cognitive approaches to motivation include:

- achievement motivation theories,
- expectancy theory of motivation,
- self-determination theory of human needs,
- self-worth theory of motivation,
- attribution theories, and
- goal theories of motivation. (See Zajda, 2023a).

Of the above six types of cognitive approaches to motivation, I would like to focus on achievement, and goal theory of motivation, as they reflect the reality of performance culture and performance schools, globally.

1.3.3 Achievement Motivation

Achievement motivation theory was initially postulated by McClelland in the 1940s. Later, achievement motivation was developed further by Atkinson & Feather (1966). Achievement motivation can be defined as 'the ability of the individual to work toward their highest performance level' (Jankielewicz, 2022). Achievement motivation also reflects one's desire for excellence, or 'the need for excellence and significant accomplishment' (Hsieh, 2011). Achievement motivation denotes students' goals and desires to improve their academic achievement. This perspective reflects the performing schools, and competitive culture, affecting students, parents, teachers and school leaders alike. It is believed that achievement motivation was influenced by individuals' two inner needs: desire to achieve success, or to avoid failure. Achievement motivation can be both intrinsic and extrinsic. It is intrinsic when 'it is sparked by an interest or enjoyment in the task itself' (OECD, 2023). Achievement motivation can be extrinsic when it 'comes from outside the person', and 'sources of extrinsic motivation among students are rewards like good marks, or praise from parents and teachers' (OECD, 2023).

Individuals, who have the need to achieve their learning and achievement goals, are likely to continue with the task, to demonstrate their success. However, individuals who wish to avoid failure were likely to select more modest, but achievable tasks, guaranteeing their realistic and moderate success (see Zajda, 2023).

Goal theories of motivation suggest that students are likely to be engaged and motivated to learn and perform if they have specific goals to achieve. Students, in general, have a choice to learn or not to learn, reminiscent of Shakespeare's 'To be or not to be?' (*Hamlet*). Overall, the goal theories of motivation, affected by intrinsic motivation, focus mainly on mastery goals, and performance goals. Mastery goals refer to students' need and desires to learn the topic well to achieve a degree of excellence. It is associated with 'persistence and effort in academic tasks' (Duchesne et al. 2022, p. 334). Students' performance goals are used to determine their desired performance in completing classroom tasks, quizzes, and tests. Some researchers believe that performance goals are defined by extrinsic factors. In my books, based on recent research findings, I argued that both extrinsic and intrinsic motivations are interconnected (Zajda, 2022a; Zajda, 2021b). Performance goals, like expectancy theory of motivation, and other theories above, may be influenced by students' prior experiences of success or failure. In addition, performance goals, including performance-avoidance goals are derived from achievement motivation and achievement goal theory (Dweck, 1986; Senko, 2016). Consequently, students may select easier tasks, in order to demonstrate their abilities and competence. This is associated with failure-avoidance strategies or performance-avoidance goals. (See Zajda, 2023b).

1.3.4 Social and Emotional Learning Intervention

Social and emotional learning (SEL) refers to the process through which individuals 'acquire and apply the knowledge, skills, and attitudes to develop healthy identities, manage emotions and achieve personal and collective goals, feel, and show empathy for others, establish, and maintain supportive relationships, and make responsible and caring decisions' (CASEL, 2020).

CASEL's five core social-emotional competencies are:

- Self-Awareness.
- Self-Management.
- Social Awareness.
- Relationship Skills.
- Responsible Decision-Making. (CASEL, 2020).

More importantly, research has demonstrated that SEL interventions are 'effective in helping students develop social-emotional competencies—and can even boost academic achievement' (Buckle, 2022). A meta-analysis of 213 programs found that social and emotional learning interventions increased students' academic achievement', and that 'the social and emotional learning programs also reduced aggression and emotional distress among students, increased prosocial behaviors in school, and improved positive relationships (Durlak et al., 2011). Durlak et al. (2011), in their research findings, based on their meta-analysis of 213 school-based, universal social and emotional learning (SEL) programs involving 270,034 kindergartens through high school students, discovered that SEL participants demonstrated *significantly* improved social and emotional skills, attitudes, behaviour, and academic performance.

1.3.5 Metacognitive Interventions in the Classroom

Metacognition is often simply defined as 'thinking about thinking'. Metacognition refers to higher order of thinking, which involves active control over the cognitive processes engaged in learning. The term 'metacognition' is most often associated with John Flavell (1993). According to Flavell metacognition consists of both metacognitive knowledge and metacognitive experiences, or regulation. Activities such as planning how to approach a given learning task, monitoring comprehension, and evaluating progress toward the completion of a task are metacognitive. Metacognitive knowledge refers to acquired knowledge about cognitive processes, knowledge that can be used to control cognitive processes. When we deal with new information, we do so in logical steps:

- Acquiring
- Retaining
- Using Information

It is an aspect of higher order thinking that involves active control over the thinking processes involved in learning in which one can regulate them and apply them to learn more effectively. *Metacognition* is one's knowledge about the operations of cognition and how to use them to achieve a learning goal. Metacognition refers to students who can, over time, instinctively control their thinking processes. This allows them to:

- Make decisions that help them to learn i.e. They think about the best way to approach a given task and are efficient thinkers and learners.
- Become strategic thinkers who can plan ahead and be aware of the consequences of their actions.
- Monitor their learning processes.
- Understand and know when to ask for help when they get stuck.

1.3.6 Five Basic Metacognitive Strategies in the Classroom

There are at least five basic metacognitive strategies that can be employed by the students in the class. These are:

1. Connecting new information to previously learned knowledge
2. Purposefully selecting thinking strategies
3. Develop concept mapping
4. Summarizing the main points
5. Planning, monitoring, with self-questioning, and evaluating thinking processes.

According to Snowman et al. (2019) learning tactics can be placed in one of 2 categories based on the tactics primary purpose:

1. *Memory-directed tactics:* Which contain techniques that help produce accurate storage and retrieval of information.
2. *Comprehension-directed tactics:* Which contain techniques that aid in understanding the meaning of ideas and their interrelationships.

Metacognitive strategies include:

Prior Knowledge (KWL)
Rehearsal
Note taking
Problem solving strategies
Cooperative learning

1.3.7 Mnemonic Devices

Some of the most common metacognitive strategies come in the form of mnemonics, which are meaningful words where the letters in the word each stand for a step in a problem-solving process. Mnemonics refers to device of or pertaining to memory. Mnemonics are often used to indicate a device that can help you remember things. A device which is a memory-directed tactic to help a 'learner transform or organize information to enhance its retrievability' (Snowman et. al 2019). Mnemonics are used to:

- learn and remember individual items of information (i.e. fact, date),
- learn sets of information (i.e. sequence of events)
- express ideas in text.

The word 'mnemonic' comes from the Greek mnemonikós, *which refers to the mind.*

Examples of mnemonics: Rhyme, acronym, (PME: planning, monitoring evaluation), acrostic (EGBDF: every good boy deserves fruit) etc. Research demonstrates that students benefit from using metacognitive strategies, as they result in improved academic performance. These include connecting new information to previously learned knowledge, or prior knowledge, purposefully selecting relevant thinking strategies, the use of the major elements of the metacognitive process to assess thinking: planning, monitoring & assessing, and selecting relevant mnemonics, and cues to retrieve information from the long-term memory (LTM).

1.3.8 Strategies for Developing Metacognitive Behaviours

Identifying 'what you know' and 'what you don't know'. At the beginning of a research activity students need to make conscious decisions about their knowledge. Initially students write 'What I already know about…' and 'What I want to learn about….' As students research the topic, they will verify, clarify, and expand, or replace with more accurate information, each of their initial statements. Talking about thinking is important because students need a *thinking vocabulary*. During planning and problem-solving situations, teachers should think aloud so that students can follow demonstrated thinking processes. Modelling and discussions develop the vocabulary that students need for thinking and talking about their own thinking.

1.3.9 Summary of Metacognitive Strategies

- A metacognitive strategy is a memorable 'plan of action' that provides students an easy-to-follow procedure for solving a particular math problem.
- Metacognitive strategies are taught using explicit teaching methods.
- Metacognitive strategies include the student's thinking, as well as their physical actions.
- Metacognitive strategies are memorable, and it must accurately represent the learning task.

Developing and enhancing metacognive skills in students, as part of metacognitive interventions in the classroom, can increase students' academic achievement Mevarech & (Kramarski, 2003; Amzil, 2013; Zajda, 2023a).

Mevarech & Kramarski (2003), in their study of metacognitive training, examined some 122 eighth-grade Israeli students, who studied algebra in five heterogeneous classrooms, with no tracking. A year later, when these participants were ninth graders, they were re-examined using the same test as the one administered in eighth grade. The researchers discovered that 'within cooperative settings, students who were exposed to metacognitive training outperformed students who were exposed to worked-out examples on both the immediate and delayed post-tests':

> In particular, the differences between the two conditions were observed on students' ability to explain their mathematical reasoning during the discourse and in writing. Lower achievers gained more under the MT than under WE condition. The findings indicate that the kind of task and the way group interaction is structured are two important variables in implementing cooperative learning. (Mevarech & Kramarski, 2003)

1.3.10 The Role of Self-regulation in the Classroom

Students' knowledge, skills, and ability to use self-regulation plays a significant part in their learning in the classroom. Self-regulation theory (SRT) is a system of conscious personal management that involves the process of guiding one's own thoughts, behaviours, and feelings to learn, remember and perform. *Self-regulation* involves controlling one's behaviour, emotions, and thoughts in the pursuit of goals, be they short-term, or long-term goals. Self-regulation theory suggests that there is a process of anchoring and adjusting our performance, both mental and physical in nature, in response to corrective feedback, within our social and physical environment. The first step to practice self-regulation is to recognize that everyone has a choice in how to react to situations. There are four basic self-regulation strategies that all students need to be able to use:

- goal-setting,
- self-monitoring,
- effective use of self-instructions or self-talk, and
- self-reinforcement.

Development of self-regulation

Student's ability to self-regulate has roots in cognitive, social, and emotional development during childhood. Learning how to self-regulate is an important skill that students learn both for cognitive and emotional maturity and social connections. In essence, maturity, in terms of cognitive development, reflects the ability and skills to face emotional, social, and cognitive threats in the environment with patience and thoughtfulness. This description reminds us of *mindfulness*, as it does relate to one's ability to self-regulate. In its most basic form, self-regulation allows us to be more resilient and bounce back from failure, while also staying calm under pressure. Researchers have found that self-regulation skills are tied to a range of positive health outcomes. This includes better resilience to stress, increased happiness, and better overall well-being.

According to Dr. Jon Kabat-Zinn, founder of Mindfulness-Based Stress Reduction (MBSR), mindfulness is 'the awareness that arises from paying attention, on purpose, in the present moment and non-judgementally.' By engaging in skills such as focused breathing and gratitude, mindfulness enables us to put some space between ourselves and our reactions, leading to better focus and feelings of calmness and relaxation. In a 2019 review of 27 research studies, mindfulness was showed to improve attention, which in turn helped to regulate negative emotions and executive functioning (higher-order thinking).

Effective strategies for self-regulation: cognitive reappraisal

Cognitive reappraisal, or cognitive reframing is a common strategy that can be used to improve self-regulation abilities. This strategy involves changing your thought patterns. Specifically, cognitive reappraisal involves reinterpreting a situation to change one's emotional response to it. For example, imagine a friend did not return your calls or texts for several days. Rather than thinking that this reflected something about yourself, such as 'my friend hates me,' you might instead think, 'my friend must be really busy.' Research has shown that using cognitive reappraisal in everyday life is related to experiencing more positive and fewer negative emotions. Some other useful strategies for self-regulation include acceptance and problem-solving. In contrast, unhelpful strategies that people sometimes use include avoidance, distraction, suppression, and worrying. One can improve self-regulation skills, by practicing mindfulness, and changing how one thinks about the situation.

Qualities of self-regulators

The benefits of self-regulation are numerous. In general, people who are adept at self-regulating tend to possess the following abilities:

- Acting in accordance with their values
- Calming themselves when upset
- Cheering themselves when feeling down
- Maintaining open communication
- Persisting through difficult times
- Putting forth their best effort
- Remaining flexible and adapting to situations
- Seeing the good in others
- Focusing on their intentions
- Taking control of situations when necessary

Cooperative and collaborative groups interventions

In general, *collaborative groups* and *cooperative learning* refer to a variety of structured classroom management techniques and grading systems developed and studied by many educational researchers, including Johnson & Johnson (2008), Kagan (1990), Slavin (1995, 1990), Zajda (2023a, 2023b), and others. Spencer Kagan (1990), for instance, in an article in *Educational Leadership*, provided an informative definition of cooperative learning, by looking at general structures, which can be applied in classroom pedagogy. His definition offered a global umbrella for the cooperative learning researchers. According to Kagan (1990), cooperative learning refers to:

> The structural approach to cooperative learning is based on the creation, analysis and systematic application of structures, or content-free ways of organizing social interaction in the classroom. Structures usually involve a series of steps, with proscribed behaviour at each step. An important cornerstone of the approach is the distinction between 'structures' and 'activities'. (Kagan, 1990)

Similarly, Nelson-LeGall (1992) captured the nature of the engagement process in cooperative learning, when she stated:

> Learning and understanding are not merely individual processes supported by the social context; rather they are the result of a continuous, dynamic negotiation between the individual and the social setting in which the individual's activity takes place. Both the individual and the social context are active and constructive in producing learning and understanding. (Nelson-LeGall, 1992, p. 52)

Studies have shown that in well-structured cooperative groups, students consistently learn many different subjects better than students in traditionally structured classrooms. Cooperative learning also has a number of psychological and social benefits, such as being exposed to other points-of-view, learning how to cooperate, having more positive feelings about school, having more positive feelings about themselves and others, and wanting their classmates to do well.

Research findings have demonstrated that all students benefit academically from cooperative learning. Successful students show modest gains in performance and achievement, while historically unsuccessful students usually show tremendous gains when taught using cooperation as the primary motivator. Cooperative grouping allows students to organize their thoughts, in a more inclusive context, than whole class discussions, and prepares students for sharing their thoughts with the class. Students can make progress on exercises that they would not be able to attempt alone.

Collaborative and cooperative group learning in the classroom

Collaborative and cooperative learning is a broad term that encompasses a variety of highly structured, yet flexible instructional strategies, management techniques, and assessment strategies that simultaneously build and enhance engagement, social and academic skills (Brady, 2006; Zajda 2018). The notion of cooperative work is broadly defined as two or more people working together for the mutual benefit of all in ways that maximize everyone's learning (Dillenbourg, 1999). It is different from individualistic learning and competitive learning. It demonstrates the shared benefits for both students and teachers. It refers to working towards shared goals and shared successes; and it is assessed on the whole group effort and group performances of tasks (Johnson & Johnson 2008). While the use of cooperative and collaborative group work in educational settings is neither original nor unique to any particular education system, contemporary education has been significantly influenced by the study of group dynamics, behaviours and practices of various education theorists (Brady 2006; Johnson & Johnson 2008; Zajda, 2023a).

There are hundreds of cooperative structures and numerous books available to help teachers to incorporate effective cooperative learning into their classrooms. The most common collaborative groups are think-pair-share, think-pair-square, and jigsaw collaborative groups, listed below:

Think-pair-share

Think-pair-share cooperative group model, for groups of two students, was first developed by Lyman (1981). This collaborative discussion strategy was designed to 'provide students with time to think and formulate their individual thoughts and ideas about a given topic or concept before forming a pair with a peer to share their thinking' (S2 TEM Centers SC, 2012). Students think about 'each question, pair off and discuss the question with a classmate, and share their answers with the class (https://srri.umass.edu/topics/collaborative-group-). Students reflect, then pair and share/discuss the question:

> Students individually THINK for a few moments about the prompt or question or observation the teacher provides to engage them. Students form a PAIR with another student to talk and compare their response to the prompt. They come to a consensus about a collective response to the prompt. Student pairs SHARE their thinking with the rest of the class as the teacher randomly calls on them or asks for volunteers to share. (S2 TEM Centers SC, 2012)

Think-pair-square

Think-pair-square cooperative group is similar to think-pair-share, but it involves groups of four students. Students are presented with a learning activity in the classroom. They can be directed and to think for few minutes before sharing their ideas. One organised in a pair, a student shares with the person next to them. The pair of students is asked to think of the 'best' answer to the question. Students first discuss problem-solving strategies in pairs and then in groups of fours.

Example 1 Discuss the meaning of 'To be or not to be, that is the question'.

Think: 'To be or not to be, that is the question'. A student thinks for 30 s of this idea…

Pair: The student then compares the idea with a partner next in the group.

Square: Students in pairs join another pair and discuss the question.

Share: What does it mean (group/class discussion).

- The think-pair-share cooperative learning strategy is used to begin discussion, and then move on to groups of four, using the think-pair-square method etc.
- In class, the think-pair-share and think-pair-square techniques are used to discuss and identify the strategies that each pair (and then each think-pair-square cooperative group square) has in common.

Jigsaw collaborative groups

Jigsaw is a collaborative or cooperative grouping strategy, involving 4–5 students, who focus on an activity, such as new approaches to education for sustainability (EfS) and develop new ideas. Jigsaw activities make it possible for students to specialize in one area and construct their new knowledge and skills to solve the problem. Cognitive, social, and emotional benefits include:

- Enhancing one's aptitude by being involved in problem-solving tasks
- Increasing one's analytical thinking, through the use of critical thinking and critical literacy
- Enhances social skill, by working with the group members.
- Activates and the use of both sides of the brain. 'The left side of the brain is used more for logical and analytical thinking and problem solving. The right side of the brain is more creative, visual, and emotional. It is used more when listening to music, recognizing people's faces, and in our spatial awareness' (see https://www.chicagoacademic.com/bid/223417/Teaching).
- Enhances one' memory, both STM (short-term memory) and LTM (long-term memory)
- Improves one's critical thinking, analytical and problem-solving skills.

Jigsaw in 10 easy steps

The jigsaw classroom is very simple to use, following the steps below, as a guide:

- 'Divide students into 4- or 5-person jigsaw groups. The groups should be diverse in terms of gender, ethnicity, race, and ability.
- Appoint one student from each group as the leader. Initially, this person should be the most mature student in the group.
- Divide the class lesson into 5 or 6 segments.
- Assign each student to learn one segment.
- Give students time to read over their segment at least twice and become familiar with it
- Form temporary 'expert groups' by having one student from each jigsaw group join other students assigned to the same segment. Give students in these expert groups time to discuss the main points of their segment and to rehearse the presentations they will make to their jigsaw group.
- Bring the students back into their jigsaw groups.
- Ask each student to present her or his segment to the group. Encourage others in the group to ask questions for clarification.
- Float from group to group, observing the process. If any group is having trouble (e.g., a member is dominating or disruptive), make an appropriate intervention. Eventually, it's best for the group leader to handle this task. Leaders can be trained by whispering an instruction on how to intervene, until the leader gets the hang of it.
- At the end of the session, give a quiz on the material so that students quickly come to realize that these sessions are not just fun and games but really count'. (https://www.jigsaw.org)

Research findings have demonstrated that in well-structured cooperative groups, students consistently learn many different subjects and topics better than students in traditionally structured classrooms (Amin, 2020; Hattie, 2009; Mendo-Lázaro et al. 2022; Slavin, 1990; van Wyk, 2012, Zajda, 2023a).

Cooperative learning also has a number of significant cognitive, affective and 'psychological and social advantages, such as being exposed to other points-of-view, learning how to cooperate', learning how to develop more positive feelings about school, developing 'more positive feelings about themselves and others, and wanting their classmates to do well' (Retrieved from https://srri.umass.edu/topics/collaborative-group

Social constructivism and improving academic achievement

Based on prolific research findings dealing with the nexus between constructivist pedagogy, quality teaching, and improvement in academic performance, I would like to suggest that effective learning environments need to offer continuous active engagement in the classroom globally. Compared with traditional methods of teaching, constructivist approach to learning and teaching has become increasingly popular and preferred pedagogy. One of the most obvious reasons for its popularity is that it offers to students much more social and cognitive interaction and engagement in collaborative groups. Constructivist pedagogy, based on psychological and social constructivism has become one of the effective classroom strategies for improving academic achievement (Richardson, 2003; Puacharearn, 2004; Kim, 2005; Rowe, 2006; OECD, 2009; Sharma & Sharma, 2012; Ayaz & Şekerci, 2015; Adak, 2017; Alt, 2017; Gupta & Tyagi, 2017; Steinmayr et al. 2019; Akpan et al. 2020; Zajda, 2023b).

There exists a causal relationship between constructivist pedagogy and students' academic achievement. Earlier, Rowe (2006), had demonstrated that that constructivist pedagogy was effective in maximising the achievement progress of students during the early and middle years of schooling. The nexus between social constructivism and academic achievement was reported by Adak (2017), Al-Rahmi & Shamsuddin (2020), Ginga & Zakariya (2020), Smritikana & Saha (2021), Bahufite et al. (2023), Umar et al. (2023), and Zajda (2023a, 2023b).

In one comparative and cross-cultural meta-analysis of constructivist pedagogy, Ayaz & Şekerci (2015) examined some 53 studies on the effects of constructivist pedagogy on students' academic achievement and concluded that 'the constructivist learning approach, compared to traditional teaching methods, has positive effects on the student's academic achievement' (Ayaz & Şekerci, 2015, p. 151). Elbaz (2015) discovered a positive correlation between constructivist approach and students' academic achievement. Ahme Qarareh (2016) demonstrated that use of constructivist strategies in the classroom had a positive impact on students' academic achievement. Similarly, Adak (2017) demonstrated that the students exposed to the constructivist pedagogy 'performed significantly higher than those exposed to the traditional teaching method in respect of their gained scores at every intelligence levels', and that the constructivist approach strategy is capable of improving 'student's mastery of content at the higher order levels of cognition' (Adak, 2017, p. 1074). Sunal & Haas (2017) showed that constructivist strategies of learning improved students' academic achievement. Ardiansyah & Ujihanti (2018) also noted that the use of social constructivist pedagogy 'significantly improved' students' 'reading comprehension achievement and vocabulary mastery in the high and low classes' (p. 463).

According to Shah (2019), constructivism is not only popular, but promoted 'significant success' in students' academic achievement:

> Constructivism has been a very powerful model for explaining how knowledge is produced in the world as well as how students learn. Moreover, constructivist teaching practices are becoming more prevalent in teacher education programs, while demonstrating significant success in promoting student learning. (Shah, 2019)

Akpan et al. (2020), in their study of social constructivism and learning, involving 154 secondary school students, concluded that their findings provided evidence of the effectiveness of the social constructivist instructional strategy in improving performance in algebra better than the conventional teaching method. Al-Rahmi & Shamsuddin (2020), argued that social constructivism contributed to improved academic achievement. This was also reported by Ginga & Zakariya (2020), in their article 'Impact of a social constructivist instructional strategy on performance in algebra with a focus on secondary school students', who demonstrated the effectiveness of the social constructivist instructional strategy in improving performance in algebra, which was proved to be better than the conventional teaching method. Similarly,

Bahufite et al. (2023) in 'The relationships between learners' academic achievement due to the use of constructivist methods in physical science and their self-esteem in Zambian secondary schools', revealed a strong interdependency between learners' self-esteem and academic achievement. Similar results were reported by Umar et al. (2023) in 'Learning activities based on social constructivism theory to promote social interaction and student's performance (EPSISM)', argued that social constructivism improved students' academic achievement.

Cano-García & Rojas-Cazaluade (2022) suggested, based on their research findings, that 'Cooperative learning has positive effects on student motivation, participation, and performance' (Cano-García & Rojas-Cazaluade, 2022). Earlier, Slavin (1980) concluded that.

> cooperative learning produces 'significantly better' academic achievement, and that 'cooperative learning techniques can achieve both cognitive and affective goals'. (pp. 337–338)

In addition, constructivist pedagogy in the classroom facilitates a good deal of students' interest, engagement, and motivation (Hunter, 2015; Shah, 2019; Zaphir, 2019; Zajda, 2023b). Constructivist pedagogy, by its focus on critical thinking and problem-solving activities during group work, promotes the development of students' cognitive, social, and emotional aspects of learning, as well as metacognition, critical literacy, and self-regulated learning strategies.

The use of homework to improve meaningful learning and retention

Grodner & Rupp (2013) in their article 'The role of homework in student learning outcomes: evidence from a field experiment' argued that that 'homework plays an important role in student learning, especially so for students who initially perform poorly in the course. Students in the homework-required group have higher retention rates, higher test scores (5–6%), more good grades (Bs), and lower failure rates' (Grodner & Rupp, 2013). There exists a consensus that homework advances study skills to a certain degree, with regard to the exams, or study skills (Pllana, 2022). Roschelle & Hodkowski (2020) in their paper 'Using research on homework to improve remote and hybrid learning' argue that homework 'improves learning when students receive the right amount of homework, with the appropriate level of challenge and appropriate supports' Roschelle & Hodkowski (2020). Similalry, Thibodeau (2023) in 'Transforming Homework in the UDL Classroom: Breaking down Barriers' suggests that homework 'strengthens classroom learning, fosters independent study habits, and offers vital practice'. (Thibodeau, 2023).

Research findings have demonstrated the relevance of above discussed strategies of effective interventions in the classroom. Lazowski & Hulleman (2016) in their article 'Motivation interventions in education: A meta-analytic review', which analyzed some 76 studies, involving some 38,377 participants, showed that interventions were generally effective, with an average mean effect size of $d = 0.49$ (95% confidence interval = [0.43, 0.56]). Clearly, research findings show that the use of effective interventions in the classroom can improve students' engagement, motivation, and performance.

1.4 Motivating Students in the Classroom

It is well known, as demonstrated by research findings, that when students feel that they belong, in an inclusive classroom environment, they are likely to be more engaged and motivated. They become 'more productive, more creative, less stressed, and more energized'. Research has demonstrated that individuals, who are 'constantly self-motivated can be more successful in life and dare to achieve their dreams'. (Self-motivation, 2022).

How motivated a student is, and how much effort a student is willing to make, is a function of the following three things:

- Internal states, such as needs or desires
- Potential outcomes
- The student's estimate of the likelihood that a specific behaviour will lead to a given outcome success.

Some effective ways of motivating students include:

- Gaining students' attention from the start, and make learning more interesting, relevant, and meaningful. You need to learn students' 'names, respond positively to students' ideas, praise their success', and 'be tactful' when commenting on their classroom work (see Chasteen, 2023).
- Using positive reinforcers (as part of behaviour medication), after a desired response is demonstrated, is likely to motivate students to give the same response in the future, because the reinforcer tells students that their responses are acceptable. For e.g. if a student puts up their hand to answer a question, the teacher says thank you for putting up your hand, the student will come to realise that this is appropriate behaviour.
- Making certain students know *what* to do, and how to determine when they achieve their designated goals. (see OECD, 2023)
- Directing learning experiences towards feelings of success, to encourage a desire to perform and achieve. For example, draw a smiley face on a student's work when they have completed it well.
- Make connections between *what* is being studied and their daily lives in school, and in the community.
- Motivation remains high when ITC (information communication technology) is perceived by the students to be relevant and used for the task.
- Promote students' self-directed learning (SDL), when students take the initiative, to meet their immediate leaning needs, and desires, to complete designated learning tasks in the classroom successfully.

Top 8 basic rules of motivation

1. Strong motivation comes from within: it is about who you are, not just about what you want and is closely related to the way you feel about yourself. (see OECD, 2023 on intrinsic motivation).

2. You can change the way you feel about yourself, by changing the way you think, and the way you act. (for self-esteem, see Zajda, 2023a).
3. Ultimately, you cannot motivate anyone else, but you can play a key role in helping other people to motivate themselves.
4. There is no 'magic formula' that will motivate everyone in the same way: we are each motivated in different ways. (see Weichert, 2022).
5. Motivation, once established, doesn't last forever; you need to work on it on an ongoing basis. (Khan, 2022)
6. Motivation requires setting realistic and achievable goals. (see Timeular, 2023).
7. Collaborative and cooperative groups in the classroom tend to generate engagement and motivation. (see Yang, 2023).
8. Competition and challenge will only motivate you if you are able to achieve your learning goals and succeed. (see Cherry, 2022).

Theories of motivation: brief overview

Effecting engagement influencing students' motivation has the following four interrelated aspects:

- Behavioural engagement
- Cognitive engagement
- Social engagement
- Emotional engagement (humanistic perspective).

Behaviourists theories of motivation and engagement

Behavioural theory of learning, as used in the classroom, as mentioned in my book (2023b) *Globalisation, and dominant models of motivational theories in education* (Cham: Springer Nature Switzerland) is one of the keys in helping students, once motivated, to engage and perform, by completing designated activities and tasks. Behavioural theory of learning can be defined as a theory of learning focusing on 'observable behaviours' (Pritchard, 2009, p. 6). Behavioural theory is based, and regulated by the **SBR** model (stimulus, behaviour, and response). Behavioural theory of learning focuses on how individuals learn, and how their visible behaviours can be observed and measured, in terms of performance. It assumes that all visible behaviours, which are influenced by the social environment, can be measured.

The prominent researchers of scientific studies of behaviourism included Edward Thorndike, John Watson, Ivan Pavlov and B. F. Skinner. Thorndike (1905) was one of the pioneers in discovering the role of operant conditioning, and reinforcement in behavioural learning. He developed his *Law of Effect*, which held that if behaviour is followed by a favourable effect (reinforcement), it is likely to be repeated. Watson (1913), like Thorndike, established behaviourism, as field of learning, in his lecture at Columbia University titled 'Psychology as the behaviourist views it.' He criticized Sigmund Freud and his psycho analytic theory for his overwhelming emphasis on the subconscious drives affecting human behaviour. Instead, he stated the opposite view that all observable behaviour is due to conscious and deliberate action.

Ivan Pavlov (1927), who won Nobel Prize for Physiology and Medicine in 1904, studied classical conditioning and discovered the concept unconditional responses and conditional responses, experimenting on dogs in the laboratory. Pavlov was able to condition the dog to form an association between the tuning fork, and the sound of the bell, if they were given food at the same time, resulting in a conditioned stimulus. Pavlov's *classical conditioning* is the 'process of repeatedly associating neutral stimulus with an unconditioned stimulus', to produce a conditioned response (Slavin, 2022). As such, classical conditioning, where behaviours are changed through the association of stimuli, like in Pavlov's dogs, is totally different from operant conditioning, where behaviours are changed because of rewards. Classical conditioning is the result of *involuntary* behaviour, with a stimulus, whereas operant conditioning is the result *voluntary* behaviour, with a consequence, like in the Skinner's **SBR** model (stimulus, behaviour, and response) model. Skinner (1953) focused on the link between behaviour and consequences. His theory of *operant conditioning* was based on the use of reinforcement to control individual's behaviour. Operant conditioning was totally dominated using 'pleasant or unpleasant consequences' to control the occurrence of individual's behaviour (Slavin, 2022).

Cognitive theories and engagement

Cognitive theories of motivation represent internal mental processes, as the origins of thought processes, and leaning outcomes. As I explained earlier in my introductory Chap. 1 (Zajda, 2023a, *Globalisation, and dominant models of motivational theories in education*), cognitive explanations of motivation refer to, by and large, as to why, what, and how students think and understand new knowledge acquired in the classroom, and how it consequently influences their attitudes, values, engagements, motivation, learning and behaviour in the classroom. Cognitive theories of motivation assume that, in general, students are cognitively alert, engaged, and active in the classroom, and are involved in the on-going meaning-making process, when confronted with new concepts and ideas. The meaning-making process refers to constructivism and constructivist theory of motivation, to be discussed later. This is also relevant to inquiry-based learning and motivation.

Cognitive approaches to motivation emphasise the individuals need to know and understand. Cognitive theories focus on the categories and labels people use to help to identify thoughts, emotions, dispositions, and behaviours. One of the key words in cognitive psychology is 'perception'. In psychology and the cognitive sciences, perception is the process of acquiring, interpreting, selecting, and organizing sensory information. The word *perception* comes from the Latin *percepio,* meaning 'receiving, collecting, action of taking possession, apprehension with the mind or senses'.

Information processing theory (or cognitive psychology) is based on the research of Atkinson and Shiffrin and other cognitive psychologists and seeks to understand how:

1. information is acquired
2. information is stored

3. information is recalled
4. current information shapes how and what a person learns.

Information-processing model-refers to a cognitive view of learning that describes and examines the processing, storage, and retrieval of knowledge in the mind. Components of the memory system: the three major components of memory are sensory register, short-term memory (STM or WM) and LTM. The three parts of LTM are: *episodic, semantic*, and *procedural memory*. The two major cognitive teaching strategies to help students learn include the use of advance organizers to assist students to achieve this task, and the use of mnemonics devices.

There are numerous examples of cognitive theories of motivation, which include:

- Identity theory of motivation,
- Inquiry-based learning of motivation
- achievement motivation theories,
- expectancy theory of motivation,
- self-determination theory of human needs,
- self-worth theory of motivation,
- cognitive dissonance theory
- cognitive evaluation theory
- metacognition
- constructivism
- discourse analysis and motivation
- self-efficacy
- attribution theories, and
- goal theories of motivation. (see Zajda, 2023).

Comparing cognitive and behavioural views

According to cognitive view, knowledge is learned, and changes in knowledge affect behavior. In the behaviourist view, behaviours themselves are learned. Both views suggest that reinforcement is important in learning, but for different reasons. Behaviourists believe that reinforcement strengthens behavior, whereas cognitivists see reinforcement as a source of feedback about what is likely to happen if behaviours are repeated or changed (thinking and metacognition).

Social-cognitive theory of motivation

Albert Bandura (1986, 2002) developed the concept of 'social cognitive theory' (initially known as *social learning theory*) and in particular the notion of 'triadic reciprocal causation'. He examined the relationship between effective learning or the ability of students to become self-regulated learners, and the *three* domains: personal characteristics, behavioural patterns, and environment. Bandura used his conception of social cognitive theory to examine how students control and regulate their learning. A social cognitive viewpoint of self-regulated learning (SRL) upheld and extended the behaviourist view to contend that behaviour is largely regulated antecedently, through cognitive processes (Bandura, 1977, 1986). Seminal work grew from Bandura's (1977) social learning theory signifying behaviour as 'a product of both self-generated and external sources of influence' (Bandura, 1986, p. 454). Hence, the social learning theory was renamed the social cognitive theory by Bandura (1986) to recognise the triadic reciprocal causation model, on which Zimmerman's (1989) social cognitive research on SRL theory was based (Schunk & Usher, 2013). Grounded in the self-regulation research from this perspective are the reciprocal interactions that suggest that learning is the consequence of personal, behavioural, and environmental influences.

The triadic reciprocal causation model

Bandura further defined the three components of his Triadic Reciprocal Model, i.e. the interaction of personal characteristics, behaviour, and environment. Personal characteristics refer to a student's mental and emotional needs such as their beliefs to perform learning goals and anxieties. It also encompasses the notion of self-efficacy, or a student's belief in their learning abilities. Behavioural patterns refer to self-observation and self-evaluation. Environment refers to a student's social and physical environment. Bandura suggested that to be effective learners, students need to exhibit self-control, self-regulation, and self-efficacy. Bandura's social learning theory has had important implication in the field of education. Today, both teachers and parents recognize the importance of modelling appropriate behaviours. Other classroom strategies such as encouraging children and building self-efficacy are also present in social learning theory.

Four key principles defining Bandura's social learning are:

a. Attention
b. Retention
c. Reproduction
d. Motivation

Four principles governing social learning are:

a. *Attention*: To learn, you need to be paying attention. Anything that detracts your attention is going to have a negative effect on observational learning. If the model interesting or there is a novel aspect to the situation, you are far more likely to dedicate your full attention to learning.
b. *Retention*: The ability to store information is also an important part of the learning process. Retention can be affected by several factors, but the ability to retrieve information later, and act on, it is vital to observational learning.
c. *Reproduction:* Once you have paid attention to the model and retained the information, it is time to perform the behaviour you observed. Further practice of the learned behaviour leads to improvement and skill advancement.
d. *Motivation*: For observational learning to be successful, you must be motivated to imitate the behaviour that has been modelled. Reinforcement and punishment play an important role in motivation. While experiencing these motivators can be highly effective, so can observing other experience some type of reinforcement or punishment. For example, if you see another student rewarded with extra credit

for being to class on time, you might start to show up a few minutes early each day.

These 4 principles were used in observational learning. Bandura (1977) believed that most learning is learned by observing others:

> Learning would be exceedingly laborious, not to mention hazardous, if people had to rely solely on the effects of their own actions to inform them what to do. Fortunately, most human behavior is learned observationally through modeling: from observing others one forms an idea of how new behaviors are performed, and on later occasions this coded information serves as a guide for action.
>
> (Bandura, *Social Learning Theory*, 1977)

Observational Learning

In his famous Bobo doll experiment, Bandura demonstrated that children learn and imitate behaviours they have observed in other people. The children in Bandura's studies observed an adult acting violently toward a Bobo doll. When the children were later allowed to play in a room with the Bobo doll, they began to imitate the aggressive actions they had previously observed. Bandura identified three basic models of observational learning:

a. A live model, which involves an actual individual demonstrating or acting out a behaviour.
b. A verbal instructional model, which involves descriptions and explanations of a behaviour.
c. A symbolic model, which involves real or fictional characters displaying behaviours in books, films, television programs, or online media.

Self-control and Self-regulation

Self-control, or the ability to control one's actions in the absence of external reinforcement or punishment.

Self-regulation, or the consistent and appropriate application of self-control skills to new situations.

The role of self-efficacy in self-regulation

- *Self-efficacy:* How capable/prepared we believe we are for handling particular tasks.

Bandura argued that self-efficacy was more powerful than rewards, or punishments.

- Students with *high* self-efficacy were more likely to use self-regulating skills
- Students with *low* self-efficacy avoid challenging tasks, depend on others, and reduce chances for developing self-regulation, and self-efficacy—a vicious circle.

Students' classroom behaviours affected by self-efficacy include:

- *Selection processes—a person with high self-efficacy will consider a variety of goals and participate in a variety of activities.*
- *Cognitive processes—high self-efficacy individuals use higher level thought process.*
- *Motivational processes—those who rate their capabilities as higher than average can be expected to work harder and longer to achieve a goal.*
- *Affective processes—when faced with a challenge, high self-efficacy individuals experience excitement, curiosity; low self-efficacy individuals likely to feel anxiety, depression.*

Effects of modelling on self-efficacy, self-regulation, and achievement

- Mathematics

  Effect of peer models
  Effect of perceived similarity in learning ability
  Effect of self-modelling
  Effect of learning-goal orientation

- Writing

  Modeling for strategy development
  Observing weak and strong models
  Modeling versus practice

Applying Social Cognitive Theory in the Classroom

The research shows that self-regulated learning (SRL) skills make a significant impact on students' academic achievement However students need adequate preparation for their own learning. Teachers can help students to become more effective self-regulated learners by using the following classroom strategies:

a. Emphasize the importance of SRL skills in learning and when they should be used.
b. Model SRL skills, including the standards one uses to evaluate one's performance.
b. Provide guided practice and corrective feedback for the SRL skills to be mastered.
c. Teach students to use both memory and comprehension tactics and taking notes.
d. Teach students how to use various forms of rehearsal and mnemonic devices (two reasons for teaching rehearsal: a useful tactic for keeping small amount of information active in STM; maintenance rehearsal.
e. Teach students how to formulate relevant comprehension questions.
f. Teach students how to take good notes.

Humanistic theories of motivation

Our emotions are important to humanists. Emotions, or what we often refer to in educational psychology as 'affect', will shape what, when, and how well we will learn something. If you are unhappy, sad, frustrated or distressed, you will not be motivated to learn. Humanistic psychologists believe we should pay more attention to emotions and ensure that our students are feeling safe, positive, relaxed, and comfortable. These are the states that are likely to make students ready to learn. Humanistic psychologists argue that other dominant educational theories, like behaviourism, and cognitive perspectives tend to ignore the nature and complexity of being, and the major role of self-actualization and emotions in learning.

Humanist approach to learning requires the teacher to consider all needs of the student to create an effective learning environment, with reference to:

social needs
emotional needs
mental needs
cognitive needs
individual differences and needs (learning styles etc.) (see Zajda, 2023b).

Humanistic approaches emphasise the importance of intrinsic motives (internal motives) such as those related to the need to be independent, to develop competence and to actualise potential. Needs-based view of motivation is a humanistic theory that views motivation as satisfying the learner's needs. The same person may have different needs at different times. (Needs, desires, emotions) Humanists are especially concerned with the personal development of students and the enhancement of positive self-concepts. Maslow's humanistic theory presents hierarchical arrangement of need systems with physiological needs at the lowest level (basic needs) and the need for self-actualisation at the highest (meta needs) these needs relate to motivation in the sense that people are motivated to meet their basic needs in order to survive and if these basic needs are not met then it is impossible to be able to meet the other needs that are higher in the hierarchy (Fig. 1.1).

Maslow's hierarchy has two broad and different types of needs:

Basic Needs: At the bottom of the pyramid are basic needs or what we sometimes call deficit needs or deprivation needs. When we don't have these needs, we're motivated to fulfil them by any means necessary.

Growth Needs: Once we have our basic needs satisfied, we work on growth needs or what we sometimes call being needs or esteem needs. These are the needs that have to be met to reach self-actualization.

Maslow's hierarchy of human needs consists of seven distinct levels of needs:

1. *Physiological Needs (a basic need):* physiological needs are the things that we *physically* need to survive. These include water, clothing, shelter, and food.
2. *Safety, Protection and Security Needs (a basic need):* We all need to be safe, to exist in life.
3. *Belongingness and Love (a basic need):* Once we have successfully met our physical and safety needs, we can start working on developing relationships. All humans need positive relationships to be fulfilled. This might include having a sense of belonging and that you are included in a classroom, that you have a loving family to go home to, and that you have a group of friends to rely on.

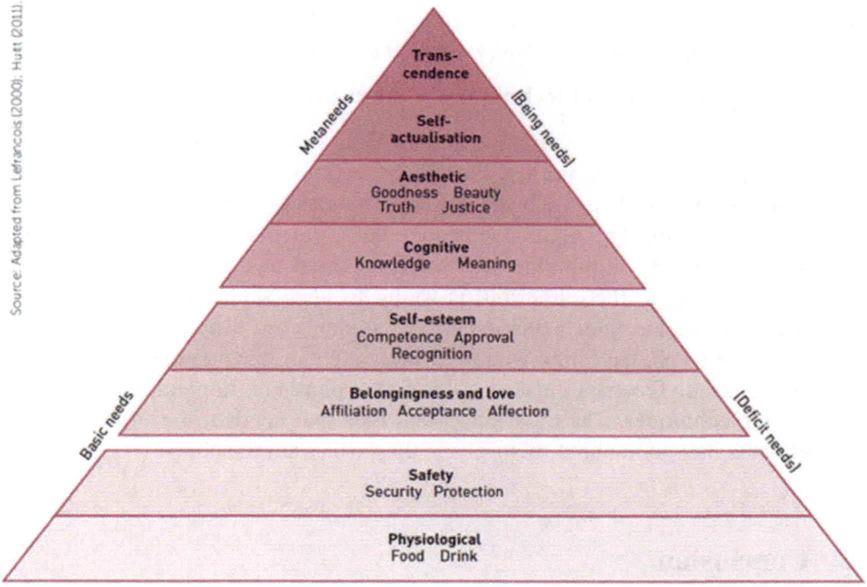

Fig. 1.1 Maslow's hierarchy of needs. *Source* Adapted from Lefrancois (2000) and Huitt (2011)

4. *Self-esteem (a growth need):* A desire 'to become everything one is capable of becoming' (Maslow, 1987, p. 64). Self-esteem means how we value ourselves. We need to think well of ourselves. If we have low opinions of ourselves, or low self-esteem, we are likely set low standards for ourselves.
5. *Cognitive needs* refer to our knowledge and understanding of the environment.
6. *Aesthetic needs* refer to one's appreciation of beauty and harmony.
7. *Self-actualization (a growth need):* The need for self-actualization is the feeling that you want to become the best you can be, now that all your needs have been met. You can go on to pursue creative pursuits and succeed to the best of your abilities.
8. *Transcendence needs:* Motivated by needs and values beyond personal self, and in helping others. Transcendence, according to Maslow, refers to the 'very highest and most inclusive or holistic levels of human consciousness, behaving and relating, as ends rather than means, to oneself, to significant others, to human beings in general, to other species, to nature, and to the cosmos' (Maslow, 1971, p. 269).

Self-actualization can be described as the complete realization of one's potential, as manifested in peak experiences which involve the full development of one's abilities and appreciation for life (Maslow, 1962). The attainment of self-actualization, as Perera (2020) explains, 'involves one's full involvement in life and the realization of that which one is capable of accomplishing' (Perera, 2020). Maslow also believed that the state of self-actualization was viewed as obtainable only after one's fundamental needs for survival, safety, love, and self-esteem are met.

Implementing motivational techniques in the classroom

Clearly, teachers cannot possibly motivate all their students all the time. However, they can help them explore and use their abilities, knowledge, skills, and feelings. As pedagogues we need to help the students to master the content and achieve classroom learning mastery goals. We need to help students to feel good about their own ideas, and work, as this and will motivate them to do their best. A key to motivating students in the classroom is trying to understand individual students, their backgrounds, and their experiences. All students are different, and therefore it is impossible to predetermine what will motivate any given student. There is no one fit all solution. Teachers must be willing to explore and implement a variety of motivational techniques. The most important idea that needs to be stressed is that when students feel good about themselves, they will want to achieve.

1.5 Conclusion

The above information provides current research and knowledge in the use of motivation in schools, to improve students' engagement, well-being, academic excellence, standards, equity, and global competitiveness. It examines the role of motivation impacting on students, schools, and pedagogy, both locally and globally, in promoting economic and social competitiveness, and academic standards. The chapter stresses that students' engagement in the classroom, plays a key role in their learning, and ability to master content knowledge in key learning areas.

Chapter 2
Increasing Engagement in the Classroom

2.1 Students' Engagement in the Classroom

The nature and the quality of students' engagement in the classroom plays a key role in shaping their attitudes, abilities, knowledge, and skills to learn new knowledge, as defined by the prescribed curriculum, and master designated key learning areas. I have argued in my recent books on motivation that for individuals to be engaged in learning, first and foremost, they must feel *positive* and good about themselves (Zajda, 2023a, 2023b). As soon as students demonstrate positive self-concepts, they can tap into their creative energy storage, and become confident learners. This contributes to the overall students' development of a positive and strong sense of self-efficacy, and the feeling that the given learning task can be learned and mastered.

To promote and increase students' engagement in the classroom, we need to consider the role of the family, peers, and teachers. Children acquire their speech patterns, attitudes, knowledge, skills, and values within the family. This represents their acquired cultural and social capital, or necessary knowledge and competencies needed for authentic engagement in the classroom.

In addition to the student's self-concept and cultural identity, I would like to stress the significance of cultural and social capital, with reference to students' engagement and motivation in the classroom (Saha, 2021; Zajda, 2024). Saha (2021), who has written numerous works on this topic, argues that cultural and social capital are closely related, and that 'both are part of a family of concepts having to do with various forms of capital' (Saha, 2021). He refers to Bourdieu (1986), who has written a great deal on the topic. Bourdieu coined the term and introduced the concept of cultural capital in his co-authored work, with Jean-Claude Passeron (Bourdieu & Passeron, 1977. The term 'cultural capital' defined dominant conceptions of what constitute knowledge, knowing, and social value, communicated by 'the symbols, ideas, tastes, and preferences':

J. Zajda, *Engagement, Motivation, and Students' Achievement*, Globalisation, Comparative Education and Policy Research 48,
https://doi.org/10.1007/978-3-031-61613-6_2

> ...the symbols, ideas, tastes, and preferences that can be strategically used as resources in social action. He sees this cultural capital as a 'habitus', an embodied socialized tendency or disposition to act, think, or feel in a particular way. (Bourdieu & Passeron, 1977)

To me, cultural and social capital refers to all the advantages, in terms of knowledge, and behaviour patterns acquired at home. Children learn desirable attitudes and values towards schooling from their parents, who represent major models of socialization. There is no doubt that parents play a significant role in the socialization process of their children, contributing to their acquisition of attitudes towards learning, knowledge, skills, and values.

2.2 Students' Self-concept and Academic Achievement in the Classroom

The 'self-concept' can be defined as the totality of a *complex, organised, and dynamic system of learned beliefs, attitudes, behaviour, and values* that each person holds to be true about his or her identity. Self-concept beliefs are hierarchical, and we have different perceptions of ourselves, depending on what we are discussing i.e. I'm a good athlete but struggling in Mathematics.

The student's self-concept, together with self-esteem and self-efficacy will invariably play a major role in the overall learning process, academic achievement, and motivation to learn and do better. Some of the factors to be considered, when defining the self-concept include:

- Conceptual variations of the definition including what an individual believes he/she is. Self-concept is more about your perception of the kind of person you are.
- It is developed primarily through one's interpretations of praise from others. We reflect in our personalities, and how we think others see us.
- These beliefs are a stabilising mechanism, which also guides future behaviour.
- People get confused between self-concept (totality of self-knowledge) and self-esteem (evaluative component of self-concept)
- Cross-cultural constructs of the self-concepts.

What factors shape and construct the self-concept? As explained above, the self is shaped by several shapers, or major agencies of socialisation. A self-image is a learnt one and is constructed by the descriptions, provided by others. G. H. Mead suggested that the self consists of two interrelated dimensions: the *subject* (the 'I') and the *object* ('me'). The picture one has of '**me**' includes what one knows about one's personality and all other things, which give one's the sense of being who one is. But is it really you or a socially constructed label of wants, needs, and desires? Some researchers have argued that the self has evolved into a global consumerist commodity. Hence, the notion of the commodification of the sel.

2.2.1 The Nexus Between the Self-concept and Academic Achievement

There exists a great deal of research demonstrating the nexus between the self-concept and academic achievement, as demonstrated by numerous researchers, including Guay et al. (2003), Marsh and Martin (2011), Ghazvini (2011), Laryea, et al. (2014), Pegalajar-Palomino (2017), Zajda (2023a, 2023b, 2023c), and others. Earlier, Guay et al. (2003) tested theoretical and developmental models of the causal ordering between academic self-concept and academic achievement. Participants in their study consisted of students in Years 2, 3, and 4 from 10 elementary schools. Their structural equation model for the total sample had proven a reciprocal-effects model, demonstrating that 'achievement has an effect on self-concept' and consequently academic self-concept effected achievement (Guay et al., 2003, p. 124). Similarly, Marsh & Martin (2011) in researching academic self-concept and academic achievement discovered the link between academic self-concept and achievement. Their findings demonstrated that increases in academic self-concept led to increases in subsequent academic achievement and other desirable educational outcomes. Their research findings confirmed that not only is self-concept an important outcome variable in itself, it also plays a central role in 'affecting other desirable educational outcomes' (Marsh & Martin, 2011, p. 59). In another study, Ghazvini (2011) examined the relationship between the academic self-concept and academic performance among 363 students from 10 high schools. The research finding demonstrated a 'close relationship between academic self-concept and measures of academic performance' (Ghazvini, 2011). It was also found that academic self-concept strongly predicted general performance in literature and mathematics. Furthermore, academic self-concept is normally enhanced by student's self-regulated learning skills and strategies. Self-regulated learning (SRL) is a central conceptual framework for understanding the cognitive, motivational, socio-cultural, and emotional aspects of learning (Panadero, 2017).

Woolfolk & Margetts (2019) argued that students' academic achievement was determined not only by intelligence and skills but also by 'how motivated one is to achieve the outcome' (p. 348). Woolfolk & Margetts (2019) also referred to Russell et al. (2005) to explain how students' engagement in the classroom can be broken down into three interdependent forms: behavioural, emotional, and cognitive engagements. Overall, engagement and motivational theories highlight the positive impact of motivation and engagement on students' academic achievement, self-confidence, and independence as learners. They remind teachers to recognise the range of student needs, cultural diversity, and students' physical and personal well-being, as well as students' perception of the links between effort and success. Factors for creating a positive and engaging motivational atmosphere include:

1. Students' positive self-esteem,
2. Engaging learning climate,
3. Positive reinforcement,
4. Inclusive classroom pedagogy,

5. Promoting positive relationships in the classroom,
6. Working in co-operative and collaborative groups,
7. High academic expectations,
8. Teachers' continuing support and respect for all students,
9. Classroom discipline, promoting engagement,
10. Teacher's self-efficacy, and
11. Teachers' use of constructivist pedagogies, to improve learning (see also Zajda, 2023a, 2023b).

This is most relevant to students' self-concept, self-esteem and self-efficacy and resultant engagement in schools, and their evolving self-concepts. The idea of belonging in the classroom is undoubtedly influenced by one's identity and self-concept. When students display positive self-concepts, they are likely to be engaged and motivated to learn. Recent research has demonstrated that some students' disengagement from learning, was due to negative self-esteem, not belonging, and being ignored by their teachers.

Students need to be 'engaged, motivated, willing to learn new things, and feel they can succeed'. (OECD, 2023). The level of students' engagement in the classroom intersects four major areas: behavioural, cognitive, social cognitive, and affective, or emotional aspects. In addition, students' engagement is also influenced by major agencies of socialization, including the family, peers, teachers, the neighbourhood, and the media. The influence of these major agencies of socialization were initially developed in Bronfenbrenner's (1979) bioecological model. It suggested that an individual's social and cultural development is influenced by a series of interconnected environmental systems, ranging from the immediate surroundings, which include the family, the peers, and teachers, to larger societal structures, such as culture and the media (Bronfenbrenner, 1979, 2005). Bandura's (1977) social learning theory, combined with Bronfenbrenner's (1979) bioecological model offer a better understanding of the factors affecting students' engagement in the classroom. Bandura emphasised the importance of social learning from role models. He also argued that students' self-efficacy played a significant part in students' engagement. Bandura (1986), using his social learning theory and his self-efficacy construct, proposed that motivation, or a lack thereof, was the result of an individual's self-efficacy related to a specific task. Bandura went on to define self-efficacy as the beliefs we have about ourselves that cause us to make choices, put forth effort, and persist in the face of difficulty. Earlier, the OECD (2009) report, *Creating effective teaching and learning environments*, analysed some of the key factors in developing motivational atmosphere and effective learning environments for all students. These factors included classroom disciplinary climate, and teachers' self-efficacy.

Research findings confirm that student engagement and motivation represent the most significant factor in all successful learning outcomes and academic achievement in schools (Marinak & Gambrell, 2010; Souders, 2020; Steinmayr et al. 2019; Zajda, 2023a). Steinmayr et al. (2019) argued that achievement motivation is not a single construct, and includes such variables as "ability self-concepts, task values, goals, and achievement motives".

The few existing studies that investigated diverse motivational constructs as predictors of school students' academic achievement above and beyond students' cognitive abilities and prior achievement showed that most motivational constructs predicted academic achievement beyond intelligence and that students' ability self-concepts and task values are more powerful in predicting their achievement than goals and achievement motives (Steinmayr et al., 2019).

2.2.2 *The Self-concept and Classroom Implications*

Do students' academic self-beliefs determine their academic achievement, or does academic achievement determine the self-beliefs? (Herrera et al., 2020). There are at least two types of motivation researchers: self-enhancement researchers, and skill-development researchers. Self-enhancement researchers believe that self-concept beliefs are a primary cause of student achievement (we do well because we feel good). Hence, fostering students' **self-esteem** should be number one priority in the classroom. Whereas skill-development researchers argue that **self-concept** beliefs are a consequence rather than a cause of academic achievement (we feel good because we do well) therefore focusing on academic competence is more useful than focusing on self-beliefs. It has been impossible so far to determine which is right, as experiments and research in this area is difficult. Some researchers currently support the idea that *both* self-belief and self-efficacy and achievement have reciprocal influences on student motivation. One could argue that both **self-concept** and **self-efficacy**, like the status and the role, are the two sides of the coin.

In addition to the student's self-concept, and engagement in the classroom, we also need to think of time, place, school's location, and country. Students globally, depending on where they are located and how they are shaped by major agencies of socialisation, are likely to display different attitudes, values, and behaviour patterns towards schooling. If you can imagine for one moment, a Brunerian spiral curriculum, as well as Bronfenbrenner's (1995) bioecological model, as concept maps, you can place the student's self at the centre of this dynamic and pulsating spiral. Each level of the spiral will contain major agencies of socialisation in the following descending order: the family, the peers, the neighbourhood, the school, teachers, the media, and the community.

2.3 Students' Cultural Identity and Engagement in the Classroom

The term 'identity' became a key word already in the 1950s, when Carl Rogers (1961), a noted humanistic psychologist, used the term to study the self-concept. In addition, Eric Erickson (1950), a prominent psychoanalyst, used the term to study adolescent personality and identity crises. Erikson, in his influential book *Childhood and Society* (1950), used a more holistic notion of 'national identities', which was his preferred term. Since then, there has been an incredible proliferation of the use of the term, across various disciplines and theoretical perspectives, referring to cultural identity, ethnic identity, racial identity, religious identity, sexual identity, and gender identity, institutional identity, interests' identity tribal identity, passport identity (as part of the documentation identity), identity credit cards, and identity politics, to name a few.

To simplify major and prolific discourses of cultural identity, I propose to delineate between global perspectives and cultural perspectives of identity. A global perspective of identity was first used by Comenius (1592–1670), when he wrote that 'we are all citizens of one world':

> We are all citizens of one world; we are all of one blood. To hate a man because he was born in another country, because he speaks a different language, or because he takes a different view on this subject or that, is a great folly. Desist I implore you, for we are all equally human...Let us have but one end in view, the welfare of humanity. (Comenius, 1649/1907)

The idea of modern global identities has been advanced in the last two decades by some researchers like Grewal and Kaplan (2001), Tomasik and Silbereisen (2011), Gensini and Triandafyllidou (2019), Rapoport (2021), Katzarska-Miller and Reysen (2022), Grimalda et al. (2023), Zajda (2023c) and many others. In numerous countries around the world, our approaches to active citizenship education, in attempting to 'reconstruct' our new *global* and national identity, are based on advancing the continuing and genuine celebration of diversity and difference, of multicultural citizenship, and of global citizenship. (Zajda & Rapoport, 2024). Due to forces of globalisation, many individuals around the world develop multiple identities, combines influences of the local culture with global influences, and ITCs. Therefore, in addition to their local identity, individuals are compelled to develop a global identity, which includes new lifestyles, based on consumerism, needs and desires, and producing the consumerist identity, and commodification of the self. Commodification of the self is based on the idea, that individuals, influenced by the media, and the ICTs, change and reconstruct their personal, social, and economic identities and lives, their needs, and desires, reflecting the impact of global economy, and the market.

A cultural perspective of identity, on the other hand, refers to local identities, defined by a particular culture, language, religion, values, and location (Zajda, 2018; Zajda & Majhanovich, 2023). Within many local communities there is a widespread consensus on what characterises their local identity. Language is intrinsically connected to personal, national, and ethnic identity.

There is no doubt that student's cultural identity, in terms of attitudes, beliefs, values, languages and practices, also affects engagement, motivation, learning and academic achievement, both locally and globally (Altugan, 2015; Ligorio, 2010; McDonald, 2007; Rodriguez et al. 2004; Zajda, 2023; Zajda & Majhanovich, 2021). Altugan (2015) argued that the identity of learners affects their motivation and concluded that cultural identity has an 'important effect on learning':

> The researcher has experienced different attitudes of learners, who seem to have different cultural identity, like one learner tried to marginalize while the other highly valued learning and have been interested in to find out if there is a link between their motivation of learning and their cultural identity. Depending on the findings, it is clear that cultural identity is an important effect on learning and should be taken into consideration while teaching and learning. (Altugan, 2015)

Rodriguez et al. (2004) also analysed the nexus between identity and academic achievement. Their research study focused on Year 10 students and the development of their academic identity and cultural awareness through the implementation of culturally responsive teaching practices. Similarly, Ligorio (2010) in her dialogical relationship between identity and learning research, argued that it is necessary to study the effects of the relationship between learning and identity.

With reference to students' self-concept and academic achievement, Steinmayr et al. (2019) concluded that students' ability self-concepts, and task values were the most important motivational predictors of students' academic achievement:

Students' ability self-concept turned out to be the most important motivational predictor of students' grades above and beyond differences in their intelligence and prior grades, even when all predictors were assessed domain-specifically (Steinmayr et al., 2019).

Finally, for students to be effectively engaged, and achieve in the classroom, one needs to think of the learner's age, stages of cognitive, social, emotional and psycho-motor development, self-efficacy, cultural background, the existing level of emotional maturity, and internal needs, desires, and rewards. Performing students need to set for themselves personally challenging, but realistic, and achievable goals, by means of their self-regulated strategies, and focus more on the task itself, rather than the grade. The amount of time spent on engagement in the classroom, and the quality of students' engagement affects their learning and academic achievement (Whelan, 2019). It is essential to engage, empower, motivate, and educate students so they can adapt, and improve in academic achievement, and become lifelong learners. Therefore, engaged, and highly motivated students are likely to strive to become independent learners, and by means of their acquired self-regulated strategies, will take active responsibility of their own learning to reach their full potential.

2.4 The Influence of Family, School, and Peers on Students' Engagement

Research findings related to students' engagement suggests that family, school, and peers, play a significant role. These three major agencies of socialization, discussed in Bronfenbrenner's student microsystem, are based on his globally influential bioecological model. To this, we can add the nature and the quality of teacher-student relationships, students' social and emotional characteristics, together with students' learning and thinking abilities, or cognitive aspect of learning, individual personality differences, and behavior.

2.4.1 The Influence of the Family in Developing Children's Thinking Skills and Education

Parents represent the first major socialization agency. As such, their role in the overall socialization process, is most significant in every area, involving cultivation of desirable attitudes towards learning, knowledge, skills, values, and acceptable behaviour. Some, parents, depending on their level of education, learn and develop a rich learning environment, with objects such as toys and children's books. Some parents spend a great deal of time reading to their children their favourite children's stories. Parents, who can play a musical instrument, or possessing other skills, such as swimming, skiing and gymnastics, as significant role models, have the power to be able to pass on these skills to their children. Here is my case study example. My son learned to play the violin and the piano, when he was six, and in his year 12, he was playing the violin in the school orchestra. He has two daughters, aged 12 and 10, and both play the piano, since they were six-year-olds. This is how it happen. One year, my wife and I, bought them a piano, as a Christmas present. The girls were very excited, when the opened their present and saw it. They immediately wanted to learn to play the piano. First the older girl was learning to play the piano, and her sister, who was watching intensely, also wanted to learn the piano. I am certain that there are many other similar examples of musical parents, encouraging their children to learn a musical instrument.

Parents, in partnership with teachers and schools, can also promote children's increased levels of engagement, in cognitive, social, emotional, and behavioural areas, influencing education, and learning new knowledge, and skills. In this way, they can help their children to be engaged in the classroom and be successful in completing class work. By showing interest in their children's schoolwork, and helping them, as needed, to complete their school's work at home, parents can be effective in improving their children's attitudes, learning and performance. Parents become, in one sense, unpaid tutors.

2.4.2 The Influence of the School Environment

Research has demonstrated that the school environment plays a significant in contributing to student engagement. Here, I want to introduce the image and the power of performance culture and performing schools, both locally and globally. We are all aware of the ubiquitous presence of the constructs of performance culture and performing schools. As I have argued earlier in my works, performance culture affecting societies and education, dictates the structure and content of economic competitiveness, competing ideologies, academic standards, and 'global monitoring of educational quality and standards' (Zajda, 2023). Current education and policy reforms globally, influenced by OECD and its PISA surveys, target academic standards, education quality and global competitiveness, in particular standards-driven and outcomes-defined standards in education.

Both the OECD and the European Union tend to base their education policies for the future, by being guided by the imperatives of the Global Educational Reform Movement (GERM). Sahlberg (2016) writes that GERM emerged since 'the 1980s and has increasingly become adopted as an educational reform orthodoxy within many education systems throughout the world, including in the U.S., England, Australia, and some transition countries':

> Tellingly, GERM is often promoted through the interests of international development agencies and private enterprises through their interventions in national education reforms and policy formulation. (Sahlberg, 2016)

The common aspects of education reforms globally, according to Sahlberg (2016), are characterised by the following five trends:

1. 'Standardization of education
2. Focus on core subjects (mainly literacy and numeracy)
3. The search for low-risk ways to reach potential goals (minimizing experimentation)
4. Use of corporate management models (borrowed from business world)
5. Test-based accountability policies to improve academic achievement'. (Sahlberg, 2016)

Similarly, Lewis et al. (2019), and Paraide et al. (2023), when examining both local and global impacts of standards-based reforms (SBR), comment critically on the global imperatives of improving standards in students' academic achievement. Lewis et al. (2019) called this push a new form of neo-colonialism, and Paraide, et al. (2023), were concerned with a '*global techno-scientific form*' of standards-based reforms globally. Paraide et al. (2023) argue that standards-based reforms, using techno-scientific rationality, tended to legitimize uncritically the nature and the context of on-going education reforms:

> The global form of SBRs thus represents the logics by which policymakers may attempt to align and create commonality across systems in the search for standardisation, even if this can never be fully realised in practice. (Paraide, et al. 2023)

All schools are affected by *standards-driven and outcomes-defined education policies*. In view of this, schools increasingly market themselves as 'performing schools', to attract students and parents alike. Most parents are aware of the existence of the schools' league tables, listing top 100 performing schools in each city, or state. Parents, informed by this information, flock to performing school areas, to enrol their children.

2.4.3 *The Influence of the Peers*

Peers play important roles in children's lives. Some children develop entrenched problems with peer relationships, in terms of 'loneliness, bullying and victimisation' (Hay et al., 2004). Children with 'good peer- relations are mentally healthy and adapt well, whereas children who do not have good peer- relations are more prone to problems in those areas. Put in another way, children who are mentally and behaviourally healthy are more likely to have good peer relationships' (Shin et al., 2016).

Pepler & Bierman (2018) in their report 'With a little help from my friends: The importance of peer relationships for social-emotional development', argued that 'positive peer relationships make critical contributions to healthy social-emotional development' and that 'children benefit from the social and emotional support that friends offer, and they learn important social skills by interacting with peers':

> All children experience occasional social stressors and peer conflicts, and 10 to 15 percent experience serious and chronic peer difficulties, including rejection, social exclusion, and victimization…Making and keeping friends, and dealing with peer group dynamics, requires both personal skills (e.g., understanding and managing one's feelings, controlling one's impulses) and interpersonal skills (e.g., understanding others, communicating effectively, negotiating and problem-solving). Interacting with peers helps to build these skills (All children experience occasional social stressors and peer conflicts, and 10 to 15 percent experience serious and chronic peer difficulties, including rejection, social exclusion, and victimization. (Pepler & Bierman, 2018)

Peer relationships in the classroom play a significant role in each student's ongoing cognitive, social, emotional, and behavioural development. Peer influence, power, and pressure in the classroom can be both positive and negative. It is positive when students form good friendship networks, and respect, and like one another. It can be negative peer pressure, when some students, 'choose to try things they normally wouldn't be interested in, like smoking or behaving in antisocial ways'. Such peer pressure and influence might result in teenagers:

- 'Choosing the same clothes, hairstyle or jewellery as their friends
- listening to the same music or watching the same TV shows as their friends
- changing the way they talk or the words they use' (Raising children network, 2021).

Effective and peer relationships can play a key role for a particular student's values development. Benish-Weisman et al. (2022) in their study 'The contribution of peer values to children's values and behaviour', based on longitudinal data on children's values from 15,008 children in Grades 3–9, and homeroom teachers' reports about the behaviours of 3476 of these children, discovered that 'peers' values were positively correlated with the strengthening of children's corresponding values' (Benish-Weisman et al. 2022) and that 'girl peers had stronger effects on both girls' and boys' values':

> Moreover, with the exception of self-transcendence values, peer values had an indirect effect on corresponding child behavior, through children's self-endorsed values. Girl peers had stronger effects on both girls' and boys' values. (Benish-Weisman et al. 2022)

2.4.4 *Bullying in Schools*

The recent emergence of cyber-bullying is one of the most painful and disturbing trends affecting peer relationship in schools. One of the threats to students' positive sense of well-being, as noted by OECD (2022d) findings, was the existence of on-going bullying in schools:

> Perhaps the most distressing threat to students' well-being is bullying...can have serious consequences for the victim, the bully and bystanders. PISA highlights a significant prevalence of all forms of bullying. What emerges clearly from the PISA data is that schools must do more to foster an environment of safety, tolerance and respect for children. Anti-bullying programmes must include both training for teachers on how to handle bullying as well as strategies to engage with parents. (OECD, 2022d)

Bullying in schools, both locally and globally, continues to be a significant factor affecting the climate of inclusive environments in schools (Armitage, 2021; Gokkaya & Sutcu, 2018; Mishna, 2012; Muijs, 2017; OECD, 2022a; PISA, 2018c; Rigby, 2007; Slee, 2016; Zajda, 2022a). Bullying, as described by Thiele (2018), is a form of behavioural, social and physical acts of aggression. Bullying can be defined as an undesirable form of behaviour, widely prevalent and increasing within primary and secondary schools (Rigby, 2007). Bullying involves repeated aggressive behaviour acts, which can manifest itself as both psychological and physical acts, against a 'less' powerful person, by a more powerful person and groups in schools (Rigby, 2007).

Bullying can become a serious health issue for individuals experiencing various forms of bullying in schools. Armitage (2021) in 'Bullying in children: impact on child health', wrote that bullying in childhood is a 'major public health problem that increases the risk of poor health, social and educational outcomes in childhood and adolescence' (Armitage, 2021). Armitage (2021) also commented on the nature and extent of cyberbullying in schools. Cyberbullying, according to Armitage (2021), is a 'relatively new type of bullying in addition to the traditional forms of direct physical, direct verbal and indirect bullying':

> The majority of victims of cyberbullying are also victims of traditional bullying, meaning cyberbullying creates very few additional victims. Overall, adverse mental health outcomes due to bullying in childhood most severely impact on bully–victims. Bullying prevention is vital for the achievement of the Sustainable Development Goals, with whole-school cooperative learning interventions having the strongest evidence base for successful outcomes. (Armitage, 2021)

Bullying in schools, as an on-going negative phenomenon impacting on some students, represents a serious threat to students' happiness, well-being, their mental health, and safety. According to PISA (2018c), bullying results in 'emotional long-term consequences for students':

> This violent behaviour can have severe physical and emotional long-term consequences for students, which is why teachers, parents, policy makers and the media are increasingly drawing attention to bullying and trying to find ways to tackle it. (PISA, 2018c)

Bullying in schools is totally unacceptable as it breaks numerous local and international conventions on human right and social justice.

2.5 Conclusion

The above analyses current research and knowledge in the use of engagement strategies in the classroom to motivate students to improve their levels of engagement, motivation, well-being, self-esteem, and self-efficacy. It examines the role of engagement impacting on students, schools, and pedagogy, both locally and globally. It also discusses the influences of students' cultural identities on engagement in the classroom, as well as the significance of the family, the school environment, and peers, and bullying in schools, as a global phenomenon.

Chapter 3
Models of Inclusive Classrooms in Promoting Motivation and Performance

3.1 Inclusive Classrooms

Over the last six decades we have acquired a significant amount of informed knowledge on the nature and context of effective learning environments in schools, globally, with reference to the student's identity, the self, motivation, performance, education quality outcomes, and some of the key factors affecting the students' engagement, and their academic achievement. These are all relevant for implementing effective and positive environments in inclusive education (Zajda, 2023a, p. 17).

To me, the most significant key idea, affecting all aspects of quality learning, and teaching in inclusive schools globally, begins necessarily with the students' *identity*. It includes students' specific self-concept, self-esteem, self-efficacy, their well-being, their sense of belonging, and their active engagement, and motivational strategies.

The OECD's longstanding programme of work on Effective Learning Environments (ELE) is significant in providing research-informed knowledge of factors defining effective learning environments. The Learning Environments Evaluation Programme (LEEP) was launched by OECD in 2013, to develop instruments and analysis of how the physical learning environment impacts learning through the continuous development and implementation of the *OECD School User Survey: Improving Learning Spaces Together*. OECD (2022c) was particularly focused on how learning environments affect improved education, health, social dimensions, and students' well-being outcomes.

One of the most significant factors defining the nature of highly effective learning environments in inclusive schools is the quality and quantity of student–teacher interactions in the classroom. As soon as students enter a new grade (e.g. Year 6), they are full of anticipation and anxieties, hoping to get kind and good teachers, who will be nice to them and appreciate them and inspire them to do their best. I have two granddaughters, aged 10 and 12, who, when they completed their classes, were very anxious to know ahead who will be teaching them in the new classes. (Zajda,

J. Zajda, *Engagement, Motivation, and Students' Achievement*, Globalisation, Comparative Education and Policy Research 48,
https://doi.org/10.1007/978-3-031-61613-6_3

2023a, p. 17). They were immensely relieved when they found that they will have nice, caring, warm, and good teachers.

Apart from the quality of student–teacher relationships and interactions in the classroom, there are other factors contributing to effective learning environments in the classroom. They also include students' expectations, the nature of classroom discussions, teacher's assessment and feedback, reciprocal learning, or questioning, clarifying, and summarising ideas, students' use of metacognitive strategies, and study skills. Hattie and Yates (2013) in their paper *Understanding Learning: Lessons for learning, teaching and research* gave the highest ratings to students' expectations, followed by classroom discussions, and reciprocal learning.

I now want to focus on the relevance of students' identities in the inclusive classroom, and the role of the self-concept, affecting students' cognitive, emotional, social, and psycho-motor domains. In addition to the student's self-concept, we also need to think of time, place, school's location, and country. Students globally, depending on where they are located and how they are shaped by major agencies of socialisation, are likely to display different attitudes, beliefs, values, and behaviour patterns towards schooling and academic achievement. If you can imagine for one moment a spiral curriculum, as a concept map, you can place the student's self at the centre of this dynamic and pulsating spiral. Each level of the spiral will contain major agencies of socialisation in the following descending order: the family, the peers, the neighbourhood, the school, teachers, the media, and the community.

3.2 The Changing Nature of Identity in the Global Age

Bostrom and Sandberg (2011), in their report, *The future of identity*, discuss and analyse various types of identities, ranging from personal identity, a narrative identity, social identity, to identities shaped by technology.

3.2.1 Multiple Identities

Back in the 1980s, postmodernist discourses reaffirmed the notion of multiple identities, created by a variety of social and technological interactions (Berzonsky, 2005; Dunn, 1998; Powell, 1997; Rattansi & Phoenix, 1997). Berzonsky (2005), like Powell (1997), and Rattansi & Phoenix, 1997) captured the notion of the multi self, when he argued, that identity was dynamic, multiplistic, relativistic, context-specific, and fragmented (Berzonsky, 2005). Earlier, Rattansi and Phoenix (1997) argued, using his theory of postmodernism, that identity was characterised by being decentred, dynamic, multiplistic, context specific, relativistic, fluid, and fragmented. In postmodernist discourses there existed a consensus of multiple identities, propelled by advances in ICTs.

There is no doubt that the power, and ubiquitous presence of information and communication technologies (ICTs) globally, have shaped the nature and context of personal identities (Bostrom & Sandberg, 2011; Davis, 2016; Granic et al., 2020; Hopkins, 2019; Mallela, 2018; Manago, 2014; Monfil, 2022; Nissenbaum, 2009; Zajda & Gibbs, 2009). It has resulted in the formation of multiple identities, and proliferation of identities online and offline. (Zajda, 2023, p. 17). There are numerous examples of this, including our use of online identities, with distinct user accounts and online persona on such platforms as a Facebook, PayPal, and Tik Tok, WhatsApp, to name a few. However, the overall effects of the ICTs on our identities, especially on our emotions, feelings, social interactions, and self-esteem, have not been fully researched.

3.2.2 Identity in the Digital Age

Davis (2016) in her chapter 'Identity Theory in a Digital Age' examined critically how social media platforms influence social media users and their identities, identity verification and the concept of multiple identities. Davis (2016) points out that those social media platforms affect the users' identities, in terms their 'identity verification processes', defining 'self-worth, self-efficacy and authenticity' in the nexus between 'digitally mediated interaction and psychological well-being' (Davis, 2016). According to Tatyana Hopkins (2019), the internet has shaped and changed people's social identities:

> The internet has not revolutionized the way people shape their identities, instead the digital age has only shifted the existing and understood building blocks on which people develop their sense of self and belonging, as argued by Eli Gottlieb, Jerusalem, a visiting scholar… he found that teens are spending less time in-person time with their friends and up to nine hours a day on average with electronic devices. (Hopkins, 2019)

Similarly, Mallela (2018) in 'Identity in the digital age: our transitioning sense of self' writes that. The 'biggest triumph of the digital age is the transference of our relationships to the digital space', and that one's social identity is now increasingly located in digital platforms and a 'significant part of our sense of self has already transitioned to our digital identity':

> This is not merely a mental transition but our bodies are online too with our pictures, voices and locations all present through an interconnected set of social platforms. So we construct our relationships based on the rules of the digital space, which places a cultural premium on broadcasting our lives…. An indicator that a significant part of *our sense of self* has already transitioned to our digital identity and future technological push is directed towards making this transition complete. (Mallela, 2018).

Granic et al. (2020), in their article 'Beyond Screen Time: Identity Development in the Digital Age', examine the nature of the process, associated with a global transition to digital screens, and suggest that adolescents live in a 'hybrid reality':

> We are in the midst of a global transition in which digital 'screens' are no longer simply entertainment devices and distractions; rather, adolescents are currently living in a hybrid reality that links digital spaces to offline contexts. Yet, psychological scientists studying the mental health impact of digital experiences largely focus on correlations with 'screen time', leading to oversimplified and atheoretical conclusions. (Granic et al., 2020)

The authors proposed their *functional* approach to studying digital screens, adolescent mental health in the digital age:

> ...one that examines *why* and *how* digital media affect adolescent development. Specifically, we suggest that understanding identity development—the core developmental task of adolescence—can help pinpoint the digital experiences that contribute to healthy versus problematic mental health outcomes. (Granic et al., 2020)

Furthermore, Monfil (2022), in 'Identity in the digital age', argues that an improvement in ICTs has contributed to the rise of biometric data.

As our technology has improved, many systems have begun replacing the signature with biometric data. Biometric data are biological measurements that can be used to identify individuals, including fingerprints, retinal scans, or facial recognition. In theory, biometric data is the perfect way to define and identify each unique individual (Monfil, 2022).

The construct of identity in the digital age, as demonstrated above, represents a complex new phenomenon, redefining our evolving identity, both on-screen and off-screen. It impacts on individuals' emotions, feelings, aspirations, mental health, and well-being. One of the effects of this is the rise in cyberbullying, and globally, one in three children had been bullied in the past 30 days (PISA, 2018c). Students, who have experienced cyberbullying, tend to be also victims of traditional bullying in schools.

Overall, adverse mental health outcomes due to bullying in childhood most severely impact on bully–victims. (PISA, 2018c). In the USA, some 20% of students, aged 12–18 experienced bullying in schools. Further 15% were bullied online or by text, and some 15% experienced cyberbullying during the last 12 months (Facts about Bullying, 2021). There is no doubt, that the internet has affected the way people shape and construct their identities, especially on digital screens. Instead of one singular social identity, defined and found in educational psychology textbooks, digital age has created opportunities for multiple dimensions of our sense of self.

3.2.3 *The Individual's Self-concept*

The individual's identity, together with self-concept, self-esteem and self-efficacy will invariably play a major role in the overall learning process, academic achievement, and motivation to learn and do better. The self-concept can be defined as the totality of a *complex, organised, and dynamic system of learned beliefs, attitudes, values, and opinions* that each person holds to be true about his or her identity. Self-concept beliefs are hierarchical, and we have different perceptions of ourselves, depending on what we do.

What factors shape and construct the self-concept? As explained above, the self is constructed by many shapers, or major agencies of socialisation. A self-image is a learnt one, and is constructed by the descriptions provided by others. G. H. Mead suggested that the self consists of two interrelated dimensions: the *subject* (the 'I') and the *object* ('me'). The picture one has of **'me'** includes what one knows about one's personality and all other things, which give one's the sense of being who one is. But is it really you, or is it a socially constructed label of wants, needs, and desires? Some researchers have argued that the self has evolved into a global consumerist commodity. Hence, the notion of the commodification of the self, which has been researched by numerous scholars globally (Davis, 2003; Silva, 2021; Zajda, 1988).

3.3 Models of Inclusive Classrooms

Guided by recent research findings on major types of pedagogies, I want to examine the following 5 models of inclusive classrooms:

- the constructivist approach,
- the collaborative approach,
- the reflective approach,
- the integrative approach, and
- the inquiry-based approach.

3.3.1 Constructivist Pedagogy in Inclusive Classrooms

One of the most popular pedagogies used in inclusive classroom is constructivist pedagogy, especially both cognitive and social constructivist pedagogies, which emphasize the idea that knowledge is actively constructed by the learner. Constructivism as a view of learning, maintains that each person, using perception, and thinking, creates meaningful knowledge and interpretations of the world. In explaining constructivists' theory Arends (1998) asserted, like other researchers, that constructivist theory of learning refers to individual's cognitive construction of meaning through experience. Richardson (2003) argued that constructivism is a 'theory of learning or meaning making' (Richardson, 2003). This meaning making process takes place during an interaction between what individuals already know and new knowledge. Shor (1992), also defined constructivism as a way of building knowledge about self, school, everyday experience, and society, through reflection and meaning making (Shor, 1992). The three principles of constructivist learning are:

- Learners are **active participants** in their learning, and learning by doing, or experiential learning is central to constructivist leaning in practice (Howe & Berv, 2000)

- Learners are **self-regulated** and they construct and monitor their learning, where meta-cognition plays an important role in meaningful learning.
- **Social interactions** is essential for meaningful learning.

Brooks and Brooks (1993) also stressed that constructivism is a theory about knowledge and learning. It emphasises how knowledge is constructed, as the result of a person's interaction in the world, either individually or with others (Oldfather et al., 1999; Packer & Goicoechea, 2000; Piaget, 1972; Thompson, 2000). Richardson (2003), however, argued that the view of constructivism as a *learning theory* has 'guided most of the developments of constructivist pedagogy' (Richardson, 2003, p. 1624).

In constructivist learning, students, when confronted with new learning tasks, are actively engaged in the meaning-making process, by deciphering and constructing their own interpretation and knowledge of the world. The concept of meaning making was initially developed and explained by Postman and Weingartner (1969) as a dynamic and dialogical process, where the focus is on the individuality and the uniqueness of the meaning maker (p. 94).

Constructivism focuses on the learner's constructing meaning from input, by processing it through cognitive structures. Implicit in constructivist views of learning is the idea that an effective learner actively monitors his or her learning and the meaning-making process, where metacognitive skills and reflection play an important role. Constructivists view learning as dependent on the degree to which learners can activate existing cognitive structures and construct new ones. Constructivist pedagogy of learning and teaching emphasizes that there are perceptual and cognitive differences in the way people perceive things and how they *form ideas* related to the linguistic, visual, logical, interpersonal, intrapersonal, environmental, and existentialist factors, as discussed in Gardner's theory of multiple intelligence (Gardner, 1993, 1999).

Constructivist pedagogy is based on the belief that *meaningful* learning occurs when learners are actively involved in a process of meaning-making and knowledge construction, rather than passively receiving and memorizing information (rote-learning). Learners become the meaning-makers, as they attempt to understand new ideas. As such, constructivist teaching is likely to promote critical thinking and create intrinsically-motivated and autonomous learners. Matthews (2000, p. 17) identified some 17 different forms of constructivism in education, and he also mentioned three major constructivist traditions: philosophical, sociological, and educational. For him, sociological or social constructivism considers '...growth of science and changes in its theories and philosophical commitments are interpreted in terms of changing social conditions and interests' (Matthews, 2000, p. 169). In addition, Phillips (2000) described two major types of constructivism: social constructivism and psychological constructivism, or cognitive constructivism. Maypole and Davies (2001), when analysing students' perceptions of constructivist learning in a community college American history course, were able to demonstrate that students 'thought more critically and independently, they developed cognitively and affectively, and they enjoyed the learning process' (Maypole & Davies, 2001). More recently, Akpan and

Beard (2016) discussed classroom teaching, using constructivist teaching strategies to enhance academic outcomes of students with special needs.

Cognitive constructivism (or psychological constructivism) draws on earlier research of Piaget (1977), Kelly (1991) and others. This approach is informed by developmental or learning theories (cognitive), which suggest that learners actively construct the meaning around concepts they encounter. By contrast, social constructivism draws on Vygotsky (1936), Bruner (1963), Bandura (1963, 1977), Kolb and Fry (1975), Hirtle (1996), Howe and Berv (2000), Kukla (2000) and many other researchers globally.

Social-cultural constructivism, as developed by Lev Vygotsky (1896–1934). Vygotsky's main relevance to constructivism derives from his theories about language and thought, and social interaction. Social constructivism emphasizes the importance of culture and context in understanding what occurs in society and constructing knowledge based on this understanding (Derry, 1999; McMahon, 1997; Watson, 2003). This perspective is closely associated with many contemporary theories; most notably the socio-cultural and developmental theories of Vygotsky, Bruner, and Bandura's social cognitive theory. Social constructivism is based on specific assumptions about reality, knowledge, and learning. Martin and Sugarman (1999), offer a meaningful description of social constructivism, as an approach to both learning and teaching, based on engagement, social interaction, and dialogue:

> We acquire, develop, convey, and confer upon others the symbolic cognitive tools through which we manage our psychological engagement with the world (Martin & Sugarman, 1999, p. 8).

Judith Watson (2003) uses examples from classroom practice to demonstrate how, within a framework of social constructivism, small changes in teachers' practice can promote effective teaching in pupils of all ages and levels of ability, across the curriculum.

Social constructivism is also based on specific assumptions about reality, knowledge, and learning. To understand and apply models of instruction that are rooted in the perspectives of social constructivists, it is important to know the premises that underlie them, namely the nature of reality, knowledge, and learning:

Reality: Social constructivists believe that reality is constructed through human activity. Members of a society together invent the properties of the world (Kukla, 2000). For the social constructivist, reality cannot be discovered: it does not exist prior to its social invention.

Knowledge: To social constructivists, knowledge is also a human product, and is socially and culturally constructed (Ernest, 1999; Gredler, 1997; Prat & Floden, 1994). Individuals create meaning through their interactions with each other and with the environment they live in.

Learning: Social constructivists view learning as a social process. It does not take place only within an individual, nor is it a passive development of behaviours that are shaped by external forces (McMahon, 1997). Meaningful learning occurs when individuals are engaged in social activities.

These two strands, namely cognitive constructivism, and social constructivism are different in emphasis, but they also share many common perspectives about teaching and learning. Before looking at the differences between cognitive and social constructivists, it might be worthwhile to look at what they have in common. As Richardson (2003) explained, constructivist pedagogy is associated with the creation of classroom environments that are 'grounded in a constructivist theory of learning, with goals that focus on individual students developing deep understandings…' (Richardson, 2003, p. 1627). Richardson also presented five dimensions of constructivism:

1. Attention to the individual and respect for student's background (informed by student-centred classroom pedagogy)
2. Facilitation of group dialogue, to create a consensus on understanding a key idea/topic (focusing on cooperative learning)
3. Introducing knowledge via text, readings, activities and ICT
4. Opportunities for students to engage in constructing their own new knowledge, based on activities
5. Developing student's meta-awareness of their own understanding (Richardson, 2003, p. 1626).

In addition, constructivist pedagogy is also characterised by cooperative/collaborative groups leaning, reflection, metacognition, teacher-initiated teaching of knowledge, skills, thinking, and the use of multi-modal models in learning, together with multidimensional view of knowledge (or *multiple* representations of reality), instead of passive and uncritical knowledge reproduction. To apply meaningfully pedagogical models that are grounded in the philosophy of social constructivists, it is important to know the premises that underlie them.

First, social constructivists believe that *reality* is constructed through human activity. Members of a society together invent the properties of the world (Kukla, 2000). For the social constructivist, reality cannot be discovered: it does not exist prior to its social invention.

Second, to social constructivists, *knowledge* is also a human product, and is socially and culturally constructed (Ernest, 1999). Individuals create meaning through their interactions with each other and with the environment they live in.

Third, social constructivists view *learning* as a social process. It does not take place only within an individual, nor is it a passive development of behaviours that are shaped by external forces. Meaningful learning occurs when individuals are engaged with other in social activities.

3.3.2 The Collaborative Approach in Inclusive Classrooms

The collaborative approach is based on the use of collaborative groups, as part of social constructivism, to promote greater engagement, motivation, and performance.

Collaborative groups and *cooperative learning* refer to a variety of structured classroom management and teaching techniques and grading systems, developed and studied by Aronson, Johnson & Johnson, Kagan, Slavin, and others since the early 1970s. Spencer Kagan in an article in *Educational Leadership* (Dec/Jan 1989/1990) provided an excellent definition of cooperative learning by looking at general structures, which can be applied to any situation. His definition offered an umbrella for the work cooperative learning specialists, including the Johnsons, Slavin, Cooper, Graves and Graves, Millis, etc. It follows below:

> The structural approach to cooperative learning is based on the creation, analysis and systematic application of structures, or content-free ways of organizing social interaction in the classroom. Structures usually involve a series of steps, with proscribed behaviour at each step. An important cornerstone of the approach is the distinction between 'structures' and 'activities'. (Kagan, 1990)

Nelson-LeGall (1992) also captured the nature of cooperative learning, when she stated:

> Learning and understanding are not merely individual processes supported by the social context; rather they are the result of a continuous, dynamic negotiation between the individual and the social setting in which the individual's activity takes place. Both the individual and the social context are active and constructive in producing learning and understanding. (Nelson-LeGall, p. 52)

The notion of cooperative work is broadly defined as two or more people working together for the mutual benefit of all in ways that maximize everyone's learning (Dillenbourg, 1999). It is distinct from individualistic learning and competitive learning, as it highlights the shared benefits, both academic and social. It refers to working towards shared goals and shared successes; and it is assessed on the whole group effort, and group performances of particular tasks (Johnson & Johnson, 2008). While the use of collaborative group work in educational settings is neither original, nor unique to any society, contemporary Western education has been significantly influenced by the study of group dynamics, behaviours, and practices by many education theorists, including Slavin (1986), Brady (2006), Kagan and Kagan (1998), Johnson and Johnson (2008), and others.

General characteristics of cooperative learning include fostering positive interdependence, ensuring that there is individual accountability, the selection of heterogeneous groups, the strong emphasis on academic and social skills, and the range of metacognitive learning opportunities, in which students can reflect on their own performance, their learning journey and their participation in the group (Boyd, 2001).

To emphasize the advantages of collaborative group work, groups are usually referred to as teams, which are well structured. Studies have shown that in well structured cooperative groups, students consistently learn many different subjects better, than students in traditionally structured classrooms.

Cooperative learning also has several psychological and social benefits, such as being exposed to other points-of-view, learning how to cooperate, having more positive feelings about school, students having more positive feelings about themselves and others, and wanting their classmates to do well.

There are hundreds of examples of cooperative structures, and numerous books available to help teachers to incorporate cooperative learning into their classrooms. The most common collaborative groups are called think-pair-share, think-pair-square, jigsaw collaborative groups, and other groups.

- *Think-Pair-Share*

Students think about each question, pair off and discuss the question with a classmate, and share their answers with the class. The concept of think-pair-share was first proposed by Lyman (1981). This is a relatively low-risk and short collaborative learning structure, and is ideally suited for teachers and students who are new to collaborative learning.

- *Think-Pair-Square*

Think-Pair-Square is like Think-Pair-Share. Students first discuss problem-solving strategies in pairs and then in groups of fours. Since problem solving strategies can be complicated, this structure may be more appropriate with experienced collaborative groups.

Example 1 Discuss the meaning of 'To be or not to be, that is the question'.

Think: 'To be or not to be, that is the question' Think for 30 s of this idea…

Pair: Compare your ideas with a partner next to you…

Square: Get together with another pair and discuss it…

Share: What does it mean? (group/class discussion).

As demonstrated above, we use the think-pair-share cooperative learning strategy to begin discussion and then move to groups of four using the think-pair-square method etc. In the classroom, teachers use the think-pair-share, and think-pair-square techniques, to discuss and identify the strategies that each pair (and then each square) has in common.

The perceived benefits of applying collaborative learning principles in teaching programs in schools are varied and range from increased cognitive stimulation, and enhanced critical thinking, to student self-management, and to pro-social skills.

Johnson and Johnson (2008) argued that it promoted higher achievement, both for specific content and general academic skills, and that it increased stimulation of cognitive development. Johnson and Johnson (2008) perceived cooperative grouping as helping to 'focus attention, organise knowledge, set expectations, create mood, ensure cognitive processing and rehearsal, summarize, pre-cue next session and provide closure' (Johnsons & Johnson, 2008, p. 476). Moreover, the higher order thinking processes of analysis, synthesis and evaluative decision-making are more stimulated in social interactions than in reading or passively listening (Borich, 2004, p. 333). The internal structure, length of cooperation, dynamics of interaction and academic aims of the group can ensure active cognitive processing of information (e.g. when working in cooperative groups) and students can gain long term support and assistance for academic progress (e.g. when working in cooperative base groups).

Cooperative group work necessarily engages students in thinking about others. At the entry level, students can identify and articulate perceived similarities and differences, and through consistent practice, students can build more positive peer relationships, and develop trust, and caring among the group members. Teachers' strategies include: How to make meaningful annotated notes, or checklists, when to intervene, and provide help, and ensuring that students are not spoon-fed, and that they are not left to feel frustrated, disengaged, and unmotivated.

Finally, an important stage in the collaborative group working cycle, is the processing and feedback time. To ensure that group work does not become unproductive, unfocused, or unreflective practice, students need enough time to reflect on their work and teachers must have a range of debriefing questions to understand new learning and evaluate further actions to be taken. Collaborative learning techniques are proven successful classroom management techniques, that help to build pro-social skills, create opportunities for developing higher order thinking, and link with constructivist pedagogy, and student-centred learning.

3.3.3 The Reflective Approach

Reflective learning involves thinking about the way one learns. It is looking back at something, an experience, and critically analysing the event. Reflective practice can be defined, according to Linda Finlay (2008). as 'learning through and from experience towards gaining new insights of self and practice' (Finlay, 2008). Melanie Jasper (2003) in her book *Beginning Reflective Practice*, offers many examples of reflective learning and practice.

Reflective approach is most relevant to *metacognition, generic learning*, and *students' self-regulated learning*. Metacognition is often simply defined as 'thinking about thinking'. Metacognition refers to higher order thinking, which involves active control over the cognitive processes engaged in learning. The term 'metacognition' is most often associated with John Flavell (1992). According to Flavell metacognition consists of both metacognitive knowledge and metacognitive experiences, or regulation. Activities such as planning how to approach a given learning task, monitoring comprehension, and evaluating progress toward the completion of a task are metacognitive.

Metacognitive knowledge refers to acquired knowledge about cognitive processes, knowledge that can be used to control cognitive processes. The three basic classroom metacognitive strategies are:

- Connecting new information to former knowledge.
- Selecting thinking strategies deliberately.
- Planning, monitoring, and evaluating thinking processes.

Research shows that metacognitive strategies resulted in increases in learning/academic achievement.

Generic learning, as opposed to surface learning, or rote learning, involves a deeper level of learning, relevant to reflective learning. Self-regulation theory (SRT), on the other hand, is a system of conscious personal management that involves the process of guiding one's own thoughts, behaviours and feelings to learn, remember and perform. Self-regulation, involves controlling one's behaviour, emotions, and thoughts in the pursuit of long-term goals.

Self-regulation theory suggests that there is a process of anchoring and adjusting our performance, both mental and physical in nature, in response to corrective feedback within our social and physical environment. There are four basic self-regulation strategies that all students need to be able to use:

- goal-setting,
- self-monitoring,
- effective use of self-instructions or self-talk, and
- self-reinforcement.

3.3.4 The Integrative Approach

Integrative learning focuses on cross-disciplinary thinking and interconnectedness of different areas of knowledge. An integrative approach combines 'biomedical sciences with social and behavioural sciences by understanding the linkages between social, behavioural, psychological, and biological factors in health' (Mullan Harris, 2010). Veronica Boix Mansilla, cofounder of the Interdisciplinary Studies Project at Project Zero (Harvard), explains 'when [students] can bring together concepts, methods, or languages from two or more disciplines or established areas of expertise in order to explain a phenomenon, solve a problem, create a product, or raise a new question they are demonstrating interdisciplinary understanding' (Boix Mansilla, 2014). Integrative approach, like interdisciplinary knowledge, learning and skills, combines relevant disciplines to generate new knowledge (see also Huber & Hutchings, 2004).

A very good example of the integrative approach, and interdisciplinary knowledge, and understanding, is the use of comparative education research, which focusses on cross-cultural and cross-disciplinary thinking Zajda & Rust, 2021). The strong comparative education heritage of the UNESCO's *International Review of Education* provided the foundation for the journal's extensive treatment of international educational policy over the years. Founded only three years after the establishment of the UNESCO Institute for Education by Walther Merck, its director, the journal sought to maintain the comparative traditions of its predecessor, *Internationale Zeitschrift fur Erziehungswissenschaft*. It aimed to promote *international understanding* and *cooperation*. The 1955 foundation issue Editorial referred to the intention 'to provide an international forum and to promote international exchange of information'. The journal aimed to 'inform readers as to educational theory and practice in various countries… and to explore the extent to which such ideas and activities have elements of validity that transcends national boundaries'. This *IRE* editorial policy emphasis on international issues, international understanding, and comparative education became its trademark for over fifty years. In the early days of UNESCO, education for *international understanding* was a significant policy initiative, and a major focus after World War II. In a later special review issue Fernig & Bowen (1980) commented on the link between international cooperation and education for international understanding in education and policy.

Cross-disciplinary research has demonstrated that critical policy issues and options, in terms of OECD's defined 'strategic challenge' and 'deliverable goals' (OECD 2001, p. 139, see also OECD, 2023) have shifted from the human capital and supply-determined (economic planning models based on enrolments, inputs and outputs, and the market forces) to a multi-dimensional model of policy analysis. The latter, in responding to the power of 'private actors', (Plank & Sykes, 1999, p. 390) remains sensitive to the political and cultural environment of the school and society.

Critical education and policy issues continue, by and large, to remain the same. The 'stubborn issue of inequality' (Coombs, 1982, p. 153), first examined in 1957 (Kandel, 1957, p. 2) is still with us (Jennings 2000, p. 113) and the prospect of widening inequalities in education, in part due to market-oriented schooling, and 'substantial tolerance on inequalities and exclusion' (OECD 2001, p. 126, see also OECD, 2023) are more than real. In 1982 the critical issues in policy directions for the next two decades included:

- 'New internal strategies (more comprehensive, flexible and innovative modes of learning) that took into account the changing and expanding learner needs,
- overcoming 'unacceptable' socio-economic educational disparities and inequalities,
- improving educational quality,
- 'harmonizing *education and culture*', and
- 'international co-operation' in education and policy directions in each country' (Coombs, 1982, pp. 145–157).

3.3.5 The Inquiry-Based Approach

Inquiry-Based Learning (IBL) or Critical Inquiry Approach, involves a consideration of problems of knowledge, skills, and values. Four most important qualities of inquiry are:

- *in-depth knowledge* of subject matter
- *critical thinking*
- *skills* in processing information
- *attitudes/reflections.*

Inquiry occurs when the learner is interested/motivated and creative. Inquiry process is associated with discovery, inductive thinking, critical thinking, and problem-solving.

Inquiry-Based Learning or Inquiry Approach model begins with students' prior knowledge and experience and moves through a deliberate process to extend this knowledge (Vygotskian perspective). In IA model, teachers select and group learning experiences & activities and under the following 6 headings:

- *Tuning in* (framing and focusing questions)
- *Finding out* (locating, organizing and analyzing evidence)
- *Sorting out* (evaluating and reporting findings)
- *Going further*
- *Making conclusions*
- *Taking action.*

Tuning in, involves the following:

- Ensure activities and learning experiences cater for a variety of learning styles.
- activities and learning experiences allow students to demonstrate current knowledge, skills and understanding.
- initial activities and learning experiences include powerful and engaging starting point.

Finding out, involves the following:

- Begin to develop student understanding of particular problems or aspects of the inquiry.
- Initial questions are investigated, students generate and frame new questions.
- Ensure activities and learning experiences allow for different student needs and learning styles.

Sorting out, involves the following:

Ensure activities and learning experiences allow students to demonstrate their understandings in different ways to accommodate personal strengths.

Going further, involves the following:

Going further activities and learning experiences provide students with alternative experiences to gain new insights into the topic. The activities and learning experiences may involve challenging ideas and early conclusions, making choices and undertaking alternative or new finding out experiences.

Making conclusions, involves the following:

This section contains the activities and learning experiences that require students to articulate new understandings, analyse, challenge, and synthesise ideas, answer and refine questions and reflect on their learning. The activities and learning experiences require the use of thinking skills such as 'compare and contrast', consider consequences, summarise, justify, generalise, synthesise, and explain. The learning experiences may involve presentations. Feedback is provided to increase understanding and to allow all students to celebrate their achievements.

Taking action, involves the following:

Students undertake reflection throughout the inquiry sequence or at the completion. Action involves doing something with or about what has been learned. Activities and learning experiences allow students to demonstrate their understandings in different ways to accommodate personal strengths. Activities and learning experiences may be individual, group or part of a whole class demonstration of understanding but allow assessment of individuals.

Guidelines for conducting IA in the classroom

- Locate and devise a topic that captures students' imagination.
- Start with an excursion as an introductory stage to the topic.
- Students are asked to bring notebooks to write the reports.
- Use the QIPE teaching strategy (question, issue, problem, and evaluation).
- Organise IA investigation groups, and give every student an opportunity to be involved with others in IA, and inquiry learning experience.

Advantages of inquiry approach (IA) include:

- *intrinsic* motivation
- *relevance*
- *the use of critical thinking*
- *the use of metacognition*
- *problem-solving skills.*

As above shows, Inquiry-Based Learning (IBL), involves a new acquisition of sets of knowledge, skills, and values. The most important qualities of inquiry for students include developing and using critical thinking, critical literacy, in-depth knowledge of subject matter, skills in processing information, and developing new values and attitudes, as well as reflections.

3.4 Conclusion

As demonstrated above, there are different models of inclusive classrooms in promoting students' engagement, motivation, and performance. The 5 popular and widely used models in inclusive classrooms discussed include the constructivist approach, the collaborative approach, the reflective approach, the integrative approach, and the inquiry-based approach. Key factors in inclusive classroom environment necessarily include the students' identities, and the use of Inquiry-Based Learning (IBL), as a pedagogical strategy for developing students' critical thinking, critical literacy, metacognition, and intrinsic motivation.

Chapter 4
Cultural Identities in the Classroom and Engagement

4.1 The Role of Cultural Identities in the Classroom

Cultural identities play a most significant role in engaging and motivating students in schooling, both locally and globally. I have argued in my books (Zajda, 2021, 2022, 2003) that student's identity is on of key factors in engagement and learning. Student's identity refers to cultural, social, emotional, and behavioural factors. It defines student's self-concept, and self-esteem. How students feel about themselves, and whether they feel that they belong, and feel that they are accepted, defines their classroom interaction and their levels of engagement. Unless students feel good and positive, and are motivated by their teachers, they are not likely to be interested, or committed to learning.

Identity

Identity, as mentioned in Chap. 2 became a key word in the 1950s, when Carl Rogers (1961), a noted humanistic psychologist, used the term to explain his idea of the self-concept.

In psychological terms, according to Tomasik & Silbereisen (2011), *identity* refers to images that we and other have of our identities:

> the image that others have of the unique personality structure of an individual, and on the other, it concerns the understanding of one's own identity, called self-awareness or self-concept. Beyond this personal aspect of identity, there also is its social aspect, which relates the self to the social ecology, be it the family, the peer group, or the macro context. (Tomasik & Silbereisen, 2011)

A modern concept of *global identity* is described as a 'consciousness of an international society or global community transcending national boundaries, without necessarily negating the importance of state, nation, or domestic society (Shinohara, 2004).

J. Zajda, *Engagement, Motivation, and Students' Achievement*, Globalisation, Comparative Education and Policy Research 48,
https://doi.org/10.1007/978-3-031-61613-6_4

Since the 1980s, postructuralist scholars popularized the idea of multiple identities and multiple subjectivities in post-modern research. This represented was a radical paradigm shift from structuralism, which accepted the single core identity. Current research has stressed that the individual is not simply defined by one identity, internalised in one's culture and environment, but many other acquired identities. I want to argue, using sociological terminology of ascribed, achieved and acquired status, that our identities, as affirmed by Bronfenbrenner's bio-ecological model, are both ascribed and constructed identities, which are embedded in our cultures. *Ascribed identities* represent characteristics we are born with, or genetically defined features such as race, ethnicity, and sex. *Achieved identities* refer to gender, occupation, values, professional mobility, power, class, status, and education.

According to Scheuringer (2016) one's identity is 'constructed and formed through contact with other individuals, groups and cultures in one's socio-cultural environment' and that there are 'numerous identities in a society that are already fixed and established' (Scheuringer, 2016).

Global identities, have been shaped by powerful and numerous social, political, economic, and technology-driven forces, resulting in globally driven multiple identities.

Cultural identity refers to local identities, defined by a particular culture, language, religion, values, and location (Zajda, 2022). Within many local communities there is a widespread consensus on what characterises their local identity (Terlouw, 2017). In addition, the construct of cultural identity is associated with a reification of culture, similar to Marx's notion of *reification*, which becomes a defining feature of the dominant discourse on identity (Bauman, 1996). Reification is the process of attributing concrete form to an abstract concept. Reification was used by Marx to describe a form of 'social consciousness in which human relations come to be identified with the physical properties of things, thereby acquiring an appearance of naturalness and inevitability' (Burris, 1988). Using the concept of reification, Marx tried to explain why workers accepted their labour and wages exploitation as natural.

Multiple identities

We all have multiple identities with reference to ethnicity, race, gender, religion, age, and occupation, to mention a few. Sarah Gaither (2019) suggests that research needs to consider 'dual identities' that combine both traditional singular social categories, and other identities.

> Moreover, some past work with adults has shown that people do in fact claim distinct and overlapping identities at different times2026A large amount of research also shows that bicultural individuals and others who have spent time studying abroad in other cultural contexts are more creative problem solvers because they have added experience reconciling their different cultural identities and social norms…. (Gaither (2019)

Similarly, Kulich et al. (2017) confirms the existence of multiple social identities, which differ how they were acquired:

> These multiple social identities differ considerably in the way they are acquired (e.g., inherited or achieved through accomplishments), in their relative stability or malleability, and in

> the value which they assign to the individual (e.g., low vs. high social status). (Kulich et al., 2017)

The authors discuss inherited identities, based on gender, skin colour, class background, etc. and in achieved identities:

> Although inherited and achieved social identities tend to correspond in their value and content over time…identities can differ in status and value, and create distressing experiences which call for a coping strategy in order to increase identity fit… When individuals face conflicting identities in terms of status or value, they use different coping strategies. Individuals may attempt to discard one of the identities, use in turn one or the other, or integrate or fuse both identities. (Kulich et al. 2017)

As shown above, research findings demonstrate the evolving nature of multiple identities, shaped by dominant forces of globalisation, instilling globally defined wants, needs, and desires, as reflected in the commodification of the self, and global consumer identity.

National identity

National identity represents a specific cultural community, whose members are united by common historical memories, values, beliefs, customs, conventions, habits, languages and practices, myths, symbols, and traditions. It denotes such elements as 'historic territory, legal-political community, legal political equality of members, and common civic culture and ideology' (Smith, 1991, p. 11). Smith (1991) argued that 'the underlying sentiments and aspirations that nationalist ideology, nationalist language and symbols evoke' relate to the three main concepts: territory, history and community (Smith, 1991, p. 78; see also Smith, 1995; Smith, 2002). Smith (2007) in his analysis of the impact of globalisation on cultural identity argued that global culture not only cannot replace national culture, but that national identity possesses the capacity to withstand the forces of globalisation (Smith, 2007, p. 30).

The idea of national identity has always been one of the ontological and teleological goals of promoting nationalism, and a defining dimension of the nation-building process. National identity has certain core characteristics, which are emphasized at varying degrees from one nation to the next. As Smith (1991) explained, the six main attributes of ethnic community, as a foundation of national identity, are:

1. a collective proper name
2. a myth of common ancestry
3. shared historical memories
4. one or more differentiating elements of common culture
5. an association with a specific 'homeland'
6. a sense of solidarity for significant sectors of the population (Smith, 1991, p. 21).

Smith (1991) suggested that 'National' identity refers to politico-economic and technological community. In a philosophical, legal, and social theory sense, nation denotes a community of people obeying the same laws and institutions within a given territory' (Smith, 1991, p. 9). Hence, the defining elements of 'national' identity include:

(a) territory, the homeland, or 'historic land'
(b) a community, or patria, a community of laws and institutions with a single political will
(c) citizenship and associated sense of legal equality among the members
(d) common values, mass culture, civic ideology, and traditions (including common historical memories, myths, symbols and traditions (Smith, 1991, pp. 9–11).

Drawing on Smith's (2007) analysis of cultural identity dynamics, Ariely (2019), suggests that globalisation not only fails to create global identity, but intensifies national feelings.

Exploring other types of identities, Zhuojun and Hualing (2014) suggested that national identity is a combination of institutional identity, interest identity, cultural identity and non-national community identity, and that national identity crisis lies in the ineffectiveness of nation states' governance. This is partly true. There are other mitigating factors relevant to national identity crisis, such as the nature of geopolitics, religious conflicts, and unstable capitalist economies legitimizing social inequality. The construction of national identity in the global age, requires a number of social, economic and political reforms, including reforming the political system, accelerating equitable economic transformation, grounded in equality and social justice, and promoting the idea of national culture, in order to 'strengthen value integration and enrich the cultural significance of national identity' (Zhuojun & Hualing, 2014).

However, globalization's effects on national identity are problematic and widely critiqued by numerous researchers. Some researchers argue that globalisation affects national identity in different ways:

> While some regard globalization as undermining national identity and increasing cosmopolitanism, others argue that it works in the opposite direction, possibly even reinforcing national feelings in the form of a backlash—or that it impacts different segments in society in dissimilar ways. (Ariely, 2019)

The problematic nature of globalisation, and its varied cultural, social, and economic influences, together with the multidimensionality of national identity are likely to produce 'the conflicting theoretical perspectives and inconsistency of the empirical findings' (Ariely, 2019).

Global cultural identities

Since the 1980s, two parallel social, political, economic, and technology-driven forces have impacted on the world. On one hand, the ubiquitous processes of globalisation affecting everything are occurring and, on the other, the transformation and reaffirmation of nation-building and cultural identities, both locally and globally, are taking place. Castells (2010) believed that globalisation, with its cultural homogenisation, was a potential threat to local cultures and to specific identities (see also Castells, 2006). This is due to globalisation perceived to be generating a global, cosmopolitan culture, and cultural homogenisation. At the same time, due to dominant political and religious ideologies, some nations wanted to preserve their historically defined identities, based on language, nationality, ethnicity, religion, territory, and other relevant identity-defining characteristics. This has resulted in the local and global cultural identity dichotomy.

One of the most powerful forces of globalisation shaping cultural identities is the ubiquitous presence of information technology, and the mass media. Every facet of culture and identity is defined by mass media and propelled by the ubiquitous presence of information technology. Global marketing of socially desirable commodities, such as clothing, fashion and global brands, perfumes, toys, and the entertaining industry, to name a few, has affected cultural identity. Global marketing affecting the formation of one's cultural identity has manufactured a new consumerist and materialistic culture, of what Rea Zajda (1988) termed it as 'commodification of the self' (Zajda, 1988).

In one major comparative and cross-national investigation, Ariely (2012), testing the relationship between globalization and national identity, and using 149 national samples across 74 countries, wished to discover, whether country level of globalisation impacts on ethnic identity, and whether globalisation moderates between patriotism and ethnic identity. He concluded that globalisation does not reduce national identity, but it does reduce their sense of ethnic identity:

> While the impact of globalization does not erode people's national identification or their sense of nationalism' it seems that it does reduce their ethnic conceptions of membership in the nation. (Ariely, 2012, p. 477)

In another study, Ariely (2019) also tested the nexus between country level of globalisation and its impact on ethnic identity and whether globalisation moderates between patriotism and ethnic identity. (Ariely, 2019). It was demonstrated that ethnic identity levels were lower in the more globalized than the less globalized countries:

> Although ethnic identity levels are lower in the more globalized than the less globalized countries, globalization has no differential effect on the strong and positive link between patriotism and ethnic identity. (Ariely, 2019)

The complexity of globalisation, and its varied cultural, social, and economic influences, together with the multidimensionality of national identity, is likely to produce 'the conflicting theoretical perspectives and inconsistency of the empirical findings' (Ariely, 2019).

4.1.1 Identity Crisis

The concept of identity crisis, which was influenced by the idea of alienation, was discussed by Berman (1991), in his influential book *All that is solid melts into air*. Drawing on Marx's *Communist Manifesto* (1848), Berman (1991) examined the identity crisis confronting various nations during the later part of the nineteenth century:

> All that is solid melts into air all that is holy is profaned, and men at last are forced to face with sober senses the real conditions of their lives... (*Communist Manifesto*, 1848).

Alienation, in a modern sense, was first examined by Émile Durkheim (1893), a French sociologist, in *The Division of Labour in Society* (translated by W.D. Halls. New York: The Free Press, 1984, and originally published in French in 1893). The crisis of materialism and the destruction of everything holy, resulting in the 'aura of holiness suddenly missing', meant that there existed an existentialist crisis and identity crisis. Berman (1991) explains it: 'We cannot understand ourselves in the present until we confront what is absent' (Berman, 1991, p. 89).

The role of language in defining and shaping cultural identity

To begin with, languages symbolise identities and are used to define identities by those who speak those languages. People are also categorised by other people according to the language they speak, and the culture they share. Byram (2013) argued that there is a very strong link 'between language and a sense of belonging to a national group'. One's language and culture affect resultant perception of national identity, and citizenship. A cultural perspective of identity refers to local identities, defined by a particular culture, language, religion, values, and location (Zajda, 2022). Within many local communities there is a widespread consensus on what characterises their local identity.

Language is intrinsically connected to personal, national, and ethnic identity. The case of Canada provides a powerful example of the nexus between language and identity. Ever since the founding of Canada as a nation in 1867 and even prior to that in the Canada Act of 1791, English and French language rights have been acknowledged. It is fair to say that Canadian identity for its citizens involves being a member of a bi-lingual state. Although most Canadians are not in fact bilingual English and French speakers, nevertheless, Canadians accept a bilingual Canada as part of their national reality. A 2012 report from the Office of the Commissioner for Official Languages shows that 72% of Canadians favour bilingualism, and a 2016 Neilsen poll showed that 86% of Canadians believe that the Prime Minister should be bi-lingual. In the latter part of the twentieth century Canadian governments spent a considerable amount of time grappling with issues of bilingualism and forging policies to address concerns (Zajda & Majhanovich, 2021).

The province of Quebec, where the largest number of Francophones resides, has been justifiably concerned about guaranteeing French language rights. Once, about one third the population of Canada, francophones, saw their numbers fall with declining birth rates, and a rise in immigration to Canada. Those immigrants, who settled in Quebec, often favoured English over French, as the official language to be learned, and wanted to have their children educated in English, rather than French. The power of English in a globalized world posed a threat to the maintenance of a solid population of French speakers in Quebec, and elsewhere in Canada. Speaking about the importance of language as part of one's place in the world, Thomas Ricento (2006) observed:

> Language is something most of us take for granted most of the time; it is usually when we discover that our language (or language variety) is different from and perhaps less valued than, the language of others, or that our options are somehow limited either because we

> don't speak/understand a language or language variety…that we begin to pay attention to languages. (p. 21)

The choice of official language in several former USSR states signals how language relates to cultural identity. The Baltic States, Latvia, Lithuania, and Estonia have all declared Latvian, Lithuanian and Estonian respectively as the official language of their post USSR nation eliminating Russian as a possible official language. In some cases, citizenship is contingent upon being fluent in the official language leaving Russian speakers who have resided in these states since before the dissolution of the USSR virtually stateless. This reflects the power of language in the construction of a national cultural identity. Belarus in contrast which identifies more with the Russian culture and traditions has designated both Belarussian and Russian as official languages (Zajda & Majhanovich, 2021).

The Balkan States provide another salient example. When Yugoslavia existed as a federation of the states of Slovenia, Croatia, Serbia, Bosnia-Herzegovina, Montenegro and Macedonia, the official languages were Serbo-Croatian, Slovenian and Macedonian and the languages appeared on the banknotes in both Cyrillic and Roman alphabets. Once Yugoslavia dissolved, the new states declared their official languages as Slovenian, Croatian, Serbian, Bosnian, Macedonian and even in some cases Montenegrin although the language is essentially Serbian and written in Cyrillic. Serbo-Croatian is no longer an accepted language even though except for the Cyrillic and Roman alphabets used (connected to the traditions of the Orthodox or Roman Catholic religions), they are almost identical languages. It is no longer permissible to recognize a language such as Serbo-Croatian related to what is now regarded as two separate cultures and ethnic identities. Bosnian language had replaced Serbo-Croatian, to reflect the Muslim culture in Bosnia Herzegovina. Under globalisation, even very small nations promote their ethnic identity through language, while embracing the economic benefits that globalisation can provide. For example, Croatia is a member of the European Union, but has chosen the Kuna as its currency, the Kuna being a traditional Croatian monetary unit dating to before the establishment of Yugoslavia (see Zajda & Majhanovich, 2021).

4.2 Cultural Identities in the Classroom and Teachers' Strategies

Techers have incredible power on their students, in promoting their identities, cultural awareness, empathy, and respect for others. All this takes place in collaborative groups, where teachers employ social constructivist pedagogy. Teachers need to develop and master cultural knowledge, competence, and skills. This will help teachers to build effective and strong trusting relationships with students, and contribute to a more positive, and engaging learning environment. Tammy

Breitweiser (2019), in her article 'Cultural identity in classrooms: ideas and suggestions for a more inclusive culture', suggests that teachers need to know and understand their students' diverse cultural identities. Her strategies for promoting cultural diversity in inclusive classroom, include:

- What are the interactions between student-to-teacher and student-to-student?
- What are the rules and who decided on them?
- Have norms been established? If so, by whom?
- How does feedback get distributed? Is it always the same format?
- The teacher must reflect how she responds to each child and may need to reevaluate her beliefs or be more aware of unconscious bias.
- Materials from different cultures, especially books should be highlighted and read often (Breitweiser, 2019).

Lorea Martinez (2021), in her article 'Five ways to celebrate your students' cultures', believes that engaging, and motivational teachers tend to 'cultivate positive relationships with students every day, no matter if the classroom is physical or virtual', and fostering 'emotional connections among students, and help them to feel a sense of belonging and purpose' (Martinez, 2021). These are some of the qualities of effective teachers, generating engaging, and motivational atmosphere in their inclusive classroom (Zajda, 2021, 2023). Martinez (2021) offers some useful and pragmatic classroom strategies for enhancing cultural diversity. These include learning 'about each student and incorporate this knowledge into classroom', promoting an 'inclusive and equitable classroom that proactively works to counter bias', and getting to 'know students' families and invite them to the classroom' (Martinez, 2021). It is essential to build a partnership with parents. Some parents may experience anxiety, and 'emotions about their children's school and teachers' and they may 'fear their child is being mistreated or bullied' (Martinez, 2021).

4.3 Conclusion

The chapter critiques dominant discourses and debates pertaining to cultural identity in the global era. It analyses current discourses related to globalisation, ideologies, cultural identity, and the state, as well as approaches to constructing national, ethnic, and local identities in the global culture. One of the most powerful forces of globalisation shaping cultural identities is the ubiquitous presence of information technology and the mass media. Every facet of culture and identity is defined by the mass media and propelled by the information technology. Global marketing of socially desirable commodities, such as clothing, fashion and global brands, perfumes, toys, and the entertainment industry, to name a few, has affected cultural identity. Global marketing affecting the formation of one's cultural identity has manufactured a new consumerist and a global materialistic culture of 'commodification of the self'. The chapter also demonstrates that language is intrinsically connected to personal, national, and ethnic identity. The case of Canada provides a powerful example of the nexus between language and identity. It has been argued, as demonstrated above, that in terms of time, location and culture, the process of re-defining and consolidation of cultural identities has been one of a continuous social, cultural, political, and historical transformation.

Chapter 5
Students' Personalities and Impact on Academic Achievement

5.1 Students' Personalities and Their Impact Learning

One of the key factors affecting students' engagement, motivation and performance is personality. According to Wang et al. (2023), 'studies have shown that personality traits are one of the important factors affecting college students' academic achievements and that personality, 'plays an important role in students' own academic achievements'. Studies have found that 'emotional stability can hinder students' learning achievement, while conscientiousness can promote higher learning achievement' (Wang et al. 2023).

To have a better, and more meaningful understanding of students' personalities, displayed in the classroom, we need to explain personality and persona. *Personality* has been defined as 'All the traits that characterize an individual over a relatively long period' (*The Macmillan Dictionary of Psychology*, 1995, p. 334). Personality can be explained as enduring individual differences in patterns of cognition, behaviour, and affect. In general, personality is the relatively *stable* organisation of a person's motivational dispositions, arising from the *interaction* between biological drives, and the social and physical environment. The term usually refers mainly to 'the affective traits, sentiments, attitudes, complexes and unconscious mechanisms, interests and ideals, which determine a human's characteristic or *distinctive* behaviour and thought' (Eysenck, 1981).

The concept of the 'personality type' was developed initially by Carl Jung (1921), referring to the psychological classification of different types of individuals. He observed that normal human behaviour is not random, but follows identifiable, and predictable patterns. Carl Jung coined the term 'persona', to describe the public face of one's personality, displayed by a person during social interaction. As such, persona signified the 'outer face that is presented to the world which he appropriated from the word for the mask worn by actors in antiquity to indicate the roles they played' (Casement, 2020). Jung believed that persona, as an archetype, was universal. Overall, personality patterns tend to arise from the structure of the mind (not the brain).

J. Zajda, *Engagement, Motivation, and Students' Achievement*, Globalisation, Comparative Education and Policy Research 48,
https://doi.org/10.1007/978-3-031-61613-6_5

However, biochemical anomalies in the brain, may affect behaviour and personalities. This could lead to 'personality disorder' in the sociology of deviance, and it refers to any disorder, accompanied by severe anxiety disorder, being a mental health disorder, that produces fear, worry, and a constant feeling of being overwhelmed. Severe anxiety in students can lead to disruptive patterns of behaviour, such as attention-seeking, being too selfish, too exhibitionist, and too disruptive. By the time a child starts school, its early temperament will be modified by learning. The 'challenging' child, and their behaviour, with teacher's attention, care, and the use of behaviour modification, may be turned around.

The process of identity development is assisted by *identification.* Identification is defined as a process, during which the person assimilates attributes, or aspects from a role model, or a major agency of socialization, be it family, peers, teachers, and the media. In terms of identification, a greater part of personality development is due to children modelling themselves on significant others, such as family members, peers, teachers, and social media.

5.1.1 Genetic and Environmental Factors Affecting Personalities

Research consistently shows that genetic factors play a significant role in human personality. Across a wide range of personality characteristics twins reared apart are almost as similar to each other as those reared together (the respective correlations are **0.49** and **0.51** for identical twins, and 0.21 and 0.23 for fraternal twins). As the child grows, temperament interacts with the environment, with cognitive factors and other maturational variables, such as physique, and physical appearance. All these, and other variables shape personalities.

If you were asked to describe your personality, you could say that you are 'Polite, friendly, and warm'. This refers to personality traits. Allport (1961) identified 4500 personality traits. To him, personality was the 'dynamic organization within the individual of those psychophysical systems that determine…characteristic behaviour and thought' (Allport, 1961, p. 28).

5.2 Four Types of Major Personality Theories

- Trait theories or personality
- Behavioural theories of personality
- Psychoanalytic
- Humanistic.

5.2.1 *Trait Theories of Personality*

The trait theory approach, according to Kendra Cherry (2023) is 'one of the most prominent areas in personality psychology'. According to these theories, 'personality is made up of a number of broad traits. A trait is a relatively stable characteristic that causes an individual to behave in certain ways. It is essentially the psychological blueprint that informs behavioural patterns' (Cherry, 2023). Hence, trait theories of personalities focus on dominant traits, defining and affecting individual's patterns of behaviour. Major types of trait theories of personalities include those of Eysenck (1981), Cattell (1986), and McCrae and Costa (1985).

The trait-based approach to personality is popular among psychologists, who use psychometry, as psychological measurement, on a large scale. Bad-tempered children become bad-tempered adults. The disadvantage of the trait approach is the weak link between personality and other variables. Correlations are often very low.

Eysenck's three-dimension theory is one of the most popular examples of trait theories of personality.

Hans Eysenck is one of the best-known psychologists for his research dealing with the three major personality dimensions and his personality tests. Eysenck defined three major personality dimensions as:

1. Extraversion (E)
2. Neuroticism (N)
3. Psychoticism (P).

All people share these qualities in different proportions. Personality tests, such as 'The Maudsley Personality Inventory (1959)', can identify the combination of personality qualities that each person has. Eysenck's other personality tests include: 'The Eysenck Personality inventory' (EPI), and 'The Eysenck Personality Questionnaire' (1975) has been widely used. I have used it in my graduate classes.

The extraversion-introversion dimension suggests that by the age of eight there is a statistically positive relationship between extraversion and academic achievement. Ten years later the relationship is reversed, so that achievement is positively related to introversion. Introversion increases and becomes more advantageous than extraversion as the learner moves through secondary and into higher education. For most learners, extraversion increases up to the age of 14, and then steadily declines towards. People tend to become more introverted as they become older.

The neuroticism-stability dimension also suggests that anxiety plays a significant role in academic achievement. Moderate levels of anxiety act as motivational energy bursts, which enhance performance. Children with high '**N**' scores will perform best in relatively unstressful environments. Why? Children with lower 'N' scores will receive optimum motivation where the pressures are severe. Young adult learners with high '**N**' scales tend to do better than those with low scales in higher education, where stresses are intense (e.g. Exam times).

High scores on '**E**' indicate that the individual is 'people-oriented', and experiences, seeks stimulation and has a high resting level of arousal. High scores on '**N**' indicate high levels of anxiety, that become more severe under stress. Individuals are likely to become excited, or depressed, over things that seem trivial to others. Such individuals are prone to anxiety. indicate high levels of anxiety that become more sever under stress. Children with high 'N' scores perform best in relatively unstressed environments, but children with lower 'N' scores are more motivated where the pressures are severe. Young adult learners with high 'N' scales tend to do better than those with low scales in higher education or where stresses are intense. A 'stable extravert' displays stability through a breezy, exuberant approach. A 'stable introvert' will do so through calmness and tranquility. An 'unstable extravert' will display instability through mood swings and volatile over-reactions. An 'unstable introvert' will do so through brooding and depression.

Cattell (1986) extended Eysenck's three personality dimensions to 16 distinct traits or factors, such as strong super-ego, excitability, shyness, conscientiousness, and guilt proneness.

Another popular example of the trait theories of personality is **The Big 5** theory, suggesting that all personalities can be characterized by five major personality dimensions: *openness, conscientiousness, extroversion, agreeableness,* and *neuroticism*, collectively referred to by the acronym **OCEAN**. The five basic personality traits theory was coined in 1949, by D. W. Fiske (1949) and later expanded upon by other researchers, including Norman (1967), Smith (1967), Goldberg (1981), and McCrae and Costa (1985). McCrae and Costa (1985), through their meta-analysis of other studies, have gained acceptance for explaining personality differences in learning. The five personality constructs assessed are:

1. *Openness to Experience*—reflected in aesthetic sensitivity, feelings, fantasy, ideas, and action.
2. *Conscientiousness*—addresses the degree of organisation, persistence, achievement, and goal-directed behaviour.
3. *Extraversion*—quantity and intensity of interaction.
4. *Agreeableness*—assesses one's interpersonal orientation.
5. *Neuroticism*—assessing the degree of emotional stability.

We need to add the significance of *self-concept* variables as a contributing factor in learning style research. Learners with high trait of self-esteem have more positive beliefs about themselves and internally consistent and stable self-concept.

5.2.2 Behavioural Theories of Personality

Behavioural personality theories, are grounded in human behaviour, when individuals respond to their environment. Behavioural theories developed by John Watson and B. F. Skinner concentrated on explanations of learning that emphasise observable changes in behaviour. Watson was a strong believer in the power of the environment in shaping people's behaviour. Watson claimed that he would be able to make anything he wished out of a dozen healthy infants if he were given a free hand in determining and controlling their environment. It was based on operant conditioning principle, and behaviour modification procedures.

Behaviourists also focused on the ways in which 'pleasurable and unpleasant consequences of behaviour change individuals' behaviour over time' (Slavin, 2020). They measured observable behaviour only and used behaviour modification strategies to shape and change behaviours. Skinner's major contribution to behavioural approaches to learning was his operant conditioning principle or learning because of reinforcement. Operant conditioning is defined as 'the use of pleasant and unpleasant consequences to change behaviour' (Slavin, 2020).

B. F. Skinner's entire system is based on operant conditioning. The organism is in the process of 'operating' on the environment, which in ordinary terms means it is bouncing around its world, doing what it does. During this 'operating,' the organism encounters a special kind of stimulus, called a reinforcing stimulus, or simply a reinforcer. This special stimulus has the effect of increasing the operant conditioning—that is, the behavior occurring just before the reinforcer. This is operant conditioning: the behavior is followed by a consequence, and the nature of the consequence modifies the organism's tendency to repeat the behavior in the future. Imagine a rat in a cage. This is a special cage (called, in fact, a 'Skinner box') that has a bar or pedal on one wall that, when pressed, causes a little mechanism to release a foot pellet into the cage. The rat is bouncing around the cage, doing whatever it is rats do, when he accidentally presses the bar and—a food pellet falls into the cage! The operant is the behavior just prior to the reinforcer, which is the food pellet, of course. In no time at all, the rat is furiously peddling away at the bar, hoarding his pile of pellets in the corner of the cage. A behavior followed by a reinforcing stimulus result in an increased probability of that behavior occurring in the future.

Operant conditioning helps us to understand why some students study hard for the test, how gold stars, money, and simple comments like 'Wonderful effort Emma!, 'Fantastic effort Sophie!' will enhance students' motivation students and keep them on completing their work. Operant behaviour is not 'elicited' (classical conditioning), but 'emitted', and 'the *consequence* of that behaviour for the organism is the crucial variable in operant learning' (Gage and Berliner, 2015). Skinner also believed that one's personality was defined and shaped by the SBR (stimulus, behaviour, and response) model. In his view, personality was essentially defined and shaped using the reinforcements and consequences.

To behaviourist, behavioural personality theories are defined and regulated by behaviour and the environment. Changing behaviour in each environment, may result in changing some aspects of one's personality.

> By changing your habits, you can begin to change your personality. This happens slowly. Say you wish you were more disciplined. That certainly doesn't happen overnight, but you can take on this trait by changing your behaviours. Start by getting up early or going through a disciplined morning routine that prepares you for success If you're having trouble performing these behaviours, incorporate some reinforcements. You don't have to punish yourself for failing to perform the behaviour, but this might help. As you perform these behaviours, you open the door for more disciplined actions. As you perform these more disciplined actions, you, and the people around you will notice that you have become more disciplined. (Behavioural theory of personality, 2024)

Students' personalities are likely to be changed by their respondent behaviour, their engagement, motivation, and performance, and the impact of behaviour modification, in the classroom environment.

5.2.3 The Psychoanalytic Personality Theory

The psychoanalytic personality theory was developed by a psychoanalyst Sigmund Freud, who theorised that an individual's personality consisted of innate instincts and parental influences. He also postulated that both nature, and nurture, worked together to form a complete personality, which consisted of 'instincts that drive behaviour such as sex, hunger, and thirst, unconscious thought processes that the person is unaware of, and childhood events, particularly parental influence' (Barowski, 2023).

Sigmund Freud suggested that personality was defined by three components, namely the id, the ego and the super-ego. Freud believed in the importance of exploring the unconscious mind to understand personality development. His theory suggested the existence of 3 forces in personality development:

First component *id*: completely unconscious; the source of basic biological needs and desires, grounded in pleasure principle, and controlling person's urgers.
Second component *ego*: the conscious, rational part of personality, based on the reality principle, and moderates the urges of both the id and superego, and controlling them.
Third component superego**:** the home of conscience, and responsible for the development of a person's morals.

All three components of personality can be visualized as a Freudian house: id represents the basement, ego is the house, and superego is the roof. Fontana argued that if one's personality is not able to produce the appropriate balance between the id, ego and super-ego, then in Freud's view, a number of ego defense mechanisms are created' (Fontana, 1995, p. 214).

5.2.4 Ego Defense Mechanisms

Ego Defense mechanisms are unconscious psychological processes which help an individual to prevent anxiety, when exposed to a stressful situation. Under stress individuals, sometimes unconsciously, resort to defence mechanisms—to protect their ego, that part of personality which is likely to suffer from the anxiety. The following represent examples of defense mechanisms:

- **Denial**: denying the seriousness of, or even the existence of a problem, or 'individuals over-emphatically deny possessing those very motives or emotions which trouble them most' (I am not killing, I am 'neutralising' the enemy).

- **Compensation**: overcoming real/imaginary inferiority in one area, by overemphasising another kind of behaviour (I can't cope with mathematics, but I will be the 'best of the worst')
- **Displaced Aggression**: becoming angry at something/someone other than the direct cause of frustration (Your friend has made you unhappy, so you take it out in your family etc.)
- **Fantasy**: withdrawing from a potentially threatening situation, taking refuge in imaginary satisfaction in place of real ones (a feature of certain forms of schizophrenia)
- **Fixation**: using immature defence mechanism
- **Projection**: ascribing our unconscious motivation to other people, or 'accusing others of acts/thoughts that are of their own making', sometimes paranoid disorders (You are a loser! Learners who think that the teachers are 'picking' on them)
- **Rationalisation**: giving socially acceptable reasons for our conduct
- **Reaction Formation**: behaving in a manner directly opposite to an unconscious wish, impulse or drive (being kind instead of cruel, a minister in the short story 'Rain' who was attracted to the prostitute, or extreme protests or moral outrage at something quite mundane, a sexy person manifests an exaggeratedly moral behaviour)
- **Regression**: retreating to an earlier form of coping behaviour, going back to earlier forms of immature behaviour which was successful in protecting the ego from disappointments, frustration and fears.
- **Repression**: exclusion of unpleasant thoughts, feelings, memories, and experiences by the ego (eg. characteristic 'amnesia' of painful memories, repression of sexual desire becomes inexplicable anger and hostility towards the parents, superiors at work and the world in general)
- **Sublimation**: basic drives, such as sex and aggression are channelled into socially approved activities (playing sport, writing romantic poetry to sublimate the sex drive).

5.2.5 Anxiety, Identification, Displacement, and Defence Mechanisms

Students' level of anxiety can influence their engagement, motivation, and performance.

The most common forms of anxiety are:

- **neurotic anxiety** (when the learner is not helped by teachers etc.)
- **realistic anxiety** (excessive demands for academic work?)
- **moral anxiety** (self-punishment, produced by repressive moral training, feelings of unworthiness, and obsessive–compulsive behaviour—excessive….)

Displacement: Children who are not happy at home are likely to be unhappy in schools. Security, safety, love, affections and belonging need to be met at home if learning is to take place.

Psychoanalytic approach emphasises the importance of ego defense mechanisms, the social learning theory, and the role of significant others. Parents, peers, and pedagogues, and significant others—as cognitive, affective, and moral role models, play a significant part in the early personality formation. Excessive restrictive practices (such as extreme discipline, regimentation, and control) may lead to cover and overt (manifest and latent) acts of deviance, resentment, hostility, and conflict.

5.2.6 Humanistic Theories of Personality

Humanism is a philosophy is a pedagogical approach that believes learning is viewed as a personal act to fulfil one's potential. Humanistic psychology emerged in the 1960s, and focused on the human freedom, dignity, and potential. Humanistic psychologists believed that it is necessary to study the person as a whole, especially as an individual grows and develops over the lifespan. It follows that the study of the self, social learning theory, social constructivism, motivation, and cooperative group learning are areas of particular interest. The following aspects represent manifestations of humanistic theories:

- The humanistic theory of teaching and learning can be defined as an educational theory that believes in teaching the 'whole' child. Humanism believes that a learner is free-willed, and capable of achieving their best when the ideal learning environment is produced. The ideal learning environment should cater to the social, emotional, and cognitive needs of the learner.
- A humanist approach will have a strong focus on students' emotional wellbeing, feelings, and potential to achieve knowledge at the highest-level self-actualization.
- A humanist teaching strategy will have at least three constructs used in teaching:
- Free Will: Learners have free choice to do and think what we want.
- Emotions impact Learning: Learners need to be in a positive emotional state to achieve our best.
- Intrinsic motivation: learners.

Humanistic theories, unlike behaviourism, focus on individuals' feelings, and emotions.

Humanistic psychologists believe we should pay more attention to emotions and ensure that our students are feeling safe, positive, relaxed, and comfortable. These are emotions that will make students ready to learn. The Humanist Approach to learning in the classroom, requires the teacher to consider all needs of their students, to create an effective and engaging learning environment, with reference to:

- social needs
- emotional needs

- mental needs
- cognitive needs
- individual differences needs (learning styles etc.).

Humanist theories, first developed by Abraham Maslow and Carl Rogers, emphasized the importance of free will. Humanist theorists promoted the concept of self-actualization, which is the innate need for personal growth, and the ways that personal growth motivates behaviour.

Maslow's (1954) hierarchy of needs, based on his 5-stage model, consisted of deficit and growth needs. Deficit, or basic needs included physiological needs needed for survival. Food, water, shelter, safety, clothing, belongingness, and love. Growth needs consisted of esteem needs and the need for self-actualization, driven by the feeling that you want to become the best you can be, now that all your needs have been met.

The humanistic personality theory was formulated by Katherine Cook Briggs and Isabel Briggs Myers, a mother and daughter. Humanistic personality theory highlights the importance of self-growth, to develop healthy personality traits. The researchers developed the test to understand the differences in personalities. Together they developed their Myers-Briggs Type Indicator, a questionnaire to help people understand their personality type. These test results split the individuals into 16 different personality groups. The goal is to place these people into careers where they are happiest and to provide them with a better understanding of themselves.

5.3 Students' Personalities and Their Impact of Academic Achievement

Moreira et al. (2020) in their article 'Students' Personality Contributes More to Academic Performance than Well-Being and Learning Approach—Implications for Sustainable Development and Education' argued that of the predictive role of personality dimensions, learning approaches, and well-being, in the academic performance of students. They conclude that 'Comprehending that personality is the strongest predictor of academic performance' (Moreira et al. 2020). Wang et al. (2023) in their article 'The influences of the Big Five personality traits on academic achievements: Chain mediating effect based on major identity and self-efficacy', discovered that such personality traits, as extraversion and conscientiousness have positive total effect on students' academic achievements. The authors noted that 'openness can also affect academic achievement through self-efficacy mediating effect and major identity to self-efficacy chain mediating effect' (Wang et al. 2023).

Tlili et al. (2023), on the other hand, in their study 'Impact of personality traits on learners' navigational behaviour patterns in an online course: A lag sequential analysis approach' examined the nexus between extraversion, neuroticism, conscientiousness, openness, and academic achievement. They discovered that learners 'high in extraversion were more likely to have navigational behaviour patterns, which were primarily influenced by extrinsic motivation', and that that learners with 'high neuroticism are usually accompanied by high levels of anxiety and stress', and those with high openness are highly engaged in discussions and learning and they expect to learn with their peers' (Tlili et al. 2023).

In another study of relationships between personality traits and academic achievement among students, involving some 285 students, Hakimi et. al. (2011), demonstrated that students' personality traits were significantly related to academic achievement. Results demonstrated that personality characteristics accounted for some '48% of variance in academic achievement. Results also showed conscientious, which explained 39% of variance in academic achievement, was the most important predictor variable'. (Hakimi et. al., 2011).

Similarly, Ossama et al. (2019), when investigated students' personalities and the impact of learners' personalities on their academic capabilities, using a sample of 180 students, demonstrated that that 'students' personalities have a direct impact on their knowledge acquisition' (Ossama et al. 2019). Finally, Fandos-Herreraa et al. (2023) in their article 'The influence of personality on learning outcomes and attitudes: The case of discussants in the classroom' discovered that 'personality directly affects the students' perceptions and attitudes' (Fandos-Herreraa et al. 2023).

Dong et al. (2022) in their article 'Emotional intelligence and personality traits based on academic performance', suggested that 'personality traits are the strong predictors of better academic performance' (Dong et al. 2022).

Similarly, Hayat et al. (2020), in their research 'The predictive role of personality traits on academic performance of medical students: The mediating role of self-efficacy', argued that in view of statistically significant correlation, of such personality traits, as 'openness ($\beta = 0.16$, $p < 0.001$), conscientiousness ($\beta = 0.22$, $p < 0.001$), agreeableness ($\beta = 0.19$, $p < 0.001$), and self-efficacy ($\beta = 0.24$, $p < 0.001$) had a significant positive and direct effect on academic performance' and 'Neuroticism ($\beta = -0.21$, $p < 0.001$) had a significant negative and direct effect on academic performance. Also, openness ($\beta = 0.47$, $p < 0.001$) and conscientiousness ($\beta = 0.33$, $p < 0.001$) had a direct positive effect on self-efficacy' (Hayat et al., 2020). The authors concluded that their research discovered the relationships between 'personality traits, self-efficacy, and academic performance of medical students', and that these results showed that 'individual differences in personality traits directly and indirectly play an essential role, through self-efficacy, in contributing to the students' academic performance' (Hayat et al. 2020).

These results demonstrate research proven causal relationship, in most cases, between students' personalities and academic achievement.

5.4 Conclusion

The above analysis of major types of personality theories, namely, trait theories of personality, behavioural theories of personality, psychoanalytic, and humanistic theories of personality, demonstrate a very complex and evolving field of personality dimensions. Personality dimensions influence individuals' attitudes, behaviour patterns, levels of anxiety and performance. In addition, personality traits influence levels of students' academic performance.

Research findings have demonstrated that personality, plays a significant role in students' academic performance., and that specific personality traits are one of the important factors affecting students' academic achievements.

Chapter 6
The Role of Intelligence and Its Impact on Academic Achievement

6.1 Intelligence Defined and Constructed

I wish to discuss the modern concept of 'intelligence' and how it is used to categorize students in terms of performance and academic achievement. The modern concept of 'intelligence' has different meaning for different individuals across cultures, time, and countries. It has many ideological, vocational, and pedagogical implications. According to a traditional definition, intelligence is *a uniform cognitive capacity people are born with.* (Anderson, 1999). Anderson (1999) argued that the 'classical view' of intelligence was derived from psychometric tests Howard Gardner (1999), suggested that intelligence refers *to the human ability to solve problems or to make something that is valued in one or more cultures.* Gardner also believes that intelligence also refers to the ability to create an effective product, or offer a service, that is valued in a culture; and a set of skills that make it possible for a person to solve problems in life; and the potential for finding or creating solutions for problems, which involves gathering new knowledge.

Recent research findings on the structure of intelligence (Deary, 2012) supports Spearman's 'g' theory, which accounts for half of the variance in intelligence tests. With reference to genetics and environment, Deary (2013) seems to support earlier findings by Eysenck, when he argues that some of the causes of intelligence differences are genetically determined:

> Twin and adoption studies provide evidence that differences in intelligence are heritable. The percentage of the variation in intelligence accounted for by genetic causes is usually given at about 50%. Heritability estimates for young children are typically lower, whereas estimates for adults are higher (up to 70–80%). (https://www.sciencedirect.com/science/article/pii/S0960982213008440).

Cattell (1987) was able to extend Spearman's 'g' model by dividing it into two spheres: crystallised and fluid intelligence. Crystallised intelligence involved culturally based, and fact-oriented knowledge, acquired through experience, and fluid intelligence demonstrated non-verbal abilities or 'mental efficiency associated with

J. Zajda, *Engagement, Motivation, and Students' Achievement*, Globalisation, Comparative Education and Policy Research 48,
https://doi.org/10.1007/978-3-031-61613-6_6

manipulation of information seeing complex relationships and solving problems' (Duchesne & McMaugh, 2022, p. 389).

Within the domain of the heredity/environment nexus intelligence has been defined as a 'general aptitude for learning or an ability to acquire and use knowledge and skills' (Slavin, 2020). Slavin argues, as expected, that experts, as demonstrated by research findings, do not share a consensus on the precise meaning of intelligence. They do agree, however, that intelligence is the ability to deal with abstractions, to solve problems, and to learn new knowledge, skills, and values.

6.2 Research on Intelligence Theories and Models

Between 1927 and 1980, several *g-centric* theories dominated intelligence theory and research. The *g* factor, also known as general intelligence, is a construct developed in psychometric research, dealing with specific cognitive abilities, and academic achievement, measured mainly by performance on tests. General intelligence (g) was first proposed by Spearman, (1904; 1927). The *g* factor defined individual differences in mental abilities. The first modern measure of intelligence was developed by the French psychologist Alfred Binet and his co-researcher Theodore Simon in 1904/5, who were engaged by the Education Department in Paris, to identify bright and 'feeble-minded' children, who could not be educated in normal schools and who needed help. Current developments in intelligence research involve the formation of more complex and diverse intelligence theories. Also, there is a corresponding trend to de-emphasise the use of standardized testing to measure intelligence. With the emergence of sophisticated genetic and neurological research methodologies, inspired by a ground-breaking discovery of the sequence of the human genome, new perspectives and dimensions on the conceptualising and measurement of the complexities of intelligence are being tested and developed.

6.2.1 Genome Research

Genome has become the first step in understanding how the instructions coded in DNA affect cognitive processes in the individual. Today, the Human Genome Project (HGP) is a worldwide research effort that has the goal of analyzing the structure of human DNA and determining the location of genes. The Human Genome Project (2016) has revealed that there are probably about 22,300 human genes (and not the estimated 100,000 human genes in the 1980s). Genome research was made possible by an earlier discovery of the double helix structure of the DNA molecule (in the form of a three-dimensional double helix) in 1953 by Francis Crick and James Watson. These significant discoveries of the structure of human genes have made it possible to research further a complex interaction between cognitive, environmental, biological, and psychological aspects of intelligence and genetics. In fact, the 'father' of this approach, where genetic and environmental variables were studied together, was Hans Eysenck (Eysenck, 1966; 1973; 1979; 1998). He defined, tested, and popularised his original and, at the time controversial theory, that general intelligence (g) was a biological phenomenon, with broad social consequences (see also Corr, 2016; Gottfredson, 2016). Recent research has demonstrated that there are shared genetic influences, as predicted by Eysenck in the 1980s, Jensen and others (Hagenaars et al., 2016).

6.2.2 Research Findings on Intelligence, Genetics, and Environment

In his recent research, Corr (2016), suggests that there are 'shared' genetic influences affecting intelligence among individuals around the world. He cites Hagenaars et al. (2016), who reported on a study of over 100,000 people, which demonstrated that there were shared genetic influences on intelligence. Eysenck's (1973) earlier research findings on IQ and genetics, like those of Arthur Jensen (1983), especially Eysenck's research dealing with intelligence, seemed to be vindicated. According to Corr (2016), Eysenck argued that general intelligence, as a broad measure of mental capacity, had a 'genetic basis, which is associated with a wide variety of life outcomes, including socioeconomic difference' (Corr, 2016). However, what is not known is that Eysenck (1982) also suggested a more interactive model of intelligence, that combined both genetic and environmental influences, which was published in *New Education* (1982). Eysenck discussed genotype, or the set of genes that the individual carries, and phenotype, or observable characteristics, which are influenced both by the individual's genotype, and by the environment, as the two major intersecting dimensions, defining and constructing the concept of intelligence. Eysenck stressed that even though some facets of intelligence were inherited, they were not fixed as such, as they were also affected by environmental influences.

The nexus between genetic and environmental influences was and continues to be an ongoing and controversial discourse in cognitive psychology, and especially in psychometric theories and biological theories concerning the nature of intelligence. Cognitive psychologists and intelligence researchers are still researching the extent of the impact of the nature/nurture theories on learning in schools.

Intelligence testing

Intelligence testing has been used as a tool for academic achievement tests, placement tests and vocational selection. It is still used to select, place, and categorise individuals into vocational/educational/career streams (vertical stratification). Some researchers have developed tests that value **process** over the final answer, such as **PAM** (Performance Assessment in Math) and **PAL** (Performance Assessment in Language).

Aptitude and intelligence

Aptitude is one of the key constructs in *Scholastic Aptitude Test Assessment* (SATA), designed to measure different abilities. Short answer tests are not used because they do not measure disciplinary mastery or deep understanding. Aptitude can be defined as 'innate or learned ability or skill, which reflects an individual's intellectual capacity to learn and attain a level of performance or academic achievement in a particular field/discipline' (Zajda & Zajda, 2013) Aptitude is a key dimension in all definitions of intelligence. Aptitude is often associated with cognitive ability, and aptitude/intelligence tests. In re-thinking of the concept of aptitude, we need to refer to the legacy of Richard E. Snow, who researched extensively human aptitudes and learning environments. In his work, Snow provided a new definition of aptitude, which differed from the cognitive abilities, as it included conative (motivational) and affective (emotional) characteristics. He also coined "aptitude-complexes" theory, which explained the nexus between personal aptitudes and situational demands, which interact to determine the level of performance. Aptitude, together with metacognition and reflection plays an important role on problem solving.

There are two opposing views of aptitude: those who maintain that aptitude is innate, like the 'g' factor, and those who believe that aptitude can be acquired over the years. The latter view represents the cognitive theory of aptitude for learning. Aptitude plays a key role in intelligence testing. Some of the widely used aptitude/intelligence tests include:

- Stanford-Binet Intelligence Quotient
- Wechsler Intelligence Scale for Children (WISCIV)
- Woodcock Johnson Test of Cognitive Ability.

Stanford-binet intelligence test

Psychometric theories of intelligence include Spearman (1927) and his concept of intelligence. In 1927 Charles Spearman developed the concept of 'g'—a model of intelligence. Spearman proposed his *two-factor theory* of intelligence (*general intelligence* factor, or 'g' and *specific ability* factors, or 's' factors) Charles Spearman, using the statistical procedure called factor analysis, concluded in 1904 that intelligence is made up of two components: a **g-factor** (general intelligence) and **s-factors** (a collection of specific cognitive intellectual skills). Spearman also used his construct of specific mental abilities (or 's') to explain individual variations in performance. In short, general mental ability, or 'g', reflected the speed and efficiency of cognitive operations, or brain processing power. On the other hand, specific mental abilities (or 's') represented the specific cognitive abilities used to solve specific tasks. This instrument, which is widely used, measures five factors of *cognitive* abilities: knowledge, working memory, quantitative reasoning, visual-spacial ability, and fluid reasoning. Each of these five factors is measured and the combined score becomes the intelligence quotient. The Stanford-Binet Intelligence Test, proved to be the most reliable test currently used in all sectors, including education.

6.2.2.1 Wechsler Intelligence Scale for Children (WISC)

The Wechsler Intelligence Scale for Children (WISC) was developed in 1949, as an adaptation of David Wechsler's 1939 Wechsler-Bellevue Intelligence Scale. This version of the Wechsler test is a psychological assessment tool that measures various aspects of intelligence and is designed to test children between the ages of 6 to 16. WISC is an IQ test. The aim of the instrument is to identify giftedness, learning disabilities, or general strengths and weaknesses a child may have in their *cognitive* abilities. The test has undergone several revisions and the current version of the test is the fifth edition WISC-V which was released in 2014. The WISC consists of a series of short sub tests that are used to assess cognitive ability. Though this test can be used as an IQ test for children, it is most often used as a clinical tool to measure *individual cognitive abilities*. The WISC is often used among a battery of other tests to assess and identify cognitive function and ability ranges which can help. WISC relies on the hypothesis that cognitive skills, or intelligence, are normally distributed throughout the population. The main benefits include:

Early identification of reading & learning issues;

Useful in identifying learning disabilities;

Understanding of an individual's learning profile;

Identification of gifted children;

The above assessment also helps schools make appropriate; accommodations and develop learning plans for individual students, needing help (http://www.school-psychology.com.au/blog/wechsler-intelligence-scale-for-children-wisc-iv/).

Woodcock Johnson test of cognitive ability

The Woodcock-Johnson Tests of Cognitive Abilities is a set of intelligence tests first developed in 1977 by Richard Woodcock and Mary E. Bonner Johnson. The Woodcock-Johnson Tests were revised most recently in 2014 and this latest version is commonly called the WJ-IV test. The Woodcock-Johnson Tests of Cognitive Abilities can be given to children from the age of 2 through adulthood. The Woodcock Johnson test covers a wide range of cognitive skills. The Woodcock-Johnson-III and Woodcock-Johnson-IV Tests of Achievement are a 22-section achievement test, which assesses both academic achievement (what children have learned in school) and *cognitive development*. It is sometimes paired with an intelligence test to qualify children for gifted and talented programs. The Woodcock-Johnson Tests of Cognitive Abilities measure the greatest breadth of cognitive abilities of any standardized body of tests. Also, the test contains new domain-specific scholastic aptitude CLUSTERS that allow for efficient and valid predictions of academic achievement, providing even more feedback for specific help that can be given for a child. The tests of academic achievement help compare a given child's levels of achievement to academic https://www.testingmom.com/tests/woodcock-johnson/).

Aptitude and achievement tests

Both aptitude and achievement tests measure cognitive development of different abilities. Aptitude tests are specifically designed to measure abilities developed over many years and predict how well a student will do in the future at learning unfamiliar material. Achievement tests measure academic performance. The IQ test is one of the most influential and widely used aptitude tests. The IQ test is a measure of scholastic aptitude. If intelligence quotient defines intelligence as being a single measurable trait affecting all mental ability, aptitudes reflect a multi-modal mental ability, suggesting that they also differ in quality as well as quantity.

More recently, the Colleges of Oxford University have introduced a *History Aptitude Test* (HAT) for use in the selection of candidates for all degree courses involving History. This test, which aims to examine the skills and potentialities required for the study of History at university, gives us an objective basis for comparing candidates from different backgrounds, including mature applicants and those from different countries. It is designed to be challenging, to differentiate effectively between the most able applicants for university courses, including those who may have achieved or can be expected to achieve the highest possible grades in their examinations.

Critique of psychometric theories of intelligence

Some critics of the psychometric approach, such as Robert Sternberg (who formulated the Triarchic Theory of Intelligence), point out that individuals in the general population have a somewhat different conception of intelligence than most experts. It can be argued that the psychometric approach measures only a small part of what is commonly understood as intelligence. Also critical of the psychometric approach were Copping, Campbell & Muncer, (2014). Other critics, such as Sir Arthur Stanley Eddington, argued that the instrument used in testing often determines the results and that proving that intelligence exists, does not prove that current instrument measures it correctly (https://www.k12academics.com/educational-psychology/intelligence/psychometric-intelligence/criticisms-psychometric-approach).

More recently, Strauss (2017), in her research, discussed numerous unresolved educational and policy-related problems associated with the use of standardised tests, especially in diverse classroom settings. She cited the Florida case, where due to policy problems, which Florida has had with its standardized testing accountability system, which became so severe that school superintendents state-wide revolted in 2015 and said they had 'lost confidence' in its accuracy (Strauss, 2017). Strauss (2017), argued, similarly to Piaget's (1950) original theory on cognition, adaptation and intelligence, the case for cognitive system changes in thinking, requiring ongoing adaptation:

> At the most fundamental level, education policy shaped by standardized test scores is at odds with the deepest of all societal needs—human survival. Inevitable environmental, demographic, technological, institutional, and cognitive system changes require continuous adaptation. Adaptation requires new knowledge. New knowledge is generated by dozens of complex thought processes—hypothesizing, inferring, relating, valuing, imagining, and so

> on. And of those dozens of complex thought processes, only two—recalling, and applying—can be quantified and measured with sufficient precision to produce a meaningful number. (Strauss, 2017)

It has been argued that standardized intelligence tests that measure specific skills are misinterpreted as measures of intelligence (Sternberg, 1999; Gardner, 1999; Copping et al., 2014; Strauss (2017). Research has demonstrated that high stakes standardized test scores are neither reliable nor valid, as they ignore the issues of individual differences, gender, and cultural differences (Jensen, 1980; Snyderman & Rothman, 1987). Another criticism refers to the use of intelligence and standardised tests, as valid and reliable indicators of academic achievement and social outcomes. Just because test scores and outcomes are correlated does not mean one causes or predicts the other, as test outcomes are influenced by a number of unacknowledged factors, including genetics, environment, and culture.

Furthermore, the very nature of hypothetical constructs, such as intelligence, intelligence quotient (IQ), and 'g' suggest that they are distinct entities. Intelligence is the term used in ordinary discourse to refer to cognitive ability. However, it is generally regarded as too ambiguous to be useful for a valid measure of the individual's cognitive abilities. The intelligence quotient (IQ) is an index calculated from the scores on test items judged by experts to encompass the abilities covered by the term intelligence. Since IQ measures a multidimensional quantity, it is a combination of diverse kinds of abilities, the proportions of which may differ between IQ tests (Intelligence, IQ, and g, 2018).

6.2.3 *Intelligence Discrimination in Schools*

According to the American Psychological Association (APA) (2015), 'Discrimination is the unfair or prejudicial treatment of people and groups based on characteristics such as race, gender, age or sexual orientation'. APA describes discrimination not only as a serious health issue, but also how it can be damaging to a person's educational and job opportunities:

> Discrimination is a public health issue. According to the 2015 Stress in America Survey, people who say they have faced discrimination rate their stress levels higher, on average, than those who say they have not experienced discrimination. That's true across racial and ethnic groups.
>
> Chronic stress can lead to a wide variety of physical and mental health problems. Indeed, perceived discrimination has been linked to issues including anxiety, depression, obesity, high blood pressure and substance abuse. Discrimination can be damaging even if you haven't been the target of overt acts of bias. Regardless of your personal experiences, it can be stressful just being a member of a group that is often discriminated against, such as racial minorities…The anticipation of discrimination creates its own chronic stress. People might even avoid situations where they expect they could be treated poorly, possibly missing out on educational and job opportunities. (APA, 2015 https://www.apa.org/helpcenter/discrimination)

Thus, discrimination is the universal practice of treating someone differently because of that person's perceived status or characteristics (Zajda, 2010, p. 3). Discrimination can be positive or negative. It can be positive when an applicant is offered a job because of that person's intelligence, qualifications, or a school tie. However, discrimination often manifests itself as a negative phenomenon—for example, when students are discriminated against each other on the bases of intelligence, abilities, academic performance, and socio-economic status (SES).

Discrimination, be it open or hidden, overt or covert, conscious or unconscious, is almost like an undeclared war by humans, against other humans in a stratified social system, by exercising power, domination, and control, (Zajda, 2023). In a world, characterized by continuing unequal distribution of socially valued commodities, especially unequal access to education, power, wealth, and privilege, humans will continue to exist in conflict-driven environments, where prejudice and discrimination are present. The very existence of social stratification, selection, and placement in society already legitimizes discrimination and prejudice in education. Such constructs as SES, intelligence, cultural capital, social class, income, education, wealth, and poverty influence both teachers' perceptions of their students' cognitive abilities and academic achievement, as well as students' overall attitudes towards schooling and academic performance.

Even though we are not born with discriminatory attitudes, we soon acquire them by observing others and imitating their prejudices. Sometimes this is internalized unconsciously, sometimes it is due to peer group pressure, or institutional constraints. Overall, discrimination and discriminatory practices in society are micro-social (classrooms) and macro social (organizations). They act as powerful and ubiquitous forces, which affect all individuals, be they at school, college, or workforce.

Discrimination, in general, will greatly affect a student's chance at success in a negative and damaging way in the long term. Students' experience can be a positive reaffirmation of what they already believe about themselves, or can be the opposite, a constant reminder that they are not considered intelligent by society's general standards. Hence, pre-conceived and biased notions about the performance or intelligence level of students, based on prejudice, creates a condition where teachers' attitude towards the students is eventually shared by the individual themselves. Teachers' perceptions and their negative reinforcement, and low expectation of certain students, in turn affect students themselves who believe their teachers and accept that they do not have the necessary abilities, intelligence and skills to succeed in schools.

Research dealing with discriminatory practices has focused on teacher bias and prejudice in predicting students' academic performance. Martschenko (2018) argues that research suggests that 'teacher perceptions and expectations of a student, which can be preconceived, have an impact upon a child's IQ scores, academic achievement, and attitudes and behaviour'. This means that teacher's perceptions play a significant role in categorizing children and can also have 'an impact on the likelihood of a child being referred for gifted or special education':

> The universal screening of students for gifted education using IQ tests could help to identify children who otherwise would have gone unnoticed by parents and teachers. Research has found that those school districts which have implemented screening measures for all children

> using IQ tests have been able to identify more children from historically underrepresented groups to go into gifted education. (Martschenko, 2018)
>
> Theconversation.com/the-iq-test-wars-why-screening-for-intelligence-is-still-so-contro.

Similarly, Ready & Wright (2011), when exploring the links between teacher perceptions and children's socio-demographic backgrounds, discovered that teachers perceive 'substantial racial-ethnic, socioeconomic, and gender differences' in children's literacy skills. Their research findings demonstrated that teachers, with reference to lower-socioeconomic-status and lower-achieving contexts were more often underestimated their students' abilities. Ready & Wright (2011) argued that teachers' subjective understandings of their students' cognitive abilities have important implications for classroom interactions, children's access to resources and opportunities, and educational equity more broadly. They also discovered that teachers in the nationally representative data perceived substantial racial-ethnic, socioeconomic, and gender differences in children's literacy skills.

Teacher bias and prejudice in predicting students' academic performance was also discovered by Thompson (2019). Thompson, as an experienced classroom teacher, argues that teachers' expectations regarding the students' abilities can result in self-fulfilling prophecy:

> The self-fulfilling prophecy begins with the expectations you have about your students. These expectations are your unconscious as well as your conscious attitudes about your students' ability to succeed. You constantly communicate those expectations to your students in many subtle ways such as though your body language, the assignments you make, the language you use, and how much time you spend with individual students. (Thompson, 2019, http://teaching.monster.com/benefits/articles/10304-the-self-fulfilling-prophecy-your-students-i-knew-you-could-do-it#comment_form)

Discrimination, based on social class, intelligence, ability, ethnicity, and gender, is a ubiquitous phenomenon in societies globally. Hence, there is an urgent need to understand and combat ethnocentrism, prejudice, discrimination, racism and other –isms, which contribute to a growing number of teachers' adverse attitudes in the classroom and beyond. If teachers are to act as true professionals and educators in the moral and humane sense, they should not bring their preconceived ideas and discriminatory attitudes into the classroom—the public space. It is important that future professionals, who aspire to become empowering pedagogues, become aware of their own attitudes toward people who differ from themselves. Being aware is certainly necessary but not sufficient. Becoming aware is one thing but acting on it is another. Treating all learners in the same fashion, as if they are at the same stage of cognitive, social and emotional development (due to standardized teaching plans, lesson plans and curricular outcomes), results in discriminating against differences in developmental, cognitive, intellectual, emotional, cultural, and individual preferences and learning modality exhibited by students. Back in the 1980s, Dunn and Dunn (1987), with reference to individual differences and learning styles, argued, that teaching which is responsive to both learning styles and individual differences, 'may help improve learning conditions for students at risk of academic and lifelong failure' (Dunn & Dunn, 1987, p. 60).

Discrimination can be felt or seen in individuals' behaviour towards other people. Discrimination is, undoubtedly, behaviour, or acts, based on bias and prejudice. Discrimination often begins in the classroom from day one. When teachers discriminate in the classroom in any one sense of the term, they are favouring the dominant and accepted ideology of knowledge, values, skills, and learning and reject and ignore other multi-modal aspects of knowledge and learning and individuals' knowledge needs in general. Instead of inclusive classrooms they have created a *stratified* and divided classroom, based on privilege, favouritism, and exclusion (see Derman-Sparks & Olsen Edwards, 1993; Gardner, 1999; Good & Brophy, 1998; Slavin, 2018).

Empowering pedagogues, just like other ethically concerned professionals, need to examine their own attitudes and either conscious or unconscious prejudicial assumptions (often based on ignorance, arrogance, phobias, and stereotypes), as to the nature of learning, ability, intelligence, gender, disability, speech patterns, physical appearance, personality, body, race, income, ethnicity, gender, religion, and lifestyles. We all suffer from some forms of biases and tend to 'filter out the reality of a situation in favour of our discriminatory assumptions' (Kussrow, 2010, p. 93). Learners from diverse cultures, with different levels of knowledge and skills and at different stages of cognitive development, are likely to exhibit different ways of learning. Yet, in a traditional classroom there is a tendency to adopt a singular, unifying and one-dimensional approach to the learning/teaching process. There is also a tendency to normalise learning using the normal curve, and by teaching to the 'average' students, which ignores individual differences. The learner's question 'Is this the right way?' already reflect the uncritical acceptance of learning.

Learning discrimination deals with numerous issues ranging from learning modes and styles to the pace of learning. Some teachers dislike 'slow' learners, who are labelled as 'slow' or 'lazy'. Yet, learning pace is a very personal and individual act, which may not be correlated with intelligence. We do assume that 'fast' learners are highly intelligent. Some learners learn best by writing it down first. Others, who are visual learners, must see it, in order to learn. These represent learning styles and modes discussed below.

Intelligence discrimination is possibly the most common discrimination in classrooms globally (Canning et al., 2019; Jacobs, 2019; Zajda, 2021b). It is based on the notion of differential intellectual abilities, where some abilities are favoured and other abilities, perceived to be not relevant, are not as valued and are completely ignored in the outcomes-driven academic achievement and performance in schools. If we add to it the notions of high and low intelligence or gifted and below average it is easy to see how these potentially damaging (but convenient tools for test administrators testing ability) labels can have significant implications for students, parents, and teachers alike, who use intelligence test scores for future career orientations (see also Martschenko, 2018). Martschenko (2018) argues that the debate concerning what it means to be 'intelligent' and whether 'the IQ test is a robust tool of measurement continues to elicit strong and often opposing reactions today' (Martschenko, 2018). Theconversation.com/the-iq-test-wars-why-screening-for-intelligence-is-still-so-contro.

Students, defined by intelligence testing (known as 'placements tests' in schools) are, consequently, streamed by abilities. According to Chmielewski (2014), the practice of grouping students by 'ability' is 'commonplace in school systems around the world and takes various forms' (see also Boaler et al., 2000; Butler & Weir, 2013). For example, in one secondary college, the most able students in Year 9 were placed in advanced mathematics classes (level 1, which was the highest), the least able found themselves doing level 10 mathematics (the lowest group, covering basic mathematics).

Most parents accept, uncritically, the political correctness of the widely perceived and accepted 'scientific objectivity' of intelligence tests, even though psychologist themselves are aware of many misconceptions concerning the nature of intelligence and the reliability and validity of its measurements. Some individuals are likely to experience significant changes in their estimated IQ, due to the nature of schooling, learning patterns, social and cultural differences, and other environmental influences.

Intelligence discrimination is a convenient way of exercising power, domination, and control over the student's life in the classroom, and society at large. Intelligence testing, as an ideology of the academic achievement syndrome for installing the gate-keeping and for sorting out students (into high and low achievers, above and below average performers, the winners and losers), becomes a powerful tool, or a weapon of the hidden curriculum, legitimizing meritocracy and educational inequality. Intelligence meritocracy creates a few winners and many losers in the classroom and later in life (see also Behar-Horenstein, 2003).

Apart from cognitive abilities and the focus on students' intelligence, there are non-cognitive abilities, or traits, which are equality relevant in academic achievement, yet they are seemed to be ignored. Alanna Bjorklund-Young (2016) defines non-cognitive traits as personality traits or 'patterns of thought, feelings, and behaviour' (Borghans et al., 2008). The term non-cognitive characteristics refer to the very broad range of knowledge, skills, attitudes, strategies, and behaviours which play a significant role in academic performance, but 'may not be captured (directly) by cognitive or achievement tests' (Farrington et al., 2012). Overall, non-cognitive skills include such traits as creativity, imagination, persistence, self-discipline, focus, confidence, organization, and other traits. Bjorklund-Young (2016), referred to the University of Chicago's Consortium on Chicago School Research, which concluded that the 'non-cognitive skills most strongly associated with academic performance are: academic behaviours (e.g. going to class and participating), academic perseverance (e.g. grit and self-discipline), academic mindsets (e.g. feeling a sense of belonging within an academic community and believing that ability and competence can grow with effort, learning strategies (e.g. metacognitive strategies and goal-setting), and social skills (e.g. interpersonal skills and cooperation)' (Farrington et al., 2012; cited in Bjorklund-Young, 2016). Some authors have already critiqued the reliability of intelligence testing in schools, as well as the 'efficacy of true intelligence measures' and 'subsequent concerns about basing our instructional approaches solely on them-as if problems in short-term memory or auditory discrimination, for example, predict lack of success in all areas of one's life' (Hearne & Stone, 1995;

see also Geddes, 2018; Zajda, 2023a). However, despite significant research findings, concerning the nature of intelligence, intelligence discrimination in schools and societies continues to exist (Eysenck, 1982; Gardner, 1999). If we define the term 'intelligence' as 'the ability to see relationships, and to use these relationships to solve problems' (Fontana, 1995, p. 95), then it is easy to infer that every aspect of one's learning is likely to be influenced by this definition of intelligence (see also Eysenck, 1998; Gardner, 1999; Richardson, 2002; Stankov & Lee, 2017; Zajda & Zajda, 2013). Despite the proliferations of definitions of intelligence, there is little consensus on the meaning of intelligence.

6.3 Self-fulfilling Prophecy and Key Principles

Self-fulfilling prophecy (SFP) is a phenomenon by which people's expectations about the future events lead them to behave in ways that, on occasion, can cause the expected event to occur. People tend to find what they are looking for. More than that, they may even tend unwittingly to create what they seek. SFP describes situations in which teachers' expectations and acts influence their own attitudes and behaviour as well as their students' behaviour. *Self-fulfilling prophecy* is a concept developed by Robert K. Merton to explain how a belief or expectation, whether correct or incorrect, affects the outcome of a situation, or the way a person (or group) will behave. A self-fulfilling prophecy occurs when a perceiver's false belief leads to its own fulfillment (Merton, 1948). Merton emphasized the role that self-fulfilling prophecies play in injustice and inequality, and research has documented the occurrence of self-fulfilling prophecies. For example, labeling someone as a low achiever, and treating that person as such, may foster low achieving behaviour in the person, who is subjected to the expectation (Brophy, 1983; Madon et al., 1997). Madon, Lee & Eccles (1997) examined the power of self-fulfilling prophecy and discovered that teacher perceptions predicted achievement more strongly for low achievers than for high achievers (see also Workman, 2012; *Teacher expectations of students a self-fulfilling prophecy?* 2018).

Workman (2012) argues that teachers are the single most important factor that affects student achievement:

> As a result, over the last decade state leaders have taken aim at increasing educator effectiveness, including requiring the implementation of new teacher evaluation systems. A growing body of research suggests that the expectations a teacher sets for an individual student can significantly affect the student's performance. Teacher expectations can, for example, be based on student characteristics such as race, ethnicity, and family income level, or indicators of past performance. These expectations can cause teachers to differentiate their behavior towards individual students. (Workman, 2012, https://eric.ed.gov/?id=ED539026)

Singhal (2018) states that what individuals believe about themselves becomes a self-fulfilling prophesy. The concept of the self-fulfilling prophecy can be summarised in these key principles:

- We form certain expectations of people or events
- We communicate those expectations with various cues.

  People tend to respond to these cues by adjusting their behaviour to match them.

- The result is that the original expectation becomes true.

This creates a circle of self-fulfilling prophecies. Earlier, Good & Brophy (1998) argued that teachers' expectations can be self-sustaining. Expectations in themselves cause teachers to be alert for what they expect and less likely to notice what they do not expect. Some expectations persist, even when they do not coincide with the facts (see also Smith et al., 1999; Van den Bergh et al., 2010). Good & Brophy (1998) developed the following 5-stage model of SFP:

1. The teacher expects 'X' to take place in the classroom (relating to academic achievement and performance).
2. In view of this expectations (true or false), the teacher behaves differently towards different students.
3. This tells each student what behaviour and achievement the teacher expects.
4. If the teacher's treatment is consistent over time, and if the student does not actively resist or change it in some way, it is likely to shape the student's performance (high achievers will remain high achievers, and low achievers will accept the failure syndrome).
5. With time, the student's achievement and behaviour conforms more and more closely with the teacher's original expectations (hence the teacher will think "Yes, I was right, Emma is…").

Research findings suggest that there are *two* types of self-fulfilling prophecies. One type is the *Pygmalion effect*, and the other type is a self-fulfilling prophecy, due to students' own perception of their abilities. The Pygmalion effect is a positive self-fulfilling prophecy, when teachers believe that certain students will perform well. These two self-fulfilling prophecies are discussed below.

The *Pygmalion effects*

It occurs when one person has a positive perception and expectations of another and treats that person in a manner consistent with those expectations. As a result, the person changes his/her behaviour, which results in the self-fulfilling prophecy (SFP). In the classroom teachers may treat certain students in a positive manner consistent with their perceptions and expectations, which are transferred to these students. If a teacher has a positive expectation or perception of the student, the teacher conveys that message both verbally and non-verbally, using non-verbal cues (NVCs) to the student. The positive expectations are likely to influence and change the student's perception and expectation and create a self-fulfilling prophecy. Wehler (2017), when examining the negative self-fulfilling prophecy cycle, argues that self-fulfilling prophecies are 'usually negative, but they do not have be':

> Perhaps the most obvious way to help students recognize and disrupt a negative self-fulfilling prophecy cycle is to make them aware of it. We would like our attempts to encourage metacognition and to quietly empower them from behind the scenes to be successful, but sometimes a direct approach is the most effective. (Wehler, 2017, https://www.facultyfocus.com/articles/teaching-and-learning/five-ways-help-students-brek-self-fulfilling-prophecies/)

Example of a positive self-fulfilling prophecy

Back in 1968, in a classic experiment, Rosenthal, a professor of social psychology at Harvard, and Jacobson worked with elementary school children from 18 classrooms. They randomly chose 20% of the children from each room and told the teachers they were 'intellectual bloomers' (a positive self-fulfilling prophecy). Apparently, the bloomers had done what was expected of them and the teachers were comfortable with them. Students gained more IQ than the other 80%, who the teachers believed to be 'average' (see Postman & Weingartner, 1971). Consequently, Rosenthal & Jacobson argued that the teachers had passed on their higher expectations to students which had produced a self-fulfilling prophecy (Rosenthal & Jacobson, 1968).

This experiment illustrated several assumptions within the 5-stage model of SFP:

- High expectations lead to higher performance
- Low expectations lead to lower performance
- Better performance resulting from high expectations leads us to like someone more
- Lower performance resulting from low expectations leads us to like someone less
- Forming expectations is natural and unavoidable.

Self-fulfilling prophecy

Self-fulfilling prophecy occurs when a perception or prophecy (prediction) is made and individuals autonomously change their behaviour to conform to the prediction. In *My Fair Lady*, the musical, Eliza Doolittle, a flower girl, who has a distinct Cockney accent, decides to have speech lessons from Professor Henry Higgins, a noted phoneticist and a speech therapist, to improve her social standing and pass as a high-class lady.

Individuals, like Eliza Doolittle, act because of their own perceptions. Another, and a more current example of this is, when the school that markets its image as a centre of high achievers and excellence, enrolls like-minded students and parents. Such targeted students come to the school with a set of preconceived ideas, and behave, in a manner, that may well turn them into high achievers. They acted because of their own beliefs, perceptions and expectations. Students already had high expectations, when enrolling at such a high-performing school.

Research has shown that SFPs exist regardless of whether the prophecies are true or false. The perception that a given student will perform well or poorly will be true if expectations are transferred from the teacher to the student. Consciously, or not, we tip individuals off, as what our expectations are (see Postman & Weingartner, 1971, Good & Brophy, 1998).

As part of non-verbal communication (NVC), we exhibit thousands of cues, some as subtle as the tilting of heads, facial expression, posture, gaze, eye contact, gestures, and the way we smile, and the raising of eyebrows. These cues are part of the impression management, or behavior of which we are aware that students will see and evaluate our words and action. And students pick up on those cues.

6.4 How Teachers Communicate Expectations

- Seating low expectation students (LES) far from the teacher and/or seating them in a group
- Paying less attention to LES in academic situations (smiling less often, maintaining less eye contact, etc.)
- Calling on lows less often to answer questions or to make public demonstrations
- Waiting less time for lows to answer questions Not staying with lows in failure situations (e g. providing fewer clues, asking fewer follow-up questions)
- Criticizing lows more frequently than highs for incorrect responses
- Praising lows less frequently than highs after successful responses
- Praising lows more frequently than highs for marginal or inadequate responses
- Providing lows with less accurate and less detailed feedback than highs
- Failing to provide lows with feedback about their responses as often as highs
- Demanding less work and effort from lows than from highs Interrupting lows more frequently than highs
- Interrupting lows more frequently than highs
- Is forming expectations natural and unavoidable in the classroom?
- What does it tell about the teacher? (See also Snow, 1995; Wehler, 2017).

6.5 Evaluation

Can we accept that individuals are born with a *fixed* amount of intelligence? If so, how such a view fit in the constructivist pedagogy, which stresses the importance of environmental factors in learning? If we accept the view that human beings possess multiple intelligences, but each person has a unique combination, or profile of various intelligences, what are we saying? Are we accepting uncritically the dominance of heredity over environment? Is it determinism over the free-will? Both the term *intelligence* and the notions of *intelligence testing*, by their nature of intended selection, exclusivity, distinction, and cognitive stratification tend to undermine the egalitarian ethos of democracy and democratic practices in the classroom and divide the learning community. Defining a very small numbers of individuals as exceptionally able due to some intelligence factors or traits seems to create unnecessary painful and prejudicial social categories and meritocratic divisions in society. We have committed numerous blunders and crimes in the name of science and progress in the past. Do we need to create a *Brave New World* syndrome to divide, conquer and rule? Some efficiency and productivity-driven functionaries, be they CEO's of corporations, institutions, or school principals, using the weapon of 'rationality' attempt to justify and legitimise intelligence testing or 'placement testing—on the grounds of natural aptitude, efficiency and differentiation in learning.

Critique of psychometric theories of intelligence, as demonstrated above, shows that psychometric approach, as used in traditional IQ tests, measures only a small part of intelligence and ignores other parts. Critique of psychometric theories of intelligence reveals both conceptual and methodological problems, not to mention ambiguities with definitions of the constructs themselves. IQ tests have been criticised by some researchers and educators for measuring only a fraction of human intelligence, as shown above, and for being culture-specific (Martschenko, 2018), and for minimizing the 'varied nature of crystallized and semi-fluid intelligence factors as described in Cattell–Horn–Carroll theory' (IQ—RationalWiki, 2018). Another serious problem with the IQ tests it relies on the normal curve of the norm-based assessment, and that it is promoted as a 'normalised measure, calibrated to have 100 as the average and 68% of people in the 86–115 range under Wechsler Adult Intelligence Scale' (IQ – RationalWiki, 2018):

> So an IQ of 140 measured now is not the same as an IQ of 140 measured 10 years ago. There are by this measure people are getting less intelligent. It was never designed to be an absolute measure. (IQ—RationalWiki, 2018)

As to the use of intelligence testing in schools and elsewhere, it can be argued that both the term intelligence and the notions of intelligence testing, by their nature of intended selection, exclusivity, distinction, and cognitive stratification tend to undermine the egalitarian ethos of democracy and democratic practices in the classroom and divide the learning community. Defining a very small number of individuals as exceptionally able, due to some intelligence factors or traits, seems to create unnecessary painful, and prejudicial social categories and meritocratic divisions in society. It seems that some policymakers and educators, by using the weapon of 'rationality' attempt to justify and legitimise intelligence testing or 'placement' testing—on the grounds of natural aptitude, efficiency and differentiation in learning.

Intelligence/aptitude testing controversy (it is still on-going), which categorizes individuals into most able versus least able, does reflect the unresolved tensions between the heredity (nature), cultural factors (language and perception in different cultures) and environment (nurture) discourses. Accepting the limitations imposed by one's genetic code could lead to a re-invented *geno-determinism*—a new 'regime of truth' of the triumph of the genetic code over free will.

The power of science, measurement and thought control rests not so much in its claims to objectivity (which could be questioned) but in its ubiquitous use of intelligence testing, as an ideology of oppression, division, and domination, which legitimizes even further the unequal treatment of individuals according to their perceived abilities, thinking and skill levels. Intelligence testing creates a deterministic (Nature over nurture), rather than voluntary (free will) view of learning, which becomes a powerful ideology of social stratification, domination and control both in the classroom and in life.

6.6 Conclusion

Students are likely to learn various forms of discrimination in the classroom and outside. Intelligence and ability discrimination, with reference to learning and assessment, tend to be common in schools globally. This is largely due to performance-based and academic assessment-driven curriculum (Zajda, 2023a). It may result, in some cases, as demonstrated above, in students' anxiety, stress and either positive or negative SFP, especially, when teachers' own biased expectations influence their attitudes and behaviour, which is communicated to their students. It also undermines the universal principles of social justice, democracy, equality, and human rights. Defining a very small number of individuals as exceptionally able due to some intelligence factors or traits seems to create unnecessary, painful, and prejudicial social categories and meritocratic divisions in society. We must resist any attempts at labelling, categorizing and dividing individuals into classes of bright, or slow learners. They are likely to contribute to students' achievement anxiety, and aggressive competition. In addition, these labels and stereotypes undermine the whole concept of holistic, and democratic schooling, based on equality, human rights, and social justice. Labelling students in term of academic achievement and performance serves to legitimize a very conservative ideology of *meritocracy* (students are judged by abilities, effort, and achievement only), so dramatically illustrated in the sci-fi novel *Brave New World*, where citizens in a futuristic society have been classified into alphas (top citizens who have the best of everything), betas (second best) and epsilons (working slaves). Progressive and inspirational teachers should offer unconditional positive regard to all students they teach. Teachers have the power, knowledge, and skills to create an effective motivational atmosphere. Genuine empowering pedagogues, who wish to implement excellence and quality learning need to monitor and control their own biases and discriminatory attitudes, to promote equality of educational opportunity and outcomes for all.

Chapter 7
Social and Cultural Factors and Their Influences on Engagement in the Classroom

7.1 Social and Cultural Factors Affecting Learning in the Classroom

Both social and cultural factors can have an enormous impact on students' engagement and learning, and, subsequently, their performance and academic achievement. Numerous social factors affect the nature and the context of students' engagement and learning. They include such factors as students' cognitive, social, affective, and psychomotor developments, their age, gender, demographic factors, the learning environment and their relationships with their peers and teachers. All these factors can influence the quality of students' engagement and learning. Similarly, cultural factors, such as knowledge, beliefs, ethnicity, language, religion, and values can affect students' engagement and the way they learn within the classroom.

7.1.1 Defining Culture

To have a better understanding of social and cultural factors affecting students' engagement in the classroom, we need to define the construct 'culture'. Anthropologist Sir Edward B. Taylor (1871) offered a broad definition of culture, stating that culture is 'that complex whole which includes knowledge, belief, art, morals, law, custom, and any other capabilities and habits acquired by the individual as a member of society.' However, culture has also been described as 'one of the two or three most complicated words in the English language.' (Williams, 1976) There is no shortage of proposed definitions—150, according to one study. The definition of culture remains elusive and contested. Both in terms of its specific meaning and broad content, the

J. Zajda, *Engagement, Motivation, and Students' Achievement*, Globalisation, Comparative Education and Policy Research 48,
https://doi.org/10.1007/978-3-031-61613-6_7

understanding of 'culture' has defied consensus among sociologists. The epistemological ambiguity is, in part, due to the difficulties in defining meaningful boundaries and deciding what resources to include/exclude.

I would like to suggest that culture can be defined as consisting of languages, beliefs and values, artefacts, ideology, religions, organisations, and technology. These are the essential major attributes of all cultures, both locally and globally.

7.2 Culture and Beliefs About Knowledge, Values, and Learning

Every society has its own rules defining behaviour and actions. This is a normative dimension of a society and its culture, consisting of norms, and values. Teachers often transmit beliefs of the mainstream culture through the 'hidden curriculum'. Hidden curriculum refers to understanding, knowledge, values and attitudes, that are implicit in school structures and in the way, material is taught (Duchesne & McCaughey, 2022). May be conveyed through:

- how teachers control interaction
- assessment and reporting practices
- teaching methods
- teaching resources (Duchesne & McCaughey, 2022).

I have argued in my books (Zajda, 2021, 2022, 2023) that student's cultural identity is one of key factors in engagement and learning. Cultural identities play a most significant role in engaging and motivating students in schooling, both locally and globally. Student's identity refers to cultural, social, emotional, and behavioural factors. It defines student's self-concept, and self-esteem. How students feel about themselves, and whether they feel that they belong, and feel that they are accepted, defines their classroom interaction and their levels of engagement. Unless students feel good and positive, and are motivated by their teachers, they are not likely to be interested, or committed to learning. (Zajda, 2023). Discourses of cultural identity suggest that national identity is not fixed, but dynamic in nature, affected by dominant forces of globalisation and the media.

One of the most powerful forces of globalisation shaping cultural identities is the ubiquitous presence of information technology and the mass media. Every facet of culture and identity is defined by the mass media and propelled by the information technology. Global marketing of socially desirable commodities, such as clothing, fashion and global brands, perfumes, toys, and the entertaining industry, to name a few, has affected cultural identity. Global marketing affecting the formation of one's cultural identity has manufactured a new consumerist and materialistic culture, of 'commodification of the self' (Zajda, 1988). Cultural identity discourses demonstrate a complex nexus between globalisation, cultural identity, and ideology. Recent research indicates that cultural identity discourses have shifted from one dimensional concept, towards a multidimensional concept of cultural identity. Hence, there is a need to position cultural identity research and various discourses surrounding cultural identity, within dominant ideologies, and identity politics.

7.3 Social and Cultural Factors and Schooling

There is a universal consensus that social and cultural factors exert a powerful influence on both learning and teaching in the classroom, particularly academic achievement. According to Duchesne & McCaughey (2022), sociocultural factors contribute to individual difference; have a basis in society and culture, exhibit social and cultural contexts in which we live, learn, and develop, demonstrate the ways they contribute to differences among individuals and show as to why some groups do not achieve equal outcomes in terms of achievement and participation in education.

For decades, policy makers, researchers and educators explored the nexus between social factors and schooling. Coleman's (1966) groundbreaking US government report *Equality of Educational Opportunity* opened educational inequality and performance debate, which continues today. Coleman's (1966) concluded that the most important predictor of a child's academic performance in school was not the school building or resources. It was home life. It was the family. As Coleman (1972) explained 'All factors considered, the most important variable—in or out of school—in a child's performance remains his family's education background' (Coleman, 1972).The educational inequality debate generated by the Coleman Report was one of many in the long history of American policy reforms to refer to education to solve *macro social*, or large scale educational and social problems, in the process encouraging us to ask too much of our schools. Why educational approaches to fighting poverty, and inequality have persistently generated so much enthusiasm, and the Coleman Report certainly generated one of one of them—when schooling was viewed as an agency of transformation and that had the power to change society, remains a pressing question for educators, policy analysts and advocates of human rights and social justice alike.

To have a more informed knowledge of the inequality debate and educational inequality one needs to consider the complex nexus between society, culture and education, and the symbiotic relationship between culture and schooling. To begin with, we need to examine critically major agencies of socialization affecting the individual situated in a particular cultural environment, beginning with *microsystem* (Bronfenbrenner, 1979). Sociologists have defined major agencies of socialization as the family, the peers, the neighbourhood, the school, the teachers, the media, community and society at large.

7.4 Bronfenbrenner's Bioecological Model of Development

Individuals' particular attitudes, knowledge, values, and behavior are acquired and shaped by a number of major agencies of socialization, such as the family, the peers, the school and the media. Urie Bronfenbrenner (1979), influenced by sociological perspectives of major agencies of socialization, developed his innovative Ecological Systems Model, to explain how individuals' attitudes and beliefs are shaped by their culture and environment and how they affect their resultant attitudes, values, and behavior patterns. According to Bronfenbrenner's Ecological Systems Theory, children are influenced by various levels in the Ecological Systems Model, beginning with the home (primary group) and then continuing at school (secondary group). Bronfenbrenner's model lists five spheres, or levels of socialization, affecting children and adults alike in different cultures:

- *Microsystem*: Interactions and activities in the child's *immediate* environment and refers to the institutions and groups that most immediately and directly impact on the child's development, including: family, school, religious institutions, neighbourhood, and peers.
- *Mesosystem*: Consists of interconnections between the microsystems, for example between the family and teachers or between the child's peers and the family.
- *Exosystem*: Involves links between social settings that do not involve the child. For example, a child's experience at home may be influenced by their parent's experiences at work.
- *Macrosystem*: Societal and cultural influences in the child's development. Describes the overarching culture that influences the developing child, as well as the microsystems and mesosystems embedded in those cultures. Cultural contexts can differ based on geographic location, socioeconomic status, poverty, and ethnicity. Members of a cultural group often share a common identity, heritage, and values. Macrosystems evolve across time and from generation to generation.
- *Chronosystem*: Includes changes in environments and processes over time which influence development. It consists of the pattern of environmental events and transitions over the life course, as well as changing socio-historical circumstances.

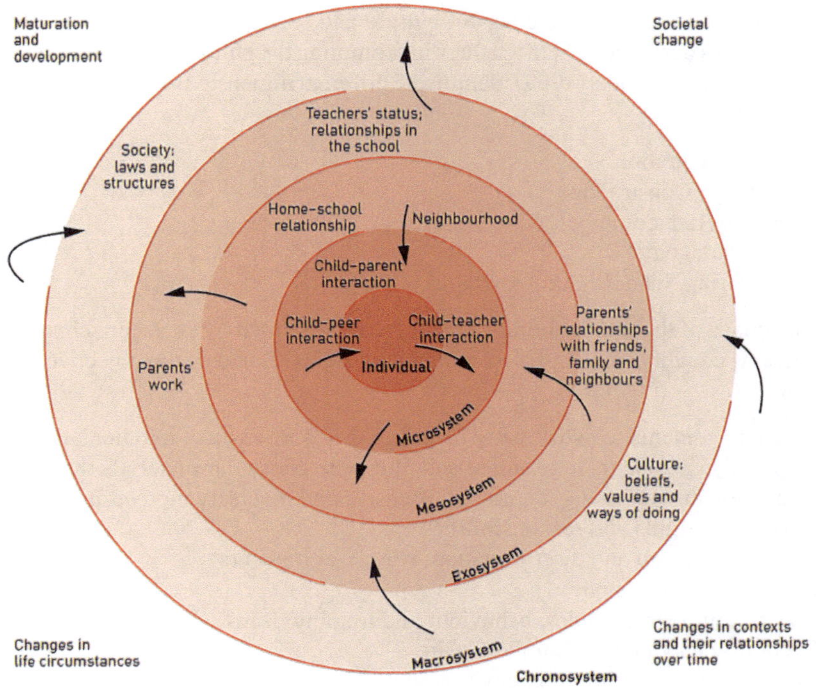

(Citation: Duchesne & McCaughey, 2022. *Educational psychology for learning and teaching*, p. 441)

7.5 Dimensions of Multicultural Education

Following Bronfenbrenner's Ecological Systems Theory, we need to consider the nature of cultural diversity and multiculturalism and implications for schooling. Multiculturalism is a term which recognizes and celebrates the cultural diversity of population. The reality and relevance of cultural diversity and multiculturalism in the USA was already addressed by Banks (2019), who analyzed the existence of a growing ethnic, cultural, social-class, and linguistic gap between many of the teachers and their students in the USA. Banks, who is a leading multicultural educator and writer in the world, has been writing on multicultural education in the USA for many decades (see Zajda, 2022). The goal of Banks' (2019) multicultural education model is to enable students from diverse racial and ethnic backgrounds to fully engage with and access the curriculum, and acquire designated knowledge, skills and values. To advance multicultural education in schools, Banks (1995a) developed his timely and relevant model of multicultural education strategy, based on his five dimensions: content integration, the knowledge construction process, prejudice reduction, equity pedagogy, and an empowering school culture and social structure (Banks, 1995a). His model was designed to help teachers in promoting the philosophy of multicultural curriculum. James Banks (1999) identified 5 different dimensions in the multicultural curriculum:

- Content Integration
- Knowledge Construction
- Prejudice Reduction
- Equity Pedagogy
- Empowering Schools culture. (Banks, 1999).

Objectives of the multicultural curriculum are informed by such core concepts as democracy, equality, social justice, and human rights. Some of the objectives could include:

- Teaching students to avoid using language that is insensitive to other students
- Encouraging students to examine and eliminate curricular materials that may be damaging, embarrassing, debasing, offensive and reversely motivating
- Know your rights and responsibilities
- Challenge racism and discrimination, whenever it occurs
- Be a positive role model
- Assess your own attitudes, behaviour and training needs
- Recognise and value cultural diversity
- Create an inclusive learning environment
- Encourage the involvement of parents and community members from all backgrounds.

My interest in multicultural education and culturally diverse environments was immensely influenced by my upbringing, my memories, my background, and experiences, as a child and pupil in the USSR, Poland, and Australia. In the USSR, we lived in a very multicultural community in Stanisławów, now Ivano-Frankivsk (Western Ukraine). Stanisławów was already a fortress built in the thirteenth century, to defend the settlement against the Mongols, who invaded the place in 1240. Stanisławów became a city in 1662, under a Polish nobleman Andrzej Potocki, who was a count and a powerful military leader. The city ratusz (town hall) was completed later in 1666. As it was within walking distance, from where we lived, I used to see it daily, as well the ruins of the fortress on the hill, as I walked to the school. I had no idea that these historic sites dated to 1240 and 1666 respectively. I suspect my teachers themselves were unaware of the historical significance of the place. Languages spoken included Ukrainian, Russian, and Yiddish. In our block of flats, where we lived, there were Russian, Ukrainian, and Jewish families. My multicultural experiences in the USSR, Poland, and Australia, speaking Polish, Russian and Ukrainian, and learning English were discussed in my book *Discourses of globalisation, cultural diversity and values education* (2023) in Chap. 3, Multicultural education globally for democracy, equality, and social justice. Urie Bronfenbrenner (1970), in his classic book *Two Worlds of Childhood*, described and analysed schooling in the USA and the USSR. However, I had experienced three worlds of childhood: the USSR, Poland, and Australia.

Overall, multicultural education is a field of study, reflects cultural diversity in societies and schools, and aims to promote and create equal educational opportunities for all students from culturally diverse backgrounds. Above all, multicultural education is built on the ideals of democracy, social justice, equality, peace, human rights, and freedom. Multiculturalism is a term which recognizes and celebrates the cultural diversity of a population. Banks (1984) defined multicultural education, as 'an inclusive concept used to describe a wide variety of school practices, programs, and material designed to help children from diverse groups to experience educational equality' (Banks, 1984, p. 182). Multicultural education involves learning about the distinctive characteristics that are representative of and are common within a particular group of people. Global education, on the other hand, is about teaching students the values, skills, attitudes, and knowledge which will enable them to be aware and empowered global citizens of the future. Bronfenbrenner (1979) in his influential bioecological model argued that individuals are shaped by major agencies of socialization: the family, the peers, the neighbourhood, the school, the media, etc. This innovative model, together with Bandura's social learning theory, helps us to understand better how we are socialized by major agencies of socialization, and how we acquire our attitudes, beliefs, knowledge, values and behaviour. Both Bronfenbrenner's and Bandura's models also explain the origins of bias and prejudice, exhibited by some individuals towards people from culturally diverse environments. In addition to Banks' multicultural education model, I want to add global education and intercultural dialogue, as two additional perspectives, to enrich our knowledge of cultural diversity. These offer additional perspectives to major discourses of multicultural education. Let me examine further their relevance and significance in culturally diverse environments.

As I have argued in my books *Globalisation and education reforms: Creating effective learning* (2021), and *Globalisation and education reforms: Overcoming discrimination* (2022), the student's 'self-concept, together with self-esteem and self-efficacy' will invariably play a major role in the overall learning process, academic achievement, and motivation to learn and do better in culturally diverse classrooms (Zajda, 2021, 2022).

7.5.1 Global Education

With reference to global education, I would like to define 'globalisation', from a social and cultural transformation perspective, as a new dominant ideology of *cultural convergence*, which is accompanied by corresponding economic, political, social, technological, and educational transformations. Such a process is characterised by increasing economic and political interdependence between nations, and which ultimately, transforms the ethnocentric core of the nation-state and national economy. The phenomenon of 'globalisation' refers, in general sense, to people around the globe being more connected to each other than ever before, to a quantum-like pace of the international flow of communication, knowledge and money, to consumer goods and services produced in one part of the world being increasingly available in all parts of the world, and to the explosion of international travel (Zajda, 2021).

Global education is built on the ideals of genuine human rights, democracy, freedom, social justice, equality, peace, and harmony. 'Global education seeks to prepare students to live in an increasingly globalised world society and to be active, participating citizens in that society, who contribute to shaping a better world. It operates in the assumption that people and communities are becoming increasingly interdependent' (Global Education Project, 2014). As such, global education aims to provide both students and teachers with opportunities to develop a better and deeper knowledge, understanding, and skills of major global issues affecting our lives. These include:

- Globalisation
- Inequality
- Slavery
- Human Rights
- Freedom
- Poverty
- Global Warming/Climate change
- Population Growth
- Food inequity
- Water quantity & quality
- Education for social justice
- Disasters etc.

7.6 Multicultural Education for Equality, Democracy, and Social Justice

What we need to remind ourselves is that the major goal of multicultural education in schools is to promote a better and informed knowledge equality, democracy, and social justice for all. We begin developing our informed critical thinking with a better and deeper knowledge and understanding of cultural diversity, which is all around us. Cultural diversity will continue to grow in its complexity, and we need to accept it. We are surrounded by individuals from culturally diverse backgrounds, who speak many languages and who display different values and lifestyles. This represents the on-going reality of growing multiculturalism and cultural diversity, both locally and globally.

One of the goals of effective multicultural education is to help transform and reconstruct society and schools globally, providing equality for all. One could practice culturally responsive teaching. This is one of the strategies which can foster the growth and acceptance of cultural diversity in multicultural classrooms. The approaches could include inquiry learning, critical thinking, role play, cooperative learning, literature-based activities, and story-writing. Effective multicultural pedagogies can help significantly reduce an on-going racism and discrimination in schools and societies (Zajda, 2022). Human rights are violated by all forms of racism, as discussed in my books *Globalisation and education reforms: Creating effective learning* (2021), and *Globalisation and education reforms: Overcoming discrimination* (2022). Multicultural education tends to focus on reducing prejudice and discrimination among groups, and works on developing equality, opportunity, and access to quality education for all. The pedagogue's key role is to provide engaging activities that promote authentic cultural diversity, where all students feel that they belong. The school curriculum for inclusive pedagogy should provide opportunities for students to learn another language, so that some students become bilingual. The school and the inclusive pedagogy should provide equal attention to all students from diverse cultural backgrounds. In addition, inclusive classrooms tend to create a classroom climate that encourages trust, tolerance, respect, harmony, and peace.

Within the discourses of multicultural education, we need to incorporate effective learning environment to promote a deeper understanding and knowledge of today's cultural diversity affecting us all. To me, the most significant key ideas and concepts affecting all aspects of multicultural education and quality learning in schools globally begin necessarily with the student's cultural identity, self-concept, values education, and active engagement. In addition to the student's identity, and self-concept, we also need to think of time, place, school's location, and country. Culturally diverse students globally, depending on where they are located and how they are shaped by major agencies of socialisation, are likely to display different attitudes, values, and behaviour patterns towards schooling (Zajda, 2021).

As a social reconstructionist pedagogy, multicultural education deals more directly with such topics as oppression and social equality, based on race, ethnicity, social class, religion, and gender. One of the major goals of a social reconstructionist pedagogy is one of preparing students to acquire the ability to reconstruct and change the future society, so that it better serves the interests of all groups of people. How can this occur in the classroom? We could encourage students to develop a sense of responsibility and critical thinking for desirable social actions, and ask them to analyse, for instance, discrimination, conflict, and inequality affecting their own lives.

7.7 Values Education in Culturally Diverse Classrooms

Values can be defined as the principles governing rules and standards for socially desirable behaviour. Such values include freedom, democracy, equality, justice, truth, and human rights. Values also provide moral standards, by which actions are judged as right or wrong (Zajda, 2018). In general, values refer to beliefs held by individuals or groups concerning moral standards defining actions that are 'good or bad', and what is desirable and what is not desirable. Global research findings have demonstrated the nexus between values education and students' academic performance in schools. Values education to be meaningful, engaging and authentic must involve a greater sense of active citizenship education, social constructivist pedagogy, and more emphasis on cultural diversity, critical thinking and a deeper and critical understanding and knowledge of democracy, equality, human rights and social justice for all. All teaching and learning in classroom settings is necessarily grounded in morality, ethics and laws, defining and directing classroom pedagogy. Ethics, derived from moral philosophy, is concerned with the study of right and wrong actions, or choosing between good or bad. While teachers are entitled to their own beliefs and **values,** in the classroom, teachers' responsibility is defined and guided by their designated school policies, classroom pedagogies, prescribed curriculum, content and its standards (Zajda, 2020). What I want to argue is that values education and effective learning environments have a positive and significant impact on students' identities and their academic achievement.

The term values education refers to a multifaceted process of socialization in schools, which transmits dominant values, to provide and legitimate the necessary link between the individual, the group and society. Values education is a structured process of instilling desirable aspects of moral education, ethical traits, and standards. Values are culturally internalized, shared, and transmitted ideas about what is good or desirable. Values may refer to: a particular belief system—believing that pluralist democracy is the best model of social/political system; a code of conduct—being honest, tolerant, and courageous; a state of existence—peace, tolerance and equality); or a moral judgment—truth, beauty, and justice.

7.8 Global Models for Values Education

The Western and non-Western models of values act as dominant agencies of socialization for values education, social identity, and nation-building. Western-informed international conventions provide value statements globally (Zajda, 2021). The United Nation's *Universal Declaration of Human Rights* (UN, 1984) was a statement by the international community of the inalienable rights and fundamental freedoms for all human beings. In Article 26, Part 2 it stressed that education 'shall be directed...to the strengthening of respect for human rights and fundamental freedom. It shall promote understanding tolerance and friendship among all nations, racial or religious groups...' (UN, 1948, p. 7). Other specific value positions are found in various international and legal treaties. For example, the four major Council of Europe treaties protecting the human rights of children combined offer a policy direction for developing and promoting a global vision for a better childhood. The four principal treaties are the European Convention on Human Rights (1950), the European Social Charter (1996), the European Convention on the Exercise of Children's Rights (1996) and the European convention on Contact Concerning Children (2003). Values associated with schooling are found in the Report to UNESCO of the International Commission on Education for the twenty-first century, *Learning: The Treasure Within* (Delores, 1996) and its four essential pillars of education for the twenty-first century: *learning to know, learning to do, learning to live together* and *learning to be*. More recently, the UNESCO Conference on Education for Shared Values and for Intercultural and Interfaith Understanding (2005) called on educational systems to incorporate common and agreed values into school curricula, to promote intercultural and interfaith understanding. Recently, the idea of 'global competence' was developed by OECD and PISA. The teaching of global competence to enhance students' knowledge and values of intercultural sensitivity was developed in *Preparing our youth for an inclusive and sustainable world the OECD PISA global competence framework* (PISA, 2018b):

> Global competence is a multidimensional capacity. Globally competent individuals can examine local, global and intercultural issues, understand and appreciate different perspectives and world views, interact successfully and respectfully with others, and take responsible action toward sustainability and collective well-being... Schools can encourage intercultural sensitivity and respect by allowing students to engage in experiences that foster an appreciation for diverse peoples, languages and cultures. (PISA, 2018b, p. 4)

Values education differs around the world both locally, regionally and nationally. Different values are transmitted, according to differences in cultural settings, be they religious, cultural or political. In some communities and societies, dominant values are defined by the ideology of religion or politics. As Huntington (1996) points out, in his book *The Clash of Civilizations and the Remaking of World Order* culturally diverse nations, divided by different and competing ideologies for global dominance, have different values priorities. In the USA, being a democratic society, the values of individualism, equality, freedom, democracy, and self-fulfilment are inculcated in schools. Values education in Europe reflect economic and social principles, which embrace student-centred learning, accompanied by dominant values embedded in cognitive, social, and emotional development, and vocational philosophies of achievement, success and work (Zajda, 2021).

7.8.1 Values Education in Schools

Values education in schools represents an essential, contested and constantly changing area of study that develops critical thinking skills that are vital for all other areas of study. A very good example of the nexus between globalisation, and values education in humanities and social sciences education is the National Council for the Social Studies. According to NCSS, social studies educators should 'teach students the content knowledge, intellectual skills, and civic values necessary for fulfilling the duties of citizenship in a participatory democracy and that 'In a multicultural, democratic society and globally connected world, students need to understand the multiple perspectives that derive from diverse cultural vantage points' (*National Curriculum Standards for Social Studies*, 2010). Carr et al. (2017) in examining the nexus between multicultural social justice education, democracy, and education for democracy, argued for the need to employ critical thinking and critical pedagogies, in order to develop a new knowledge and skills of 'transformative education for democracy':

> Our findings underpin the need to include critical pedagogies that focus on reflexivity, transmediation, autobiography, and self-positionality throughout the educational process. A broad, multi-pronged framework for conceptualizing a critical, engaged, transformative education for democracy is proposed, in which multicultural social justice education is inextricably interwoven. (Carr et al., 2017)

The current debate on values education has become an overtly partisan political issue producing a dominant ideology of teaching values and character education. I am reminding the readers that what we call values education was known as 'character education' in most schools during the nineteenth and twentieth centuries. Values education has also became a 'metaphor and code' for pedagogy pursuing the neo-liberal and conservative social and cultural agenda (Purpel, 1999, p. 83). In some ways, according to Purpel (1999), the values taught in schools are traditional rather than modern:

> ...the values taught in the schools are very much in line of Puritan tradition of obedience, hierarchy, and hard work, values which overlap nicely with the requirements of an economic system that values a compliant and industrious work force, and a social system that demands stability and order. (Purpel, 1999, p. 89)

Virtues such as freedom, justice, truth telling and kindness are general moral principles, or abstractions. They, in themselves, cannot explain daily applications. Hence, values education needs to be practical, as individuals confront their values, societal values, choices, and their applications in everyday life. Furthermore, a critical understanding, analysis, and evaluation of moral principles such as freedom, human rights, social justice and responsibility in classroom pedagogy constitutes the essence of morality and value education and should form the foundation of moral education of an individual. Here, the focus is on translating abstract moral principles into everyday life (Zajda, 2021).

7.9 Factors Contributing to Engagement and Academic Achievement in Schools

When examining major factors affecting academic achieving in schools, researchers have listed the following major variables: school environment, social factors, instruction, teaching, students, method of teaching, learning strategies and the school. Research findings of Hattie, Biggs & Purdie (1996) demonstrated that the most significant factors impacting on students' academic achievement were:

1. Students' learning strategies, specifically reinforcement (0.49 correlation)
2. Teaching, specifically questioning techniques (0.47 correlation)
3. Students' cognitive development (0.44 correlation)
4. Social and cultural factors at home (0.31 correlation)
5. Teachers' Feedback (0.31 correlation)
6. Classroom environment and the school (0.20 and 0.12 correlations respectively).

Originally, Hattie studied six areas that contribute to learning: the student, the home, the school, the curricula, the teacher, and teaching and learning approaches. The updated list also includes the classroom. But Hattie (2009) did not only provide a list of the relative effects of different influences on student achievement. He also explains the data. He found that the key to making a difference was making teaching and learning visible. He further explained this story in his book *Visible learning for teachers* (2009).

John Hattie updated his list of 138 effects to 150 effects in *Visible Learning for Teachers* (2011), and more recently to a list of 195 effects in *The Applicability of Visible Learning to Higher Education* (2015). His research was based on nearly 1200 meta-analyses—up from the 800 when *Visible Learning* came out in 2009. According to Hattie the story underlying the data has hardly changed over time even though some effect sizes were updated and we have some new entries at the top, at the middle, and at the end of the list.

7.9.1 Visible Learners

Visible classrooms are committed to five key educational principles: that learning is purposeful, social, emotional, empowering, and representational.

1. Show how to make learning happen in relation to others, spark emotional connections, give students power over their learning, and express ideas in multiple ways
2. Illustrate Reggio-inspired principles and approaches via quotes, photos, student and teacher reflections, and examples of student work.
3. Offer a new way to enhance learning using progressive, research-based practices for increasing collaboration and critical thinking in and outside the classroom.

7.10 Race and Ethnicity Discrimination

Other social and cultural factors include race and ethnicity and their impact on individuals' access to quality education. In *Globalisation and education reforms: Overcoming discrimination* (2022), in Chap. 2, dealing with dominant discourses of race and ethnicity discrimination in education, I examined racial stratification and inequality and argued that it is one of the 'most serious inequality issues confronting societies and schooling globally':

> Racial prejudice is one of the greatest obstacles for achieving authentic pluralist democracy, equality, human rights and social justice. Race, as a construct, continues to be a significant dimension of social inequality, and discrimination, contributing to entrenched racial stratification in society, and education, and affecting academic achievement in the USA and elsewhere. (Zajda, 2022, p. 17, p. 24)

Ethnocentrism is very difficult to overcome in the classroom. If we define 'ethnocentrism' as a particular view of culture, then we have created the majority/minority divide in the classroom. Ethnocentrism can range from an open intolerance of other people, based on their race, ethnicity, language, religion, and life styles, to dislike of people's looks, beliefs, attitudes, and values. While Nelson (2002) reviewed unequal treatment and reducing racial and ethnic disparities in health care in the USA (Nelson, 2002, p. 668), Zajda & Freeman (2009) examined race and ethnicity research globally and evaluated the interplay between state, ideology and current discourses of race, ethnicity and gender in the global culture. They discovered that race continued to be a significant dimension in education and academic achievement in the USA and elsewhere. In the USA, only one-quarter of community colleges can be considered racially integrated, where on average 37 percent of their students are from minority groups. One recent study by Goldrick-Rab & Kinsley (2013) reported that some 75 percent of the variation in 'racial composition in the two-year sector is directly attributable to the racial composition of their surrounding geographic locales':

> The problems of those communities resulting from neighbourhood segregation and the concentration of poverty are simply transferred up the educational pipeline. Segregated community colleges with large shares of needy students not only receive fewer monetary resources, but they likely produce less student learning. (https://www.insidehighered.com/news/2013/05/28/consequences-racial-and-economic-stratification-community-colleges)

Carnevale (2013) argued that U.S. higher education is 'colour blind' in theory, it 'in fact operates, at least in part, as a systematic barrier to opportunity for many African-Americans and Hispanics'. He demonstrated that since the mid-1990s, student enrolment in American higher education has grown increasingly stratified along racial lines with White students overwhelmingly populating the '468 most well-funded, selective four-year colleges and universities while African-American and Hispanic students were more and more concentrated in the 3,250 least well-funded, open-access, two- and four-year colleges' (http://diverseeducation.com/article/54956/).

Hence a better and more meaningful understanding of race and racialisations in education are needed in order to see the real experiences of minority groups in educational systems, as they negotiate inequitable and discriminatory social and cultural conditions in increasingly stratified societies (see Baker, Keller-Wolff & Wolf-Wendel, 2000; Rezai-Rashti & Solomon, 2008). Gosa & Alexander (2007) demonstrated how the dimension of race still matters in schooling and success. They argued that racial discrimination affects both working-class and middle-class African Americans. Well-off African American children, in general, were not as successful in academic achievement as white American students:

> While the educational difficulties of poor black students are well-documented and have been discussed extensively, the academic performance of well-off African American children has received much less attention. However, despite economic and educational resources in the home, well-off African American youth are not succeeding in school at the levels of their white peers. (Gosa & Alexander, 2007)

Freeman (2006), in attempting to explain under-achievement of black children argued that this was due to the process of cultural assimilation and the loss of social identity (Freeman, 2006, p. 51).

By examining the socialisation process in schools, assimilation, prejudice and stereotypes, one could argue that the schools' ethos and classroom environment contribute to black children's low self-esteem; low motivation and lack of desire and interest in maximising their educational and human potential (see also Briggs, 2014). Some researchers have demonstrated that the relationship between self-esteem and student outcomes is limited, at best. Hansford & Hattie (1982) demonstrated in their meta-analysis of 128 research studies that the average correlation was in the range of 0.21 to 0.26, which means that differences in self-esteem can account for only about 4 to 7% of variation in academic performance. These studies represented a total sample of 202,823 persons and produced a data base of 1136 correlations between self-ratings and performance measures. A range in the relationship of 0.77 to 0.96 was reported with an 'average' correlation of 0.21.

Furthermore, since African Americans lagged behind Whites in college attendance, they lacked 'access to many of the necessary skills that higher education provides' (Freeeman, 2006, p. 48). Gosa & Alexander (2007) suggested that cultural capital, education, income, and other SES indicators were insufficient to explain these differences in academic achievement. Instead, it may well be that the perception of race itself in the society is the real issue. Both whites and non-whites have constructed and internalised their racial identities:

> [T]he race at issue is a social construction, imbued with meaning through its particularhistory and current place in the social fabric. The liabilities that prevent black parents from passing on advantages to their children are racial, in the sense that they follow from the contemporary and historic social ecology of race. Closing the black-white education gap, and keeping it closed, necessarily will involve strategies that acknowledge and address the continuing significance of race ... differences in school quality, segregative patterns *within* schools, and teacher relationships intersect to hinder the academic development of better off black **youth. Conse**quently, the family background advantages that middle-class whites enjoy in positive schooling outcomes are not realized to the same extent by middle-class blacks. (Gosa & Alexander, 2007)

Rezai-Rashti and Solomon (2008) have examined racial identity models and the notion of racial identity in social settings. Their findings indicated that 'people of colour' have 'different orientations, understandings and experience of race, racism and race privilege' in institutional settings (2008, p. 184).

I have argued previously that there is a need to reassert the relevance of intercultural dialogue in an increasingly interdependent world of globalisation and social change, to address ethnic and racial discrimination in education both locally and globally (Zajda, 2009). In *Understanding Others, Education Ourselves* (National Research Council, 2002, p. 9), it was argued that comparative and international discourses surrounding other cultures, can often lead us to 'identify and question beliefs and assumptions that are taken for granted', by 'making the familiar strange' and the strange familiar', and questioning the 'universality' of our beliefs and assumptions. Informed and balanced intercultural dialogue can help us to define, explain and critique what is achievable, especially within the current imperatives of globalisation.

By focusing on topic social and cultural factors and their influences on engagement in the classroom globally, I wish to answer one of the most pressing global questions:

Are social, economic, and cultural divisions between the nations, between school sectors, between schools and between students growing or declining? To answer this question, we need to re-examine and re-assess current evidence concerning the nexus between intercultural dialogue, cultural transferability and human rights, and democracy models (Zajda, 2023). We need to examine such topics as education for all, language issues in cross-cultural research and education, and issues of race and ethnicity in the regional and global cultures. We also need to focus more on the unresolved tensions between religion, politics, and values education, and the implications for equity, access, and democracy. We need to critique the overall interplay between intercultural dialogue, education, and the state. This can be accomplished by drawing upon recent major and significant studies in the areas of education, intercultural dialogue, and transformational and global pedagogies. By referring to Bourdieu's call for critical policy analysts to engage in a 'critical sociology' of their own contexts of practice, and poststructuralist and postmodernist pedagogy, we need understand how central discourses surrounding the debate of intercultural dialogue and education are formed in the contexts of dominant ideology, power, and culturally and historically derived perceptions and practices defining the processes of nation-building and cultural identity in the global culture.

Critical discourses surrounding race, ethnicity and gender in education need to reflect a cross-cultural perspective. Discourses surrounding other cultures, nation-building and identity politics can often lead us to identify and question beliefs and assumptions that are taken for granted, by making the familiar strange and the strange familiar, and questioning the 'universality' of our beliefs and assumptions. It is not enough to depict cultural differences in intercultural research, and there is now a need to rediscover to what degree such cultural differences can be 'generalised' across cultures. The issues to be addressed in future research should include: What kinds of roles do our perceptions concerning identity (in this case perceptions of race, ethnicity and gender) and the nation state play in intercultural dialogue and conflict analysis, and the relationship between globalisation, social change and emerging cultural values.

7.11 The Role of Equity in Schooling

Aristotle's conception of equity is that of a corrective of justice which sits within the law but allows for the interpretation of phenomena to uphold a greater good. As he wrote in *Rhetoric*, "It is equitable to pardon human failings and look to the lawgiver and not the law, to the spirit and not to the letter…to the whole and not to the part" (I: 13). From these early iterations, equity has come to mean that which is in the best interest of the individual and community while upholding justice, though not in a tight and narrow sense (see also Zajda, Majhanovich, and Rust, 2006). The equitable man "is one who chooses and does equitable acts, and is not unduly insistent upon his rights, but accepts less than his share" (Aristotle, c. f. Beever, 2005). Such a notion of civil morality suggests that it is incumbent on all citizens, but especially those with means, to take less than they are entitled to so that others may have enough.

Rather than a principled, rights-based argument that fixes justice solely on what one is due by right, equity tempers justice by considering what all are due through a larger, moral criterion than what is fixed in law. Equity is what fills the gap between where the law or civil society is ambiguous, silent, or even non-existent, as a means of weighing what actions will promote justice and serving the best interests of the community and the individuals within it. Equity discourse is vital since those who advocate social equality in an era of globalization rely on appeals to equity, justice, and fairness rather than codified law. Education scholarship, particularly within multicultural education, often invokes equity as both a pedagogical principle and a rationale for public education. Christine Bennett (2003) differentiates equity from equality, as the latter requires identical treatment and the former "different treatment according to relevant differences" (p. 16). Gloria Ladson-Billings (1996) refers to equity pedagogy as ensuring equal access to knowledge for all students, which requires an intimate knowledge of the child (p. 196).

7.12 The Role of Cultural Capital in Schooling

Cultural capital refers to dominant conceptions of what constitutes knowledge, knowing, and social value. By upholding a single standard of what it means to be knowledgeable, educational systems both reinforces the differentiated achievement status of class groups while rewarding those who are conversant with implicit rules of dominant ideology (see Saha, 2005). Sociologist Pierre Bourdieu is widely recognized for his groundbreaking work on cultural capital. In *Distinction* (1979) Bourdieu argues that children develop from their parents a *habitus*, or unconscious orientations towards ways of being that fit their class position and thus reproduce social classes. He argues that these outlooks are cast at birth and even attempts to *add-on* cultural capital later in life will convey the sense that the child is an outsider. Schools, in a sense, are markets wherein children enter with various stores of capital that can be exchanged for enhancement of one's capital, and thereby, their life-chances. Children who lack the *habitus* of educated parents, or the working or poor classes, are simultaneously viewed as devoid of valued knowledge and filled with useless or detracting family baggage, or what Bourdieu described as an organic culture.

7.13 Poverty

Recent research findings show that children and young people living in disadvantage have access to fewer books and learning materials in the home. Access to support and resources forms the foundation for learning. In many cases, the parents of disadvantaged children may not have the necessary level of formal education, knowledge, skills, or experience to support their child's education. As these children get older, they have fewer opportunities to get ahead. Disadvantaged students are on average

2–3 years behind in reading and maths by the time they are 15 years old. The reading gap between the lowest socio-economic status (SES) students and the highest SES students is equivalent to almost three years of schooling. Year 12 completion rates are significantly lower (60%) for students from low SES backgrounds than for students from high SES backgrounds (90%). University students from high SES backgrounds are three times more likely to attend, than students from low SES backgrounds. https://www.thesmithfamily.com.au/poverty-in-australia.

7.13.1 UNESCO Study Reveals Correlation Between Poverty and Education

A study conducted by UNESCO (the UN Educational, Scientific, and Cultural Organisation) in June 2017, examined the correlation between poverty and the accessibility of education. Due to the high rates of children and adolescents who are out of school, or have not completed their education, the global poverty rate may not see a reduction. According to the UNESCO Institute for Statistics (UIS), the global number of children, adolescents, and youth out of school in 2015 was 264 million. From that, 61 million are children who are of primary school age. 62 million are young adolescents and 141 million are young people of upper secondary school age.

The study also showed that the majority of these out of school populations are in poorer countries. These countries generally have lower incomes and are in regions including Sub-Saharan Africa, Central and Southern Asia, Eastern Asia and South-eastern Asia, and Western Asia and Northern Africa. Poverty rates also have an impact on gender disparities in education, showcasing that more females than males are likely to be out of school in low-income and lower-middle income countries. As the study itself stated, low levels of education and acquisition of that education can hinder economic prosperity, which would, in turn, slow down poverty reduction. According to the study, if all adults received two more years of schooling or completed secondary school, it would lift nearly 60 million people out of poverty. The study postulates that economic growth would see an increase in their income. This could be achieved through effective education policies that address the issues of drop-out rates. Universal access to primary and secondary education is necessary to decrease the out of school rates, and therefore, decrease the poverty rate. (https://www.unaa.org.au/2017/06/28/unesco-study-reveals-correlation-between-poverty-and-education/).

In the global culture, international conventions provide policy statements, defining democracy, equality, human rights, and social justice. The United Nation's *Universal Declaration of Human Rights* (UN, 1948) was the first global policy document, by the international community, reaffirming the inalienable rights and fundamental freedoms for all human beings. In Article 26, Part 2 it stressed that education 'shall be directed…to the strengthening of respect for human rights and fundamental freedom. It shall promote understanding tolerance and friendship among all nations, racial or religious groups…' (UN, 1948, p. 7).

7.14 Conclusion

As demonstrated above, social, and cultural factors, together with cultural diversity and multiculturalism, and values education in schools can play a significant role in promoting democracy and active citizenship education. Teaching such core values as democracy, freedom, active citizenship, intercultural understanding, human rights, social justice, and peace, consolidates our ideal of participatory democracy. In schools, both locally and globally, where cultural diversity, values education and critical literacy are taught, values should be discussed and critiqued, within the paradigm of cultural diversity, and pluralist democracy, grounded in human rights and social justice discourses. Multiculturalism and values education have a potential to affect and change individuals in every sphere: cognitive, social, emotional, moral, and educational. Values education in schools ought to represent our quest for the ideal of the morally good society, to promote a deeper, meaningful, and critical understanding of democracy, equality, human rights, and social justice for all. Values education to be meaningful, engaging, and authentic in schools globally, must involve a greater sense of active citizenship education, grounded in pluralist democracy.

Chapter 8
Social Learning, Self-efficacy, and Self-regulated Learning in the Classroom

Albert Bandura (1986, 2002) pioneered and developed the concept of 'social cognitive theory' (initially known as *social learning theory*) and the notion of 'triadic reciprocal causation'. He examined the relationship between effective learning, or the ability of students to become self-regulated learners, and the associated three domains affecting students' learning: personal characteristics, behavioural patterns, and environment. Bandura used his conception of social cognitive theory to examine how students control and regulate their acquisition of knowledge, skills, and learning. Bandura further defined the three components of his Triadic Reciprocal Model, i.e. the interaction of personal characteristics, behaviour, and environment. *Personal characteristics* refer to a student's mental and emotional needs such as their goals and anxieties. It also encompasses the notion of self-efficacy or a student's belief in their learning abilities. *Behavioural patterns* refer to self-observation and self-evaluation. *Environment* refers to a student's social and physical environment. Bandura suggested that to be effective learners, students needed to exhibit self-control, self-regulation, and self-efficacy. Bandura's social learning theory has had important implication in the field of education. Today, both teachers and parents recognize the importance of modelling appropriate behaviours. Other classroom strategies such as encouraging children and building self-efficacy are also rooted in social learning theory. Self-control refers to controlling one's behaviour without external rewards or punishments. Self-regulation is the consistent use of self-control in new contexts. Self-efficacy refers to how one perceives one's ability to complete a given activity and therefore influences self-regulatory skills.

Bandura argued that self-efficacy is more powerful than rewards/punishments. Students with **high** self-efficacy were more likely to use self-regulating skills. Students with **low** self-efficacy tended to avoid challenging tasks, depended more on others, and reduced their chances for developing their self-regulation and self-efficacy skills—a vicious circle.

Bandura's three basic models of observational learning, consisted of:

J. Zajda, *Engagement, Motivation, and Students' Achievement*, Globalisation, Comparative Education and Policy Research 48,
https://doi.org/10.1007/978-3-031-61613-6_8

a. A live model, which involves an actual individual demonstrating or acting out a behaviour.
b. A verbal instructional model, which involves descriptions and explanations of a behaviour.
c. A symbolic model, which involves real or fictional characters displaying behaviours in books, films, television programs, or online media.

In his book *Social Learning Theory* (1977) Bandura stressed that 'most human behaviour is learned observationally through modelling: from observing others one forms an idea of how new behaviours are performed, and on later occasions, this coded information serves as a guide for action.' (Bandura). Bandura, like behaviourists, believed that students' acquisition of new knowledge and skills occurs by observing others' desirable behaviour to be copied, or modelled. The significant revisions to his social learning theory, included adding the central role of self-efficacy and the importance of individuals' actions and behaviours, to achieve desirable outcomes. Bandura was the 'first person to make this connection, and the main pillars of social learning theory were revised to make the following arguments:

- Learning is *both* behavioural *and* cognitive. It also occurs in a social context.
- Learning occurs through vicarious reinforcement–observing a behaviour *and* its consequences (which have social ramifications).
- Learning involves observation, drawing conclusions from observations, and making subsequent decisions (that do not necessarily result in an observable change in behaviour).
- While reinforcement is critical to learning, it is not the sole cause of learning.

Furthermore, Bandura suggested that the six major factors influencing students' observational learning, included:

1. Developmental status (cognitive development)
2. Learning from 'significant other' (role model)
3. Vicarious leaning
4. Outcome expectations
5. Self-efficacy
6. Goals.

Students' behaviours affected by self-efficacy include such factors as:

- Selection processes—a person with high self-efficacy will consider a variety of goals and participate in a variety of activities.
- Cognitive processes—high self-efficacy individuals use higher level thought process.
- Motivational processes—those who rate their capabilities as higher than average can be expected to work harder and longer to achieve a goal.
- Affective processes—when faced with a challenge, high self-efficacy individuals experience excitement, curiosity; low self-efficacy individuals likely to feel anxiety, depression.

Through the concept of reciprocal determinism, cognition, environment, and behaviour all influence each other and the learner.' (TeachThought Staff, 2022).

There is no doubt that Bandura's revisions to his dominant and popular social learning theory, which included the significant role of self-efficacy in students' acquiring new knowledge and skills, and stressing, that both behavioural and cognitive domains affect students' learning, were relevant and necessary. Recent research findings demonstrate the importance of students' cultural identities in learning, and engagement in the classroom (Castells, 2006; Ariely, 2019; Breitweiser, 2019; Zajda, 2023a). In addition, the affective domain is equally relevant to students' learning, especially emotional intelligence.

One of the most important emotional skills that connect us to others is the *capacity for empathy and sympathy*. Empathy is the ability to detect others' emotions. Increasingly, educational psychologists and researchers acknowledge that emotions are central to learning and teaching, and that an understanding of their role in the learner's experience is essential (Pekrun & Stephens, 2012). Emotional development plays a central role in our capacity to understand ourselves and others. An **emotion** is a mental or physiological state associated with a wide variety of feelings, thoughts, and behaviours. We usually experience emotions as a type of mental state that is closely connected to our actions and sense of wellbeing. It is well accepted that humans are born with a biological capacity for experiencing a range of **basic emotions** and that emotions are also shaped by interaction with the social environment, including cultural and social forces (Fischer et al., 1998; Menon, 2000; Panksepp, 2004). Recent theories of emotional development can be organised around functionalist and social constructivist perspectives.

The functionalist perspective

The **functionalist perspective** maintains that emotion is a central force that directs shapes and organises our behaviour (see Fischer, Wang, Kennedy & Cheng, 1998; Lazarus, 1991). This perspective includes the study of emotion in relation to cognitive processing; in other words, emotion helps us make meaning of our world in ways that cold, hard, rational thinking cannot (Dalgleish & Bramham, 1999). Emotions such as fear can redirect our thinking to work out safer solutions to a problem; a certain level of anxiety can sometimes direct us to focus on a task, but just a little too much anxiety can tip us over the edge into poor cognitive processing.

Functionalist perspectives also examine the role of emotion in shaping our social behaviour. For example, our ability to interpret and understand emotional expressions plays a critical role in our survival. By the time infants are three months of age, they and their mothers have developed a complex array of signals to convey and respond to emotion, including the ability to convey 'stranger danger' and fear, along with warmth and security (Boccia & Campos, 1989). Another critical area of research in the functionalist approach concerns the interaction between emotion and health. For example, states of psychological stress can depress the body's immune system, leading to ill health and development of the common cold virus (Cohen, Tyrell & Smith, 1991). Emotional deprivation in the mother–child relationship has

Table 8.1 Skills of emotional competence

- 'Awareness of one's own emotions,
- Ability to discern and understand other's emotions,
- Ability to use the vocabulary of emotion and expression,
- Capacity for empathic involvement,
- Ability to differentiate subjective emotional experience from external emotion expression,
- Adaptive coping with aversive emotions and distressing circumstances,
- Awareness of emotional communication within relationships, and
- Capacity for emotional self-efficacy'.(Saarni, 1999)

been associated with the child's failure to thrive and develop at an expected rate (Iwaniec, 2006).

The social constructivist perspective

The **social constructivist perspective** is largely reflected in the work of Carolyn Saarni and colleagues. This perspective incorporates elements of the functionalist perspective but also emphasises the role of the context in shaping our interpretation of situations. In this view, emotion allows an individual to maintain or change a relationship with their environment on a matter of importance to that person.

Emotional competencies and their development

The development of emotional competence is closely connected to our relationships with other people. For example, the earliest relationship in the child's life is characterised by attachment to a primary caregiver. this attachment relationship is critical for the development of social and emotional processing regions of the brain. It is within this earliest relationship that the foundations of emotional competence are formed. The following section explores several features of emotional development that hold important implications for learning and relationships with others. Each of the emotional competencies presented in Table 8.1 are interdependent; this means that skill or ability in one area is dependent on the development of skill in another area.

The first of Saarni's (1999) eight emotional competencies requires *awareness of our emotional state*. The ability to be aware of one's emotional state is also referred to as the development of *self-conscious emotions* (Lewis, 1993b; Saarni et al., 1998). Self-conscious emotions vary with age. They first appear between 18 and 24 months, when babies can experience pride, shame, and embarrassment. By about three years of age, children can experience emotions of envy and guilt (Lewis, 1993a; Sroufe, 2000). In the early years, these emotions are evoked primarily through adults' influence, such as when adults' praise for a job well done evokes pride in a child. Alternatively, parents or caregivers punish children for lying, making them feel shame and guilt for being deceitful (Zahn-Waxler & Robinson, 1995). Later in life, as a sense of self develops, external agents are no longer necessary to arouse these emotions. We usually feel proud of our accomplishments or ashamed of our weaknesses. These are known as 'higher-order' emotions because they require higher-order cognitive processing such as metacognitive awareness and because they depend on our capacity to reflect on our self. Self-conscious emotions are associated with our core values, such as the valuing of good academic results, or the valuing of others' opinions of our honesty or trustworthiness (Turner et al., 2002). To experience self-conscious emotions, we require an awareness of our self and of the ways in which that self might be harmed or enhanced. Higher-order emotions develop with adults' encouragement. For example, we experience the emotion of pride when we feel positive about ourselves for doing a good job. Thus, if a teacher praises a student for doing well on a test, the student feels proud of his achievement. Conversely, that student may feel shame if he fails a test, and his parents are disappointed or even angry. The student's sense of self is harmed, and he feels negative about.

Awareness of our emotional state is part of understanding of emotions. It is possible to experience more than one emotion at a time. Ability to discern the emotions of other people is equally necessary for developing a good sense of empathy. Empathy is an ability to read situational and expressive cues, such as facial expressions, that hold a clear emotional meaning. Capacity to be empathic and sympathetic, means to be involved in others' experiences by showing care and concern. Ability to use the vocabulary of emotion. Our culture and subcultures have a common language to describe emotion, and cultural scripts. One needs to understand that inner emotions need not match outward emotional expressions. It is possible for the self and others to hide emotions; awareness that our emotional expression can affect other people and ability to alter our presentation if necessary. It is also the ability to cope with unpleasant and distressing emotions. Individuals use self-regulation skills to soften or lessen the effect of their emotional states. It results in an awareness that relationships are partly defined by immediate and honest emotional expressions. There is an expectation in mature, close relationships of the mutual sharing of genuine emotions. Emotional self-efficacy results in feeling confident and satisfied with our emotional state, and being capable of achieving a balance in our emotional state.

Relying on the emotional signals and cues of others is called *social referencing*, as infants look to caregivers and other adults for clues about their social world. It seems that the easiest facial expressions to interpret are positive ones, such as happiness, whereas negative emotions such as fear, anger or sadness are more difficult for children to interpret (Fabes et al., 1991; Gross & Bailiff, 1991). As children grow older, they are more able to incorporate additional information to help them make sense of the emotions of others. For example, older children have a greater capacity to infer or predict a person's likely emotional response based on knowledge of that person's previous response in a similar situation. Younger children tend to rely on current contextual information to judge a person's likely emotional response (Gnepp, 1989). This difference appears to be attributable to the abstract and higher-order thinking skill associated with being able to infer or predict an outcome by transferring information from one time point to another.

The skill of discerning emotions has important implications for children's relationships with peers. Children who are very good at discerning emotions are better accepted by their peers (Cassidy et al., 1992; Walden & Knieps, 1996). In contrast, children who are rejected by their peers sometimes misinterpret or misread the social cues conveyed in the emotional responses of those peers (Crick & Dodge, 1994).

8.1 Social Learning in the Classroom

Bandura (1977) popularised the concept of modern idea of social learning globally. It suggested that individuals, in various settings, tend to acquire new ideas and behaviours, by simply observing significant others. Earlier researchers of social learning included Vygotsky (1934), Clark Hull and his associates (1941), Julian (1954), Skinner (1957), and Noam (1959). Vygotsky (1934), when examining thinking, language, and environments, argued that individual's thinking was strongly influenced by social and cultural factors. He also believed that social interaction played a key role in language development, speech, and cognition. However, the term *social learning* was used for the first time by Hull et al. (1941) in their path-finding book, *Social learning and Imitation.* They were followers of behaviorist stimulus–response theories, and suggested a new idea, in their drive theory, where a drive stimulates a behavioural response, and a drive for imitation, which was reinforced by social interaction. Rotter (1954), in his book, *Social Learning and Clinical Psychology*, argued, like Vygotsky, for the interaction between the individual and environment. Some believe it to be the first development of social learning theory. Skinner (1957), on the other hand, in his book *Verbal behaviour*, using his stimulus–response theories to describe language use and development, which was defined, and controlled by operant conditioning and behaviour modification, suggested that the process of acquiring language and speech was affected by one's environment. Chomsky (1959), however, rejected stimulus–response theories of behaviour in explaining speech and language acquisition, as it could not account for the process of language acquisition. Noam Chomsky, a linguist, in his innovative book *Syntactic Structures* (1957), proposed a new idea that 'all human beings may be born with an innate understanding of how language works' and that 'we *can* acquire language *because* we're genetically encoded with a universal grammar—a basic understanding of how communication is structured' (Chomsky, 1957). Jackendoff (2002), in his chapter 'Universal grammar' examined further Chomsky's, theory that one's ability to learn language is dictated by genetically encoded universal grammar, and that 'universal grammar is wired into children's brains' (Chomsky, 1957).

Bandura (1977) also suggested, as already mentioned in my Chap. 1, four key steps in observational learning in the classroom: attention, observation, retention, production, and motivation. These steps became accepted as the key principles of social learning theory.

The above works on social learning represent a complex nexus of behaviourism, cognitivism, social learning, environment, and genetics. Anna (2022), in her article 'How students can benefit from social learning, suggested five steps: be a role model, metacognitive teacher modelling, multiple modelling to scaffold, deepening modelling, and peer modelling. Teacher, as a role model, must communicate desirable attitudes, values, and behaviour patterns. There should be zero tolerance for aggressive behaviours and bullying in the classroom and school grounds.

Metacognition is often simply defined as 'thinking about thinking'. Metacognition refers to higher order thinking, which involves active control over the cognitive processes engaged in learning. The term 'metacognition' is most often associated with John Flavell, (1993). According to Flavell metacognition consisted of both metacognitive knowledge and metacognitive experiences, or regulation (Henrick, 2014). Activities such as planning how to approach a given learning task, monitoring comprehension, and evaluating progress toward the completion of a task are metacognitive. Metacognitive knowledge refers to acquired knowledge about cognitive processes, knowledge that can be used to control cognitive processes.

Metacognitive strategies

Metacognitive teacher strategies are designed to promote critical thinking, critical literacy, and generic, rather than surface learning. Metacognition involves the use of metacognitive strategies, which represent 'sequential processes that one uses to control cognitive activities, and to ensure that a cognitive goal (e.g., understanding a text) has been met' (Henrick, 2014). Henrick (2014), explained that met cognitive strategies help the learner to plan and monitor learning activities in the classroom:

> ...help to regulate and oversee learning, and consist of planning and monitoring cognitive activities, as well as checking the outcomes of those activities. For example, after reading a paragraph in a text a learner may question the concepts discussed in the paragraph. Her cognitive goal is to understand the text. Self-questioning is often a common metacognitive comprehension monitoring strategy. (Henrick, 2014)

The three basic classroom metacognitive strategies are:

1. Connecting new information to former knowledge.
2. Selecting thinking strategies deliberately.
3. Planning, monitoring, and evaluating thinking processes.

Developing metacognitive strategies may commence with: Identifying 'what you know' and 'what you don't know.' At the beginning of a research activity, or a task to be completed, students need to make conscious decisions about their knowledge. Initially students write 'What I already know about…' and 'What I want to learn about….' This is like KWL model: What student knows (K), what student wants to know (W), and what student learned about a topic (L). As students research the topic, they will clarify and expand it, or replace it with more accurate information. The process involves talking about thinking, which is important, because students need to build their own *thinking vocabulary*. Modelling and discussion in cooperative and collaborative groups, using both cognitive and social constructivist pedagogies, helps students to develop the vocabulary needed for thinking, and talking about their own thinking.

Metacognitive strategies consist of:

1. A 'metacognitive strategy is a memorable 'plan of action' that provides students an easy-to-follow procedure for solving a particular math problem.
2. Metacognitive strategies are taught using explicit teaching methods.
3. Metacognitive strategies include the student's thinking as well as their physical actions

4. Some of the most common metacognitive strategies come in the form of mnemonics which are meaningful words where the letters in the word each stand for a step in a problem-solving process' (Metacognitive strategies, 2002).
5. Metacognitive strategies need to be memorable, and they must accurately represent the learning task.

Following metacognitive teacher strategies, described earlier, teachers' use of multiple modelling strategies are likely to cater for diversity in social learning, including the use of cooperative and collaborative groups, with cognitive and social constructivist pedagogies, where students share with each other their new knowledge. Peer modelling is based on the idea that students tend to copy their desirable peers, or 'significant others', which they respect and value. These strategies can improve performance, as students think about their thinking, and monitor their progress. It can be used to reduce disruptive behaviour of students, as they are involved in self-guidance.

8.2 Applying Social Cognitive Theory in the Classroom

Bandura's (2012) social cognitive theory explains such factors as individual learning, development, acquisition of knowledge, and self-regulated competency, within a social context, in which 'parents, peers, and teachers play a significant role as social models' (Bembenutty et al., 2016). A unique contribution of social cognitive theory, according to Bembenutty et al. (2016), is its 'emphasis on the triadic interaction between the person, behaviour, and the environment' (Bembenutty et al., 2016). Using cognitive and social constructivist models and strategies, in social learning, together with critical literacy and critical thinking for improving students' engagement, and quality learning, I want to argue that they have the power to influence and change the learner in every sphere: cognitive, social, emotional, and academic achievement. An effective and engaging inclusive classroom environment affects students' knowledge, particularly in having a more meaningful and relevant knowledge, skills, and understandings of such key concepts as democracy, cultural identities, belonging, evolving cultural diversity, human rights, and social justice.

Self-regulated learning (SRL) strategies play a significant role in students' learning and their engagement, motivation, and academic achievement. In examining major factors contributing to students' improved learning in the classroom and their academic achievement, one needs to analyse students' use of (SRL) specific strategies. Self-regulated learning is a way of students' learning, and is influenced by a set of personal, cognitive, social, emotional, and behavioural factors. It consists of the ability to set a realistic and achievable goal for a given task. Students also use metacognition or thinking about the task (also self-monitoring), completing a task (performance), and self-evaluation. Zimmerman (2000) defined self-regulated learning as 'learners' beliefs about their capability to engage in appropriate actions, thoughts, feelings, and behaviours in order to pursue valuable academic goals, while self- monitoring and self-reflecting on their progress toward goal-completion' (Zimmerman, 2000; see also Zimmerman, 2015). In other words, Zimmerman (2000), in defining self-regulated learning, concentrated on learners' beliefs, their self-efficacy, and performance, accompanied by self-monitoring, designated task completion, and desirable performance, all resulting in high achievement. Self-regulation theory represents a deliberate and conscious activity that involves the process of guiding one's own thinking, feelings, values, performance goals, and appropriate behaviours, to achieve high performance. Students' demonstrated ability of self-regulation can be found already in cognitive, social and emotional development stages during childhood. Acquiring self-regulation knowledge and skills represent an important step, which students learn and employ for enhancing cognitive, emotional, and social dimensions. Teachers also play a significant role of promoting students' SRL in the classroom. Alvi & Gillies (2020) examined the primary school teachers' role in supporting students' SRL. The authors employed their integrative and ecological model of SRL-in-context, to analyse teachers' role. The authors concluded that teachers' 'abilities and skills enhanced students' levels of SRL, in terms of motivation, critical thinking and feedback:

> Overall, the teachers stressed multiple factors that influence their efforts to promote SRL. These include their own beliefs, abilities and motivational levels, the environment in which they find themselves, curriculum, students' home and family background and community. On the other hand, effective practices employed by the teachers to support students' SRL include: Providing instructional, motivational, behavioural, instrumental/strategic, and recreational support, fostering critical and independent thinking, continuous monitoring and feedback, and involving the community. (Alvi & Gillies, 2020, p. 16)

The research shows that self-regulated learning (SRL) skills make a significant impact on students' engagement, motivation and academic achievement (Chou & Zou, 2020; Cheng, 2021; DiBenedetto, 2018; Panadero, 2017; Schunk & Zimmerman, 2011; Zajda, 2023a). The significance of students' self-regulating learning (SRL), and its impact on academic achievement was examined by numerous scholars. The role of SRL in enhancing students' learning performance was analysed by Cheng (2021), who evaluated some 6524 students from schools in Hong Kong. His research findings demonstrated conclusively that 'students' learning motivation, goal setting, action control and learning strategies played a significant role in their learning performance' (Cheng, 2021). Panadero (2017), in 'A review of self-regulated learning: Six models and four directions for research', suggested that self-regulated learning (SRL) includes the 'cognitive, metacognitive, behavioural, motivational, and emotional/affective aspects of learning' which represents a 'core conceptual framework to understand the cognitive, motivational, and emotional aspects of learning' (Panadero, 2017).

Karen Peel (2019), in 'The Fundamentals for self-regulated learning: A framework to guide analysis and reflection', goes further, and examines critically a framework for self-regulated learning (SRL). Peel discusses the three principles of SRL, namely, a rationale for learning, a responsibility for learning, and a capability for and from learning. Peel suggests that in exploring opportunities that promote SRL in educational contexts, it is necessary to frame conceptually the influences that empower individuals to think and feel as active participants in their learning processes. The SRL fundamentals, namely 'individual, environmental and behavioural, tend to clarify how learners construct and rationalise their goals, and accept responsibility for monitoring cognition, motivation, and behaviour, to realise their capabilities (Peel, 2019). As a result, Peel (2019) concludes that the conceptualisation of the three SRL fundamentals presented in her research encompasses the personal, environmental, and behavioural influences, that support opportunities for learning to be self-regulated (see Zajda, 2023, Chap. 3). Teachers can help students to become more effective self-regulated learners by using the following classroom strategies:

a. Emphasize the importance of SRL skills in learning and when they should be used.
b. Model SRL skills, including the standards one uses to evaluate one's performance.
c. Provide guided practice and corrective feedback for the SRL skills to be mastered.

However, students need adequate preparation for their own learning. There is a need to teach students to use both memory and comprehension strategies and taking notes. Students need to use various forms of rehearsal and mnemonic devices (two reasons for teaching rehearsal: a useful tactic for keeping small amount of information active in STM; maintenance rehearsal is something young children can learn to use; remind them to use no more than seven items/chunks at a time). Students need to learn how to formulate comprehension questions. Students need to learn how to take good notes, etc.

8.3 Advantages of Social Learning for Teachers and Students

For teachers, social learning results in numerous advantages for students' levels of engagement, motivation, and performance. To enhance the quality of their pedagogy, teachers could consider implementing the following steps:

1. Adressing cultural diversity
2. Practicing the pedagogy of inclusive classroom
3. Advancing critical thinking
4. Using constructivist pedagogy
5. Promoting principles of democracy, equality, and social justice
6. Teaching global perspectives and education for sustainability.
7. Acting as a role model. (Zajda, 2023).

Addressing cultural diversity and multiculturalism represent the most significant step for progressive pedagogues. Acknowledging cultural diversity and implementing culturally responsive curriculum, prejudice reduction, an equity pedagogy, result in the acceptance of all students, tolerance, democracy, and social justice. (See Banks, 1995, 2017).

Practicing the pedagogy of inclusive classroom is also significant, as it enables students to feel that they belong, that they are valued, and their voices are respected. The inclusive classroom promotes a sense of democracy, equality, and social justice. Using the tools of constructivist pedagogy, teachers have the power to advance critical thinking and critical literacy, essential for maintaining and preserving participatory democracy, peace, and harmony.

It is equally important for pedagogues to promote global perspectives and education for sustainability. It helps to overcome ethnocentrism, bias and prejudice within the classroom, and the school community. At the same time, students begin to gain new knowledge regarding sustainability, both locally and globally.

For students, social learning produces many positive outcomes, in terms of knowledge, attitudes, values, and behaviour patterns. First, and foremost, they learn, by observing and imitating their desirable role models. Second, they learn to use metacognition, and self-regulated learning (SRL) skills. Third, they develop their emotional intelligence, and empathy. Fouth, they improve their critical literacy and critical thinking skills, by working in small cooperative, or collaborative groups, where cognitive and social constructivist pedagogy is used. Fifth, they develop a new knowledge of global perspective, and education for sustainability.

First, in social learning settings, students observe and learn from one another, at times imitating their role models. This represents Bandura's (1977, 1986) social learning theory, and his Triadic Reciprocal Model, of the interaction of personal characteristics, behaviour, and environment.

Second, students learn to use metacognition, metacognitive skills, and self-regulated learning (SRL) skills. Metacognition, as mentioned earlier, refers to students' higher order thinking, and their active control over the cognitive processes engaged in learning. SRL refers to the way of students learning takes place, which is influenced by many personal, cognitive, social, emotional, and behavioural factors. Students' SRL results in their ability to set a realistic and achievable goal for a given task. Students also employ metacognition in terms of self-monitoring, performance, and self-evaluation.

Third, students develop their emotional intelligence, and empathy. Emotional development as noted earlier, plays a key role in our capacity to understand ourselves and others. It is related to one's Emotional Intelligence (EI), or the ability to understand, manage and control emotions, as well as understanding 'the emotions of people around you'. Accordingly, there are 'five key elements to EI: self-awareness, self-regulation, motivation, empathy, and social skills' (Mental Health America, 2022).

Fouth, students improve their critical literacy and critical thinking skills, by working in small cooperative, or collaborative groups, where cognitive and social constructivist pedagogy is used.

Fifth, students develop a new knowledge of global perspective, and education for sustainability. Using 'Global Education Project', designed by Diana Boase and her team, students acquire new knowledge and understanding of such topics as

Australia's engagement with Asia and other places, and sustainability. Here the focus is on identity and cultural diversity, interdependence and globalisation, peace building and conflict resolution, sustainable futures, social justice, and human rights.

8.4 Conclusion

In schools, both locally and globally, where social, and emotional development are taught, they should be discussed and critiqued, within the paradigm of cultural diversity, and pluralist democracy, grounded in human rights and social justice discourses. Social, and emotional factors have the potential to affect and transform individuals in every sphere: social, emotional, moral, and academic. New research findings demonstrate the nexus between neuroscience, feelings, emotions, and values education. They also show that that good practice pedagogy must be directed to the whole person, and that it is the process of cognition itself that activates a whole range of intersecting emotional, social, and moral impulses, which affect resultant attitudes and behaviour. Social, emotional, and moral development, and values education in schools ought to represent our quest for the ideal of the morally good society, to promote a deeper and critical understanding of democracy, equality, human rights, and social justice for all.

Chapter 9
Engagement in Collaborative Groups in the Classroom and Improved Academic Achievement

9.1 Engagement in the Classroom

As I have argued in my Chap. 7 in this book, social and cultural factors can have the most significant impact on students' engagement, motivation, and learning, and, subsequently, on their performance and academic achievement. Many social and cultural factors affect the nature and the context of students' engagement and learning. They include such factors as students' cognitive, social, affective, and psychomotor developments, their age, gender, demographic factors, the learning environment, and the nature and quality of their relationships with their peers and teachers. All these factors can influence the dynamics and quality of students' engagement and learning. Similarly, cultural factors, such as knowledge, beliefs, ethnicity, languages, religion, and values, can affect students' engagement, and the way they learn and perform within the classroom.

I want to argue that the best and the most effective way to engage students in learning new knowledge, is by using collaborative groups, and by combining both cognitive and social constructivist pedagogies. They enhance further, social, cognitive, emotional, and behavioural aspects in the classroom. Collaborative groups have the power to affects students' attitudes, knowledge, values, skills, and behaviour patterns. From a social learning perspective, Slavin (2020), described a variety of perspectives on peer learning, including social-psychological, sociocultural, cognitive development, and cognitive-elaboration approaches, or the nexus between new information and prior knowledge.

In collaborative learning, group members must work on individual tasks, develop their ideas into concrete solutions, share it with others, and combine their work with others in the group. Group members in the classroom display their specific social, and cultural factors, their self-esteem, levels of their cognitive, social, emotional, and psychomotor developments, their beliefs, values, and the resultant behaviour outcomes. While patterns of behaviour for most students is normal, reflecting the

J. Zajda, *Engagement, Motivation, and Students' Achievement*, Globalisation, Comparative Education and Policy Research 48,
https://doi.org/10.1007/978-3-031-61613-6_9

school's ethos, and acceptable standards of behaviour, behaviour of some individuals in school settings can be challenging, especially bullying. Some parents had to remove their children from such schools, because of the prevalence of bullying. An effective and authentic collaborative group, by generating quality students' engagement, motivation, and performance, is likely to produce a very harmonious environment, where students treat each other with respect, and empathy. It would certainly eliminate any forms of bullying. In this way, the inclusive pedagogy employed in collaborative groups can create an atmosphere of peace, and harmony.

9.2 The Role of Collaborative Groups in Engagement

Collaborative learning (CL) is a student-centred approach to learning in the classroom. Collaborative learning is a pedagogical strategy to teaching and learning in the classroom, involving students working together to solve a problem, complete a task, or create a new idea (see also Chap. 3). There is a sharing of authority and acceptance of responsibility among group members for the group's actions. The underlying assumption of collaborative learning is consensus building through cooperation by group members, in contrast to competition, in which individuals best other group members. In short, in collaborative group learning, it is the students who organize their efforts among themselves. It is group structured.

Cooperative learning, on the other hand, can be defined by a set of procedures which help people interact together to accomplish a specific learning and performance goal. It is a teacher-centred strategy. In cooperative learning, students are divided by the teacher into groups and the teacher assigns specific roles and tasks to each student, and so it is a teacher-structured activity.

The use of both collaborative and cooperative learning groups in the classroom is based on the principle of constructivism, with particular attention to the contribution that social constructivism and social interaction can make. In essence, constructivism rests on the idea that individuals learn through building their own knowledge, connecting new ideas and experiences to existing knowledge and experiences to form new or enhanced understanding (Zajda, 2021, 2023a, 2023b). In collaborative learning, group members are asked to organise their joint efforts and negotiate among themselves who will perform group roles as the group critiques a student essay (student-centered).

Collaborative learning in the classroom

Lev Vygotsky was one of the first researchers, who examined the relationship between cognitive processes, the environment, and social activities, developing his unique sociocultural theory of development. The sociocultural theory of development suggests that learning takes place when students solve problems beyond their current developmental level, with the support of their instructors or their peers. Thus, both the idea of a zone of proximal development, supported by positive group interdependence, is the basis of collaborative learning.

Collaborative learning groups in the classroom, synthesise all key ideas from educational psychology: behavioural, cognitive, social learning, affective, and humanistic approaches to classroom pedagogy. Students' self-esteem, self-efficacy, values, and achievement motivation are also relevant here. Recent research findings demonstrate that collaborative groups result in improved academic achievement (Adak, 2017; Alt, 2017; Akpan et al., 2020; Brame & Biel, 2015; Gupta & Tyagi, 2017; Tran et al., 2014, Zajda, 2023a, 2023b). Studies have shown that in well-structured cooperative groups, students consistently learn many different subjects better than students in traditionally structured classrooms.

The small groups are essential to this process, because students can both be heard and interact with their peers, while in a traditional classroom setting students may spend more time listening to what the teacher says. In collaborative learning, students work together in small groups on a structured activity. They are individually accountable for their work, and the work of the group is also assessed. In small groups, students can share strengths and develop their skills, such as

1. They develop their interpersonal skills.
2. They learn to discuss a topic.
3. They learn to research a topic.

9.3 Major Benefits of Collaborative Learning

Major benefits of collaborative learning can be divided into four distinct categories of: cognitive, social, affective, and pedagogical advantages.

Cognitive benefits of collaborative learning

Cognitive benefits of working in small groups result in enhancing students' thinking abilities and skills, including their critical thinking and critical literacy. Students take active part, with their peers, in learning new knowledge and skills. The pioneering research of Piaget (1959), Vygotsky (1962), Bruner (1963) and others, stressed that collaborative interactions with peers has benefits for children's cognitive development. Small collaborative group activities are used in schools to 'promote the development of verbal, cognitive and social skills' (Gillies, 2006). Sills et al. (2016) suggested that 'collaboration is a key facilitator of cognitive development in early childhood', and that knowing 'which factors influence cognitive development during collaborative exercises for young children has implications for educators' and educational outcomes (Sills et al., 2016). Sills et al. (2016) argued that collaborative interactions are 'beneficial for tasks measuring visual perception, problem-solving and rule-based thinking, but not for word-reading and spatial perspective-taking':

> Collaboration is particularly beneficial for low-ability children when there is an ability asymmetry. High-ability children either regressed or did not benefit. Overall, the studies included within this review indicate that brief one-off interactions can have a significant, positive effect on short-term cognitive development in children of infant school age… (Sills et al., 2016)

There is no doubt, as demonstrated by numerous research findings that cognitive benefits of collaborative groups enhance development of verbal, and cognitive skills, such problem-solving and critical thinking skills. Sills et al. (2016) reported 'positive effects of collaborative-working, compared to individual working, were reported on a range of cognitive measures, including visual discrimination, visual perception and problem-solving. Higher quality studies reported benefits of collaborative-working on card-sorting, language ability and rule-based thinking tasks' (p. 14)/

More specifically, one of the benefits of collaborative learning is, that it lessens the cognitive load of students and teachers alike. (Kinney, 2022). Cognitive load theory suggests that when excessive demands are made on the limited capacity of working memory (WM), we are likely to experience cognitive overload, or the condition, where the brain is trying to process far too much information, which will affect the pace of learning, working memory, long-term-memory, and learning results. According to Duchesne et al. (2022), there are at least three types of cognitive load aspects, affecting knowledge acquisition:

- Level of complexity of knowledge, or intrinsic aspect of cognition.
- Extraneous cognitive load, or the load influenced by the information presented.
- Germane cognitive load, or the amount of WM devoted to solving a task, and linking new information, with the already stored information in the long-term memory (LTM) (see Duchesne et al., 2022, pp. 244–245).

Duchesne et al. (2022) suggested that the implications of cognitive load theory for teachers means to promote germane cognitive load by 'engaging and motivating the learner, reducing intrinsic load by simplifying complex material, and building automaticity of skills, and reduce extraneous load by attending to instructional design' (Duchesne et al., 2022, p. 245). Research by cognitive load theories focused on how teaching, and relevant instructional design can effectively reduce extraneous cognitive load and maximise the transfer of new information into long-term memory (LTM). Earlier research by Sweller et al. (2011) regarding cognitive load theory, suggested that cognitive capacity and resources were limited, which implied that teachers must be aware of it, and design their pedagogy to maximise the acquisition of knowledge and its transfer into long-term memory (LTM) storage.

Social learning advantages of learning in collaborative groups

Social learning theory was elaborated in Bandura's (1974) revised social cognitive theory, which is a concept of learning through modelling. Albert (1974) described '*modelling*' as a learned behaviour that comes naturally by observing what happens to others, within the context of social interactions, experiences, and media influences. Social cognitive theory (SCT) combines both behavioural and cognitive explanations for human behaviour. Central to SCT is the idea that 'humans do not passively respond to past or current environmental influences but possess the ability to foresee the consequences of their actions' (Oei & Hasking, 2013).

According to Bandura (1986), while self-efficacy is one of the key factor underlying the human agency central to social cognitive theory, Oei and Hasking (2013) argued that 'intention to act and a desired outcome are not sufficient to enact behaviour; rather individuals must possess self-regulatory mechanisms that allow them to exert control over their behaviour'. In addition, 'regardless of what other factors may affect behaviour, unless someone believes they have the ability to perform a behaviour or change their circumstances, they will not attempt to do so' (Oei & Hasking, 2013). Consequently, self-efficacy is effective only if individuals possess self-regulatory strategies, and self-esteem.

The most obvious advantage of social learning in collaborative groups in the classroom, is that students must work together, learn from one another, share their existing knowledge and skills, and learn from their role models. This social interaction facilitates a sense of belonging, engagement, and motivation, and overcomes 'feelings of isolation' (Kinney, 2022).

Albert Bandura (1974, 1986), apart from Vygotsky (1978), is regarded as one of the most prominent theorists of social learning, who developed his concept of 'social cognitive theory', initially known as *social learning theory*, and in particular the notion of 'triadic reciprocal causation' (see my Chap. 1 in this book). He examined the nexus between effective learning, or the ability of students to become self-regulated learners, and the *three* key domains: personal characteristics, behavioural patterns, and environment. As a result, Bandura used his conception of social cognitive theory to examine how students can control and regulate their learning. This became the foundation of his social cognitive viewpoint of self-regulated learning (SRL), and his self-efficacy theory (SET). According to self-efficacy theory, the two key determinants of human social behaviour are self-efficacy and outcome expectations. Outcome expectations refers to the perceived possible positive, or negative consequences of performing the behaviour, to achieve desirable outcomes.

To Bandura, the key factor affecting students' learning in his social cognitive theory (SCT) was the concept of self-efficacy. Bandura developed the concept of self-efficacy, to 'explain the role it played in his theory of social learning' (Zajda, 2023a, p. 44). Self-efficacy can be defined as 'individuals' belief in their ability to perform a behaviour, to achieve specific performance attainments' (Bandura, 1986). Self-efficacy demonstrates one's confidence in the ability to exert control over one's own motivation, behaviour, and social environment. Similarly, I have argued in my books (Zajda, 2022, 2023) of the significance of students' self-concept, self-esteem, and self-efficacy.

For social learning to be effective in the classroom, first and foremost, students need to have a positive image of themselves, and their self-concept, together with self-esteem and self-efficacy. In other words, students need to feel confident and good about themselves. This is reflecting Bandura's idea of the significance of self-efficacy in social learning. Unless students feel positive about themselves, and confident of their abilities, they would not be able to be engaged and motivated to complete their designated work in the classroom.

Affective benefits of collaborative learning

Affective domain of collaborative learning focuses on enhancing individuals' feelings and emotions, which draws on humanistic psychology. Humanism is a pedagogical approach that maintains that learning is viewed as a personal act to fulfil one's potential. Humanistic psychology emerged back in the 1960s, as a reaction against behavioural psychology, and focused on the human freedom, dignity, and potential. Humanistic psychologists believed that it is necessary to study the whole person, especially as an individual grows and develops over the lifespan. It follows that the study of the self, social learning theory, social constructivism, motivation, and cooperative group learning are areas of particular interest. The humanistic theory of teaching and learning is an educational theory that believes in teaching the 'whole' child.

Humanism believes that a learner is free-willed, and capable of achieving their best, when the ideal learning environment is produced. The ideal learning environment should cater to the social, emotional, and cognitive needs of the learner. A humanist approach has a strong focus on students' emotional wellbeing, feelings, and potential to achieve knowledge at the highest-level of self-actualization. A humanist teaching strategy will have at least three constructs, used in effective teaching:

- Free Will: Learners have free choice to do and think what we want.
- Emotions impact Learning: Learners need to be in a positive emotional state to achieve our best.
- Intrinsic Motivation: Learners generally have an internal desire to become our best selves (Zajda, 2023a).

The two prominent humanist theorists were Abraham Maslow and Carl Rogers. Maslow (1962) and Rogers (1961) became the most influential humanists, who suggested the ideas of **self-concept** and **self-actualization**, as being part of the overall positive nature and development of people. Humanistic psychologists also believe we should pay more attention to emotions and ensure that our students are feeling safe, positive, relaxed, and comfortable. These are emotions that will make students ready to learn. Humanistic psychologists argue that other dominant educational theories, like behaviourism, cognitive and socio-cultural perspectives tend to ignore the major role of emotions in learning. The humanist approach to learning requires the teacher to consider all needs of the student to create an effective learning environment, with reference to:

- social needs
- emotional needs
- mental needs
- cognitive needs
- individual differences need (learning styles etc.).

Emotions, or what we often refer to in educational psychology, as 'affect', will shape how, what, when, of the teaching and learning environment, and how well students will learn something new in the classroom. If students feel sad, anxious, frustrated, or distressed, they will not be engaged and motivated to learn. When students are worried about something, they tend to spend all their time thinking about it—and are unable to concentrate on their work.

We can study further feeling and emotions, as part of one's emotional intelligence. Emotions can be defined as 'conscious mental reactions (such as anger or fear) subjectively experienced as strong feelings usually directed toward a specific object and typically accompanied by physiological and behavioural changes in the body' (APA, Adapted from Merriam-Webster). Emotions deal with happiness, pleasure, or fear. Cowen and Keltner for their study, collected some 2185 short videos that aimed to elicit particular emotions, displayed in five to ten second clips, and as a result discovered some 27 emotional states (see Lee, 2017). These emotional states included admiration, adoration, aesthetic appreciation, amusement, anxiety, awe, awkwardness, boredom, calmness, confusion, craving, disgust, empathetic pain, entrancement, envy, excitement, fear, horror, interest, joy, nostalgia, romance, sadness, satisfaction, sexual desire, sympathy, and triumph. To these, one can also add 'anticipation'. I am certain, given the complexity of emotional intelligence, and emotional states, cultural differences, and individual differences, more can be added.

Individuals with emotional intelligence traits tend to be somewhat 'empathetic, tuned in, and perceptive'. They also have high levels of 'emotional awareness, self-control, and situational skill'. These emotional intelligence traits help them to 'perceive, understand, use, and manage emotions in their personal lives, careers, and other situations' (Maven, July 2023). Here are at least seven common characteristics of emotional intelligence, that have been observed in a wide range of people.

1. 'Emotional Resilience: emotional fortitude, the ability to recover from personal setbacks and manage negative emotional experiences.
2. Emotional regulation: the ability and willingness to manage, regulate, and control one's own emotions.
3. Self-awareness: awareness of one's emotional state and nature.
4. Social awareness: awareness of other people's emotions, behaviours, needs, and psychology.
5. Communication: excellent communication that's appropriate for the situation and people.
6. Interpersonal skills: skilful in social situations and personal interactions.
7. Conflict management: socially aware and agile enough to detect, mitigate, and resolve conflicts' (Maven, 2023).

In addition, the 5 elements of emotional intelligence, also include:

- 'Self-awareness.
- Self-regulation.
- Motivation.
- Empathy.
- Social skills' (ICAEW Insights, 2021).

The above listed characteristic of emotional intelligence helps us to have a better understanding and knowledge of the complexity of the concept.

Affective advantages in collaborative group, or cooperative learning, include developing feelings, empathy, and emotional intelligence. Rivera-Pérez et al. (2020) in their article 'Linking cooperative learning and emotional intelligence in physical education: Transition across school stages', using their sample of some 1332 students (682 males, 650 females), demonstrated that the existence of positive and significant associations between cooperative learning (CL) and emotional intelligence (EI) in all school stages. On a similar note, Simpson (2023), in his thesis 'The effects of social-emotional learning, classroom relationships, and collaborative learning on students' emotional relationships, and collaborative learning on students' emotional intelligence and academic achievement, intelligence and academic achievement', argued that 'ultimately, emotional intelligence is a key component for collaborative learning to have a positive effect on academic achievement' (Simpson, 2023). The author concluded that overall, the results of his action research indicated that 'growth in emotional intelligence, through social-emotional learning relationship development, and collaborative learning activities may increase academic achievement for students. (Simpson, 2023).

In another study, by Torrego-Seijo et al. (2021), 'The effects of cooperative learning on trait emotional intelligence and academic achievement of Spanish primary school students', where the participants were primary education students (n = 692) and teachers (n = 24) from eight public schools in Madrid, Spain, investigators studied the impact of cooperative learning on emotional intelligence. The instruments used consisted of the Emotional Quotient-Youth Version questionnaire, and internal and external assessment tests. Torrego-Seijo et al. (2021), argued that cooperative learning improved scores of one dimensions of trait in emotional intelligence, and students' academic achievement.

The above findings demonstrate that effective collaborative learning environments are likely to provide students with opportunities to develop, enhance and practise their emotional intelligence, and, above all, empathy.

Pedagogical benefits of collaborative learning

Pedagogical advantages of collaborative learning include cognitive, social, and emotional development, as well as enhanced oral communication, social interaction, critical literacy, critical thinking, creativity, and metacognition. One of the key teacher's roles in the inclusive classroom, at the cognitive level, is to develop in their students higher-level thinking, which is embedded in critical thinking and critical literacy. According to Alber (2017), when creating a highly effective collaborative classroom, 'teachers need to frequently model listening, paraphrasing, artful questioning, and negotiating' (Alber, 2017). Teachers promote collaborative learning in their inclusive classroom, 'which in turn encourages higher-level thinking' (Padayichie, 2023). It is suggested that teachers, should focus on developing twenty-first century skills, and which should be taught in all aspects of teaching and learning. These skills, according to Padayichie (2023), need to encompass the '7C's: Communication, collaboration, critical thinking, and problem solving, creativity and innovation, change, and citizenship, character' (Padayichie, 2023).

There are many pedagogical benefits of collaborative learning, covering various aspects of the teaching and learning process, and reflecting behavioural, cognitive, social cognitive, humanistic, and affective domains. Pedagogical benefits of collaborative learning in the inclusive classroom tend to include the following **12** advantages:

- Improving oral skills and communication (cognitive and social cognitive aspects)
- Promoting acceptance of cultural diversity (multicultural pedagogy)
- Developing students' positive self-image, self-esteem, and self-efficacy (cognitive skill)
- Enhancing students' problem-solving skills (cognitive skills)
- Developing critical thinking and critical literacy skills (cognitive skills)
- Promoting students' metacognition, metacognive strategies, and self-regulated learning (SRL)
- Developing relevant knowledge, skills, and understanding of diverse perspectives (see also Cornell University Centre for teaching innovation: Collaborative learning)
- Constructing meaningful peer relationship groups (social skills)
- Promoting trust, tolerance, acceptance of others, and a sense of belonging in the peer group environment (social skills)
- Enhancing creativity (cognitive skills)
- Creating quality learning environment (pedagogic strategy)
- Encouraging for both teachers and students effective and meaningful social interaction and engagement (social skills).

The above 12 pedagogical benefits of collaborative learning focus mainly on cognitive, social, cultural diversity, and inclusive pedagogy. In effective collaborative groups, teachers have the power to create and influence positive students' attitudes, authentic engagement, and to deliver relevant and curriculum defined knowledge, values, skills, and acceptable behaviour patterns.

9.4 Benefits of Collaborative and Cooperative Groups in the Classroom

The perceived benefits of applying cooperative and collaborative learning principles in teaching programs are varied and range from increased cognitive stimulation to student self-management, to pro-social skill building to the wide relevance and applicability of this instructional strategy. Cooperative group work engages students in thinking about others. Students learn to understand more effectively cultural identities, accepting and learning from each other, and sharing their knowledge and skills. Recent research has demonstrated the nexus between cooperative groups and improved academic standards. Benefits of effective collaborative groups in the classroom include the following five characteristics:

1. *Celebration of multiculturalism and cultural diversity.* Collaborative group interactions within the classroom environment allow students to work with all types of students from diverse cultural backgrounds. Students are provided with an opportunity to understand the diverse responses that peers, and the questions being raised.

2. *Acknowledgement of individual differences.* The varied responses from the students can help the group to create a new knowledge that reflects a variety of responses and a more comprehensive discussion of the topic, or issues.
3. *Interpersonal development.* Students with developmental differences in social skills can benefit from learning social kills in the inclusive, and safe collaborative group environment. As the group works together on solving a problem, students are practicing cognitive and social skills, by interacting with their peers, while working in a structured collaborative group environment.
4. *Actively involve students in their learning.* Students have more ownership for their work, when they have been actively engaged in its development, and have been asked to think critically about related topics, while working in a team. Within collaborative group environment, each member has an opportunity to contribute.
5. *Greater opportunity for frequent and constructive feedback.* Within the discussion nature of collaborative group learning, where social constructivist pedagogy is used, relevant, meaningful, and constructive feedback to the students' ideas and responses needs to be immediate and frequent, as well as feedback from their peers.

9.5 Values Education in the Global Culture

Collaborative groups, using both cognitive and social constructivist pedagogies are ideal for teaching values education. In my books, I have demonstrated that values are best taught in small collaborative groups. (Zajda, 2023a. *Discourses of globalisation, cultural diversity and values education.* Cham: Springer Nature Switzerland; Zajda, 2023b. *Discourses of globalisation and values education for equality, democracy, and social justice.* Cham: Springer Nature Switzerland). Here is an examples of teaching values in collaborative groups in the classroom.

Values refers to moral and ethical decisions and choices: ***Moral***- to do with the right or wrong conduct; ***ethical***-concerning universal standards and codes, moral principles.

Teaching values education involves deciding which values, whose morality, and how to assess or judge moral character (exams for moral character?). Good teachers, exemplify virtues such as honesty and fairness. One example of teaching values is the 3Ms of moral education, developed by Straughan (1982). Straughan (1982), in his critique of dominant approaches to the content of values education and the structure of values education, and the contested areas and boundaries between moral reasoning and the content of morality, suggested a pragmatic approach to values education, based on what I call the 3Ms of moral education:

- *teaching* ***that*** informed decisions must be made in making moral choices
- *teaching* ***how*** to think for themselves as autonomous moral agents
- *teaching children* ***to*** **want** to be moral (to guarantee moral goodness in an individual) (see also Winch & Gingell, 1999, p. 149).

To achieve this, students need to act and behave morally themselves.

9.6 Presenting a Moral Dilemma in *Collaborative Groups*

Example: Sophie's Choice

In the novel *Sophie's Choice*, by William Styron (Vintage Books, 1976–the 1982 movie starred Meryl Streep & Kevin Kline), a Polish woman, Sophie Zawistowska, is arrested by the Nazis and sent to the Auschwitz death camp. On arrival, she is 'honored' for not being a Jew, by being allowed a choice: One of her children will be spared from the gas chamber if she chooses which one. In an agony of indecision, as both children are being taken away, she suddenly does choose. They can take her daughter, who is younger and smaller. Sophie hopes that her older and stronger son will be better able to survive, but she loses track of him and never does learn of his fate. Did she do the right thing? Years later, haunted by the guilt of having chosen between her children, Sophie…

Teaching values education, including role plays, moral dilemmas and values clarification involve all students (in a non-didactic way) in exploring their feelings, attitudes, and prejudices.

9.7 Conclusion

Major benefits of collaborative learning include a better knowledge and understanding of cultural identities in culturally diverse classroom settings. Collaborative learning techniques are proven to be effective and successful classroom management techniques, that help to build pro-social skills, create opportunities for developing higher level thinking skills, and metacognition, which reflect the outcomes of cognitive and social constructivist pedagogies, and student-centred pedagogy. It offers quality learning experiences for all students, that will cognitively, socially, emotionally, and behaviourally engage students, and improve their academic performance. The benefits of collaborative learning include the development of higher-level thinking, oral communication, metacognitive strategies, and self-regulated learning skills.

Chapter 10
Teachers' Role in Promoting Engagement, Motivation, and Students' Achievement

This chapter analyses current research and knowledge in the teachers' role in improving students' engagement, well-being, academic excellence, standards, equity, and global competitiveness. It examines the teachers' role of improving students' motivation impacting on their educational outcomes, both locally and globally, promoting economic and social competitiveness, and academic standards. The chapter argues that one of the most significant teachers' roles is in establishing an inclusive classroom environment, characterized by an atmosphere of belonging, safety, and acceptance of students' voices. Teachers, who use constructivist pedagogy, based on cognitive and social constructivist approaches in collaborative, or cooperative groups in the classroom, are likely to offer supportive environment, and offering the necessary cognitive scaffolding for students to solve a given task and achieve designated classroom outcomes.

10.1 Teachers' Role in Promoting Engagement and Motivation

As I have argued in my recent books, dealing with motivation, *Globalisation, and dominant models of motivational theories in education* (2023a), and *Globalisation and inclusive schooling*: *Engaging motivational environments* (2023b), teachers represent a major socializing agency, impacting on students' engagement in the classroom. This socialization process also consists of the family, peers, and the social media, which are other significant agencies of socialization, discussed by Bronfenbrenner (1979) in his groundbreaking and innovative ecological and bioecological models. (Bronfenbrenner & Morris, 2007). As Bronfenbrenner & Morris (2007), noted their new bioecological model 'is not a paradigm shift, but rather represents a transition from a focus on the environment to a focus on *proximal processes* as engines of development'. Proximal processes were described as 'the engines of development,

J. Zajda, *Engagement, Motivation, and Students' Achievement*, Globalisation, Comparative Education and Policy Research 48,
https://doi.org/10.1007/978-3-031-61613-6_10

the transfer of energy between individuals and their environments in a bidirectional way' (Bronfenbrenner & Evans, 2000). Proximal processes are described as the activities that individuals engage with, as they learn and develop.

As teachers have an incredible power to influence their students' attitudes, engagement, and behaviour towards learning in school settings, I wish to focus more on teachers' specific roles in contributing to students' increased engagement in schools, and effective models of inclusive schooling. Teachers have the power to promote quality engagement, accept cultural identities, and have a powerful impact on the nature of students' engagement in the classroom. Teachers also contribute to students' evolving social learning in the inclusive classroom. Specific teachers' roles in contributing to students' engagement, consist of a variety of cognitive, socio-cultural, emotional, and behavioural aspects.

10.2 Effective Teachers

I would like to suggest the following qualities defining engaging and effective teachers:

1. Effective teachers demonstrate *teacher efficacy*, or a belief that all students are capable of quality learning, and that teachers have the necessary and relevant knowledge, the skills, and the means in creating effecting learning environments in the classroom.
2. Effective teachers believe that all students have a potential to learn. They devote much of the day to quality teaching, and learning, by means of variety of tasks and methods.
3. Effective teachers create supportive and inclusive classroom learning environments that are well managed to allow diversity of learning to take place.
4. Effective teachers individualize classroom teaching environment, to meet diverse needs of each student, and keep students continually engaged, and motivated to perform.
5. Effective teachers demonstrate the quality and value-added learning in ways that emphasise higher level thinking skills and involve active engagement by most students.
6. Effective teachers develop and maintain students' effective engagement, using cooperative learning strategies, collaboration, and student-centered approaches to learning.
7. Effective teachers encourage the application of new learning, monitor individual student performance, and provide relevant feedback and scaffolding, to ensure that all students master the concepts being taught.

Slavin (2020), on the other hand, proposed his popular model of effective teaching, based on the following 4 core characteristics: quality of teaching, appropriate level of teaching, incentive, and time:

1. *Quality of Instruction*: The degree to which information or skills are presented so that students can easily learn them. Quality of instruction is largely a product of the quality of the curriculum and of the lesson presentation itself.
2. *Appropriate Levels of Instruction*: The degree to which the teacher makes sure that students are ready to learn a new lesson (that is, they have the necessary skills and knowledge to learn it) but have not already learned the lesson. In other words, the level of instruction is appropriate when a lesson is neither too difficult nor too easy for students.
3. *Incentive*: The degree to which the teacher makes sure that students are motivated to work on instructional tasks and to learn the material being presented.
4. *Time*: The degree to which students are given enough time to learn the material being taught (Slavin, 2020).

Furthermore, Slavin (2020) also summarises good and effective pedagogy in term of the following four dimensions:

- Knowledge of subject and teaching resources
- Knowledge of students and their learning (these are related to self-knowledge and self-regulation)
- Critical thinking and problem-solving skills (reflection)
- Communication skills and decision making (Slavin, 2020).

By synthesising research findings dealing with effective teachers and quality schooling we can summarise the following **5 main** factors contributing to quality teaching in schools: teacher's self-efficacy, lesson structure, and awareness of cultural diversity, positive motivational atmosphere, and teacher's self-efficacy and mastery skills. These are described below:

1. Effective teachers demonstrate a sense of *self-efficacy*, or the belief and confidence that they can successfully influence the learning of students
2. Structure their lessons as constructivist and student-based learning experiences (using advanced organisers, executive summaries, metacognition, etc.)
3. Sensitive to cultural diversity and employ global/cross-cultural perspective
4. Maintaining positive classroom climate and positive expectations
5. Exhibit mastery of teaching skills, by demonstrating high level of knowledge, and skills, excellent communication, effective questioning, and the use of effective motivational strategies.

Thus, effective teaching is likely to be shaped by the teacher's *self-efficacy*, attitudes, beliefs, knowledge, skills, and values. It includes teacher's content knowledge, organisation, clarity, teaching pace, classroom control and management, effective lesson planning, realistic and achievable objectives, the use of engaging questioning techniques, and above all, showing students how to learn best (see Fontana, 1995; Zajda, 2018; Zajda, 2023).

10.3 Teachers Developing and Promoting Engagement in the Classroom

Teachers represent, by far, the most powerful role models in the classroom. Teachers' professional knowledge, their skills, their values, combined with their high self-esteem and self-efficacy contribute to their overall image as role models. Teachers, as role models, have the power to promote effective engagement in the classroom. Student engagement, according to 'The Glossary of Education Reform' (2016), refers to the 'degree of attention, curiosity, interest, optimism, and passion that students show when they are learning or being taught, which extends to the level of motivation they have to learn and progress in their education'. (The Glossary of Education Reform, 2016). Students' engagement and motivation is dependent on their self-concept, attitudes, and desire to learn. First, and foremost, students, like their teachers, need to feel positive about themselves. This positive image will influence their initial level of engagement and motivation in the classroom. As soon as teachers provide and maintain a positive climate in their classrooms, students will also feel good about themselves and their abilities to learn. (See Chap. 2 of this book). To cultivate a positive climate in their classrooms, teachers need to promote a genuine sense of democracy and equality, there students feel they are accepted, and that they belong, and that their voices are valued during cooperative or collaborative classroom activities.

10.4 Classroom Discrimination and the Self-fulfilling Prophecy

What is discrimination?

The term 'discrimination' can be defined as a distinction made in favour or against a person or thing based on an unfavourable opinion beforehand. The notion of discrimination based on an adverse judgement or opinion formed beforehand—without facts or knowledge is also very similar to the definition of 'prejudice' defined as an adverse judgment or opinion formed beforehand or without knowledge or examination of the facts. classroom from day one. When teachers discriminate in the classroom in any one sense of the term, they are favouring the dominant and accepted ideology of knowledge, values, skills, and learning and reject and ignore other multi-modal aspects of knowledge and learning and individuals' needs in general. Instead of inclusive classroom' they have created a *stratified* and divided classroom, based on privilege (and favouritism), distinction and exclusion. Empowering pedagogues, just like other ethically concerned professionals, need to examine their own attitudes and prejudicial assumptions (often based on ignorance, arrogance, phobias, and stereotypes) as to the nature of learning, ability, intelligence, gender, disability, speech patterns, physical appearance, personality, body, race, income, ethnicity, gender, religion, and lifestyles. We all suffer from some forms of biases and tend to 'filter out the reality of a situation in favour of our discriminatory assumptions' (Kussrow, 2002, p. 93).

We can distinguish between the following types of discrimination in the classroom, and relate them to the concept of labelling:

- Learning and learning styles discrimination
- Modality discrimination
- Intelligence discrimination
- Disability discrimination
- Race and ethnicity discrimination
- Language and speech patterns discrimination
- Gender discrimination
- Age discrimination
- Body discrimination
- Personality discrimination
- Income and wealth (SES, or **classism**) discrimination
- Cultural and lifestyle discrimination
- Values discrimination.

Discrimination can be felt or seen in individuals' behaviour towards other people or 'the practice of making a difference in treatment or favour on a basis other than individual merit' (Kussrow, 2002, p. 93). Discrimination is, undoubtedly, behaviour or act based on prejudice. Discrimination often begins in the discriminatory practices, be they open or hidden, overt, or covert, conscious or unconscious. These acts are almost like an undeclared war by humans, who are in the position of power, domination, and control, against other humans in a stratified social system. In a world, characterised by continuing unequal distribution of socially valued commodities, and unequal access to education, power, wealth, and privilege, humans will continue to exist in conflict-driven environments, where prejudice and discrimination rule. The very existence of social stratification, selection, and placement, already legitimizes discrimination and prejudice. As Kussrow (2002) stated 'There are many kinds of discriminations, and we have all been discriminated against in more ways than we know' (p. 93). Even though we are not born with discriminatory attitudes, we soon acquire them by observing others and imitating their prejudices. Sometimes this is internalised unconsciously, sometimes this is due to peer group pressure.

Learning discrimination

Learners from different cultures, with different levels of knowledge and skills and at different stages of cognitive development are likely to exhibit different ways of learning. Yet, in a traditional classroom there is a tendency to adopt a singular, unifying and one-dimensional approach to the learning/teaching process. There is also a tendency to normalise learning using the normal curve, and by teaching to the 'average' students, which ignores individual differences. The learner's question "Is this the right way?" already reflect the uncritical acceptance of learning.

Recently, multiple perspectives models in learning and intelligence have been used. There are literally hundreds of major learning theories, representing specific approaches to the teaching/learning process. Numerous learning theories were identified by various scholars dealing with learning and pedagogy. These include many variants of behaviourism, cognitivism, social cognitivism, constructivism, humanism, existentialism and connectivism.

More recently, social constructivist and transformationalist approaches to learning have received a good deal of prominence and attention.

Overall, learning discrimination deals with numerous issues ranging from learning modes and styles to the pace of learning. Some teachers dislike 'slow' learners, who are labeled as 'lazy'. Yet, learning pace is a very personal and individual act, which may not be correlated with intelligence. We do assume that 'fast' learners are highly intelligent. Some learners learn best by writing it down first. Others must see it to learn. These represent learning styles and modes discussed below.

Learning Styles

We learn in different ways. How and what we learn is influenced and determined by a variety of factors and variables that can be grouped under affective, cognitive, psychomotor, intelligence, perception, cultural, and environmental domains. The unresolved **nature-nurture** discourse is just as relevant to the learning process today as it was at the turn of the century.

Learning styles are used by different learners in different settings and across different cultures.

Furthermore, learning styles are usually considered to be bipolar dimensions whereas abilities are unipolar (ranging from zero to a maximum value). Having more of ability is usually considered beneficial while having a particular cognitive style simply denotes a tendency to behave in a certain manner. Cognitive style is usually described as a personality dimension, which influences attitudes, values, and social interaction.

Learning modes

In addition to the above-mentioned learning styles, Bernice McCarthy (1990) suggested **four** learning modes, known as the **4MAT** framework:

- Analytic
- Imaginative
- Common Sense
- Dynamic.

The 4 MAT framework has been widely used in learning and teaching. Also, the learning styles framework developed by Dunn (1999) seems to be useful in terms of creating teacher awareness of individual differences in learning.

Learning modality discrimination

The modality preferences of learners cover **visual** (cortical tissue at the back of the brain), **auditory**, and **sensory** (touch) or tactile/kinaesthetic. It affects more than 70%

of school age children and their ability to learn (Dunn et al., 1989, p. 50). Research shows that most students are visual rather than auditory. As Kussrow (2002) observed, only '30% of the population is auditory, 40% are visual, and 15% are tactile' (Zajda, 2021). Most researchers agree that 'lecturing' is the least effective way to teach. While kinaesthetic learners prefer to move around in the classroom during a session, autistic (a category of disability) children are withdrawn and prefer to be left alone.

Like the multiple intelligences, one teaching modality does not meet all individual needs and learners should be taught in multi-modal and multi-sensory learning environments. Pedagogues need to be acutely aware of the 'biological and developmental nature of other learner's modalities' (Zajda, 2023). Research has shown that the link between sensory abilities (in this case colour and sound discrimination) and general intelligence (the *g* factor) is weak, suggesting that sensory abilities are quite distinct from general intelligence (Acton and Schroeder, 2001).

Intelligence discrimination

Intelligence discrimination is based on the notion of differential intellectual abilities, where some abilities are favoured and other abilities, perceived to be not relevant, are completely ignored in the outcomes-driven academic achievement and performance. If we define the term 'intelligence' as 'the ability to see relationships, and to use these relationships to solve problems' (Fontana, 1995, p. 95) then it is easy to infer that every aspect of one's learning is likely to be influenced by it.

If we add to it the notions of high and low intelligence, or gifted and below average it is easy to see how these potentially damaging (but convenient tools for test administrators testing ability) labels can have significant implications for students, parents, and teachers alike, who use intelligence test scores for future career orientations. Students, defined by intelligence testing (placements tests in schools) are, consequently, streamed by abilities. For example, the most able are placed in advanced mathematics classes (level 1, which is the highest), the least able find themselves doing level 10 mathematics (the lowest group, covering basic mathematics).

Most parents accept, uncritically, the political correctness of the widely perceived and accepted 'scientific objectivity' of intelligence tests, even though psychologist themselves are aware of many misconceptions concerning the nature of intelligence and the reliability and validity of its measurements. Some individuals are likely to experience significant changes in their estimated IQ, due to the nature of schooling, learning patterns, social and cultural differences and other environmental influences (Zajda, 2023a).

Intelligence discrimination is a convenient way of exercising power, domination, and control over the student's life in the classroom, and society at large. Intelligence testing, as an ideology of the academic achievement syndrome for installing the gatekeeping and for sorting out students (into high and low achievers, above and below average performers, the winners and losers), becomes a powerful tool, or a weapon of the hidden curriculum, legitimising meritocracy and educational inequality. Intelligence meritocracy creates a few winners and many losers in the classroom and later in life.

Disability discrimination across cultures

Understanding attitudes towards students with disabilities is essential in order to shape an educational system that aims at building an integrated society. Negative attitudes towards students with disabilities are likely to lead to exclusion, biased and cruel treatment. There are numerous ways in which both students and teachers contribute to prejudice against students with disabilities in the classroom. At times, students with disabilities may have very low self-esteem, and experience negative personal, social, and academic attitudes that teachers are ignorant of. It has been suggested that some teachers may even desire that these students be removed from their classroom so that they can focus on helping the more able students.

Research was also conducted to determine the attitudes that teachers hold towards their students. The four categories that students were placed in were as follows: attachment (characterized by high achievement and diligence), concern (students who stand out because of academic problems), indifference (students who are quiet and unnoticeable), and rejection (low achievers who require a great deal of time and effort by the teacher). This study showed that children with disabilities were greatly over-represented in the category of rejection and under-represented in the category of attachment. Unfortunately, teachers often view these children as hopeless. Furthermore, rejected students receive fewer turns to participate in class and are more likely to be criticized by the teacher. Ultimately, teachers' attitudes towards their students directly impact the quality of the students' educational experience. These stereotypical views held about students from minority groups, including those with disabilities, affect the development of students. who experience discriminatory treatment.

Race and ethnicity discrimination

Ethnocentrism is very difficult to overcome in the classroom. If we define 'ethnocentrism' as a particular view of culture, then we have created the majority/minority divide in the classroom. Ethnocentrism can range from an open intolerance of other people, based on their race, ethnicity, language, religion, and lifestyles, to dislike of people's looks, beliefs, attitudes, and values.

Language and speech patterns discrimination

Teachers and students are likely to develop dominant languages stereotypes, which are promoted by social learning and learning from the role models. Here, one needs to introduce the term sociolect, defined as 'language variations produced by the effects of education, socio-economic class, systems of belief (ideologies), occupation and membership of any other social groups. Also, we need to define the term dialect. Dialects are 'language varieties where grammar and vocabulary identify the regional and social background of the user'. One should not confuse dialect with accent, which is (relatively) a much simpler and narrower feature of the spoken language.

The way one speaks English, for instance, due to social variations, or the sociolect (a class dialect variation), for example, or regional variation, becomes an SES indicator of one's education, class, and wealth. The BBC and the upper-class sociolect in the UK is a very good example of the way our speech patterns in a given language can contribute to a division in our society. Basil Bernstein's pioneering work on linguistic codes (the restricted and the elaborate codes) was an attempt to find the link between social classes and linguistic codes.

Some teachers, on the basis of the child's speech patterns, make erroneous judgements and labels—poor speech patterns are equated with underachievement and 'losers'. I can imagine the peer pressure that is felt by a child in an exclusive boarding school, who may come from a poor working-class background. The 'in-group' of rich and privileged upper-class girls will create a life a misery for the less fortunate students.

The following represent other major dimensions of discrimination in the classroom:

- Gender discrimination
- Age discrimination
- Body discrimination
- Personality discrimination
- Income and wealth: SES or *classism* (see also Edith King, 1999, *Looking into the Lives of Children*, where she is using the term to explain social class discrimination and prejudice
- Cultural and lifestyle discrimination
- Assessment and evaluation discrimination
- Values discrimination.

10.5 Self-fulfilling Prophecy in the Classroom Today

Self-fulfilling prophecy (SFP), as explained earlier, is a phenomenon by which people's expectations about the future events lead them to behave in particular ways that, on occasion, can cause the expected event to occur (for a more detailed discussion, see my Chap. 6).

Self-fulfilling prophecy and social prejudice

If teachers want to control students—as passive, obedient, and conformist learners, they will teach in such a way that self-fulfilling prophecy will condition students to do nothing unless closely supervised. If teachers want students to assume responsibility, they will teach in such a way that self-fulfilling prophecy will condition learners to assume responsibility for their own learning. There is need for teachers to understand and combat ethnocentrism, prejudice, discrimination, racism, and other examples, which contribute to a growing number of adverse attitudes in the classroom and beyond. If teachers are to act as true professionals and educators in the moral and humane sense, they should not bring their preconceived ideas and discriminatory attitudes into the classroom.

10.6 Teachers' Role in Promoting in Promoting Cognitive, Social Cognitive and Emotional Skills

As powerful role models teachers can advance their students' development of relevant and necessary cognitive, social cognitive, emotional knowledge, and skills.

Cognitive knowledge and skills

Teachers need to explain to their students the three stages of the information-processing theory, which includes sensory memory, short-term memory, or working memory, and long-term-term memory. It is important to stress the nature of short-term memory, and the fact that the second memory store can hold up to 7 (7 plus or minus two) chunks of information for about 20s. It is also the place where encoding organisation, and retrieving of information occurs. The working memory is more highly related to learning than any other factor. Working memory predicts performance in: comprehension, reasoning, concentration, and effort.

Terms, such as advanced organizers, or summaries, memory processes, and memory enhancing strategies need to be taught to all students. memory processes contain such stages as recognition, attention, maintenance rehearsal, elaborative rehearsal, meaningful learning, and dual coding theory etc. Recognition is a process by which the mind identifies the key features of a new piece of information and compares it to information that is already stored.

This process partly depends on the new information an individual receives and partly on the information stored in the **long-term memory**.

The attention stage is the process by which the mind focuses on a portion of the available information. The world often provides too much information to process all at once.

The brain deals with this by prioritising and reducing information. That is, using attention.

The maintenance rehearsal stage, also commonly known as rote rehearsal and repetition, is a process by which the learner uses mental and verbal repetition to hold information in the working memory for immediate use.

The elaborate rehearsal stage is also called elaborative encoding. It is a process by which new information is consciously related to information stored in the long-term memory (LTM). It is an important analytical process because it uses information in the long-term memory to add new details to newly acquired information. It is used to:

clarify meaning of a new idea
make inferences, or deductions
construct visual images
create analogies.

Overall, meaningful learning refers to information that makes sense (learners can relate to it, using their existing knowledge), and it is more meaningful than rote learning. Meaningful learning stage is slightly like the elaborative rehearsal because learning new information is enhanced by relating it to personal interests and prior knowledge, and experiences. Meaningful learning occurs when a learner is presented with clear and logically organised new information and tries to relate it to ideas and experiences stored in the long-term memory. According to *schema* theory individuals' meaningful knowledge is constructed of networks and hierarchies of schemata, or concept 'files'.

How do cognitive approaches help students learn? Students learn to use advance organizers, or summaries, which help students to process new information. Analogies, information elaboration, organizational schemes, cues, mnemonics, questioning techniques, and conceptual models are also other examples of teaching strategies based on cognitive approaches to *meaningful* classroom learning.

The *dual coding theory* states that concrete information (such as car, house, chair) is more easily remembered than abstract information (such as existence, beauty, symbolism, modernism, and futurism in art). This is because concrete information can be encoded in the memory as images, **and** verbal labels, whereas abstract words can only be encoded as verbal labels.

Schemata, or mental folders, consist of an abstract structure of information. A schema summarises many different parts of information about the same topic and structures this information to display how it is all interrelated. Many cognitive psychologists believe that information is stored in the long-term memory in a series of schemata, or folders.

Why we forget? There are, depending on individual differences, at least four basic reasons why we forget:

1. The information in the working memory was never effectively transferred to the long-term memory.
2. The information is not used over a long period, and so the memory appears to fade.
3. We cannot retrieve the relevant cues for information that is in the long-term memory.
4. Our retrieval of specific information is interfered with by similar information, causing confusion.

To overcome the problem of forgetfulness, we need to teach students how to use various forms of rehearsal and mnemonic devices (two reasons for teaching rehearsal: a useful tactic for keeping small amount of information active in STM; maintenance rehearsal is something young students can learn to use; and remind them to use no more than seven items/chunks at a time). This process also involves:

a. Teach students how to formulate comprehension questions.
b. Teach students how to take notes.

Improving Attention and Memory involves:

1. Breaking activities into smaller segments, alternating among various types of class activities, allowing opportunities for movement, using reinforcement, and teaching self-recording may also help improve.

2. Attending.
3. Using pictures, enhancing meaningfulness, using activities, providing sufficient practice, and promoting active learning all help promote better memory for students with disabilities.
4. The use of mnemonic strategies to improve memory.

Mnemonic strategies provide visual, auditory, colour, or verbal cues for students, who experience some difficulty retaining information. There are various types of mnemonic strategies, including peg word mnemonic, acronyms, acrostics, rhymes, coding mnemonics, the story method etc.

The peg word mnemonic uses numbers and letters, instead of places. These numbers are transformed into visual images by means of the following simple rhyme:

one is a bun

two is a shoe

three is a tree

four is a door

five is a hive

six is sticks

seven is heaven

eight is a gate

nine is a line

ten is a hen

There are two types of **first-letter** mnemonics:

1. acronyms in which the initial letters form a meaningful word—such as FACE for the notes in the spaces of the treble staff.
2. acrostics in which the initial letters are used as the initial letters of other words to make a meaningful phrase—such as *E*very *G*ood *B*oy *D*eserves *F*ruit for the notes on the lines of the treble staff.

The story method is an effective means of learning lists. Classroom examples include:

Calendars and Time

30 days hath September, April, June, and November. All the rest have 31 (Except for February Which Has 28);

History

Divorced, Beheaded, Died, Divorced, Beheaded, Survived (A very popular mnemonic for the six wives of Henry VIII).

Social cognitive knowledge and skills

Teachers, by working with their students in the classroom, in cooperative and collaborative groups are developing social cognitive skills. Social cognitive knowledge and skills were developed earlier by Albert Bandura (1986), who suggested that to be effective learners, students need to exhibit self-control, self-regulation, and self-efficacy. Self-control refers to controlling one's behaviour without external rewards or punishments. Self-regulation is the consistent use of self-control in new contexts. Self-efficacy refers to how one perceives one's ability to complete a given activity and activate self-regulatory skills.

Today, students, teachers and parents recognize the importance of modelling appropriate behaviors, and values. Building self-efficacy, as concept, was regarded to be very significant in Bandura's social cognitive theory. Bandura (1977), by examining personal characteristics, behavioural patterns and environment, argued in his *Social learning theory* that individuals control and regulate their learning, and that human behaviour is learned mainly by observations and modelling:

> Learning would be exceedingly laborious, not to mention hazardous, if people had to rely solely on the effects of their own actions to inform them what to do. Fortunately, most human behavior is learned observationally through modeling: from observing others one forms an idea of how new behaviors are performed, and on later occasions this coded information serves as a guide for action".
>
> (Albert Bandura, *Social Learning Theory*, 1977)

Both self-efficacy and self-regulated learning (SRL) play a significant part in students' learning. The research shows that self-regulated learning (SRL) skills make a significant impact on students' academic achievement. However, students need adequate preparation for their own learning. Teachers can help students to become more effective self-regulated learners by using the following classroom strategies:

a. Emphasize the importance of SRL skills in learning and when they should be used.
b. Model SRL skills, including the standards one uses to evaluate one's performance.

Teachers need to provide guided practice and corrective feedback for the SRL skills to be mastered. Teachers need teach students to use both memory and comprehension tactics and taking relevant notes:

a. Teach students how to use various forms of rehearsal and mnemonic devices (two reasons for teaching rehearsal: a useful tactic for keeping small amount of information active in STM; maintenance rehearsal is something students can learn to use; remind them to use no more than seven items/chunks at a time).
b. Teach students how to formulate meaningful comprehension questions.

Emotional knowledge and skills

Teachers, by working in cooperative and collaborative groups in their classroom have the necessary professional knowledge and skills to develop their students' emotional knowledge, reflecting their emotional intelligence. From a humanist perspective, emotions refer to individuals' feelings. More recently, there has been a good deal of research on emotional intelligence, adding to other forms of multiple intelligences, identified by Howard Gardener (1993) and others. Emotional intelligence is the knowledge of being aware of emotions and feelings, and recognize one's 'emotions, understand what they're telling you, and realize how your emotions affect other people' (Mind Tool, 2022). Furthermore, emotional intelligence is the ability to 'understand, use, and manage your own emotions in positive ways to relieve stress, communicate effectively, empathize with others, overcome challenges and defuse conflict':

> Emotional intelligence helps you build stronger relationships, succeed at school and work, and achieve your career and personal goals. It can also help you to connect with your feelings, turn intention into action, and make informed decisions about what matters most to you. (Segal et al., 2024)

Teachers, have the power to enhance their students' emotional knowledge, skills, and emotional intelligence, by using both cognitive and social constructivist pedagogies in their classrooms.

10.7 Teachers' Role in Promoting in Promoting Cultural Diversity

Promoting cultural diversity in the classroom, is one of the most significant professional roles of all teachers. It simply reflects the acceptance of the ubiquitous existence of multiculturalism, and culturally diverse societies, both locally and globally. *Cultural diversity* refers to many cultures and many ways of life in our world. Given this diversity, we can refer to cultural diversity, as a mosaic of intersecting cultures. Language, religion, customs, and social class define the various dimensions of cultural diversity.

Multiculturalism as a social and educational policy, refers to educational programs, which recognise past and present *cultural diversity* in each society, and which are designed to promote the *equality* of all cultural traditions. Multicultural education, as an ideal of pluralist and participatory democracy, expresses the ideology of pluralist democracy, equality, social justice, and *egalitarianism.*

Cultural diversity of Australia is central to our evolving cultural and national identity. In 'Reconciliation and Multiculturalism: Towards Human Rights', Chap. 1, *Education and Society* (pp. 1–110), George Smolicz (2001) argued that Australia is a culturally diverse society, which is based on pluralist democracy and multiculturalism: 'One of the features of a multicultural society is...the phenomenon of social and cultural interaction among members of different social groups' (Smolicz, 2001, p. 7). As children enter the classroom, they have absorbed many dimensions of culture, such as language, attitudes, beliefs, mores, ways of behaving, and values.

One of the most problematic terms in researching cultural diversity is 'national identity'. Defining the term, in terms of its epistemology, ideology and culture, presents several challenges. 'National identity', according to Anthony Smith (1991), 'involves some sense of political community, history, territory, patria, citizenship, common values and traditions' (Smith, 1991, p. 9). He argued, using a structuralist perspective, that 'nations must have a measure of common culture and a civic ideology, a set of common understandings and aspirations, sentiments and ideas that bind the population together in their homeland' (Smith, 1991, p. 11). Accordingly, national identity is a type of 'collective identity grounded in past symbols, memories, and values linked to a specific territory that distinguishes itself from other nations and also projects into the future' (Guibernau, 2001). Guibernau (2001) argued that national identity referred to 'the set of attributes and beliefs shared by those who belong to the same nation'. Accordingly, the political aspect of national identity, when applied to the nation-state, focused upon those state's strategies—often referred to as 'nation building'—destined to foster a cohesive, loyal and, up to a point, homogeneous citizenry (Guibernau, 2001, pp. 242–68).

The reality and relevance of cultural diversity and multiculturalism in the USA was already addressed by Banks (2019), who analyzed the existence of a growing ethnic, cultural, social-class, and linguistic gap between many of the teachers and their students in the USA. Banks, who is a leading multicultural educator and writer in the world, has been writing on multicultural education in the USA for many decades (see Zajda, 2022). The goal of Banks' (2019) multicultural education model was to enable students from diverse racial and ethnic backgrounds to fully engage with and access the curriculum, and acquire designated knowledge, skills, and values. To advance multicultural education in schools, Banks (1995a) developed his timely and relevant model of multicultural education strategy, based on his five dimensions: content integration, the knowledge construction process, prejudice reduction, equity pedagogy, and an empowering school culture and social structure (Banks, 1995a). His model was designed to help teachers in promoting the philosophy of multicultural curriculum in the classroom:

- *Content Integration*: Teaching diversity
- *Knowledge Construction*: Teaching how knowledge is created
- *Prejudice Reduction*: Developing positive relationships among students from culturally diverse backgrounds
- *Equity Pedagogy*: Promoting high academic achievement for all students
- *Empowering School Culture*: Inclusive classroom environment that is conducive to the academic and emotional needs and growth of all students (Banks, 1995; 2019).

The creation of a more equitable, tolerant, and peaceful society for everyone on this planet is a dream for all empowering and egalitarian pedagogues. But it will remain a mere hollow rhetoric, or magic words, unless we debate more vigorously social inequality in the global culture (Zajda & Majhanovich, 2021). We need to critique the existing status quo of stratified societies, and cultures:

> As numerous educational researchers have documented, existing schools are profoundly unequal, stratified by race and class, and increasingly driven by the standardized testing of students and teachers and the deskilling of teachers through the introduction of packaged curricula geared to standardized tests. (Weiler & Maher, 2002)

We need to critique the overall interplay between intercultural dialogue, education, and the state. This can be accomplished by drawing upon recent major and significant studies in the areas of education, intercultural dialogue, and transformational and global pedagogies. By referring to Bourdieu's (1990) suggestion for critical policy researchers to engage in a 'critical sociology' of their own contexts of practice, and poststructuralist pedagogy, we need to understand how major discourses surrounding the debate of cultural diversity, intercultural dialogue and education are formed, in the contexts of dominant ideology, power, and culturally and historically derived perceptions and practices defining the processes of nation-building and cultural identity in the global culture.

By focusing on the competing discourses surrounding global political, social, and religious conflicts we need to evaluate critically both the reasons and outcomes of dominant ideologies, education reforms, and policy change, with respect to intercultural dialogue in the global culture. A new understanding and a more effective use of intercultural dialogue could be seen as a means for delivering an authentic and empowering paradigm of peace, tolerance, and harmony in the world. It is likely to offer a more informed and compelling critique of the place of the Other in the Western-driven models of intercultural dialogue, surrounding identity politics, liberty, and democracy.

10.8 Conclusion

As demonstrated above, teachers play a powerful role in promoting engagement and motivation and thereby influencing students' cognitive, social cognitive, affective, and behavioural dimensions. As argued earlier, one of the most significant teachers' roles begins in establishing an inclusive classroom environment, characterized by an atmosphere of belonging, safety, well-being, and acceptance of students' voices. Teachers, who use constructivist pedagogy, based on cognitive and social constructivist approaches in collaborative, or cooperative groups in the classroom, are likely to offer supportive environment, and provide the necessary cognitive, social, and emotional scaffolding for students to solve a given task and achieve designated classroom outcomes.

References

Acton, G. S., & Schroeder, D. H. (2001). Sensory discrimination as related to general intelligence. *Intelligence, 29*(3), 263–271. https://doi.org/10.1016/S0160-2896(01)00066-6

Alber, R. (2017). Deeper learning: A collaborative classroom is key. [Online] In *Edutopia*. Available at: https://www.edutopia.org/blog/deeper-learning-collaboration-key-rebecca-alber

Ali, M., & Hassan, N. (2018). Defining concepts of student engagement and factors contributing to their engagement in schools. *Creative Education, 9*, 2161–2170.

Allport, G. W. (1961). *Pattern and growth in personality*. Harcourt College Publisher.

Altugan, A. S. (2015). The relationship between cultural identity and learning. *Procedia—Social and Behavioral Sciences, 186*, 1159–1162.

Amzil, A. (2013). *The effect of a metacognitive intervention on college students reading performance and metacognitive skills*. https://www.researchgate.net https://pdfs.semanticscholar.org/8909/

Anwar, Y. (2017). *Emoji fans take heart: Scientists pinpoint 27 states of emotion*. https://news.berkeley.edu/2017/09/06/27

Ariely, G. (2012). Globalization and the decline of national identity? An exploration across sixty-three countries. *Nations and Nationalism, 18*(3), 461–482.

Ariely, G. (2019). *The nexus between globalization and ethnic identity: A view from below*. https://journals.sagepub.com/doi/full/10.1177/1468796819834951

Armitage, R. (2021). *Bullying in children: Impact on child health*. https://bmjpaedsopen.bmj.com/content/5/1/e000939

Artino, A. (2012). Academic self-efficacy: From educational theory to instructional practice. *Perspectives on Medical Education, 1*(2), 76–85.

Bandura, A. (1974). Behaviour theory and the models of man. *American Psychologist, 29*(12), 859–869. https://doi.org/10.1037/h0037514

Bandura, A. (1977). *Social learning theory*. Prentice-Hall.

Bandura, A. (1986a). *Social foundations of thought and action: A social cognitive theory*. Prentice-Hall.

Bandura, A. (1986b). *Social foundations of thought and action: A social-cognitive theory*. Prentice-Hall.

Bandura, A. (1997a). *Self-efficacy: The exercise of control*. Freeman.

Bandura, A. (1997b). *Self-efficacy: The exercise of control*. W H Freeman/Times Books/Henry Holt & Co.

Banks, J. A. (1995). Multicultural education: Historical development, dimensions, and practice. In J. A. Banks & C. A. M. Banks (Eds.), *Handbook of research on multicultural education* (pp. 3–24). Macmillan.

J. Zajda, *Engagement, Motivation, and Students' Achievement*, Globalisation, Comparative Education and Policy Research 48,
https://doi.org/10.1007/978-3-031-61613-6

Banks, J. A. (2008). Diversity, group identity, and citizenship education in a global age. *Educational Researcher, 37*(3), 129–139.
Barowski, J. (2023) Personality theories. *Definitions and types*. https://study.com/academy/lesson/personality-theories-types-lesson-quiz.html
Bauman, G. (1996). *Contesting culture*. Cambridge University Press.
Bembenutty, H., et al. (2016a). *Applying social cognitive theory in the development of self-regulated competencies throughout K-12 grades K-12*. https://www.researchgate.net/publication/301337814_
Bembenutty, H., et al. (2016b). *Applying social cognitive theory in the development of self-regulated competencies throughout K-12 grades K-12*. https://www.researchgate.net/publication/301337814_Applying_Social_Cognitive_Theory_in_the_Development_of_Self-Regulated_Competencies_Throughout_K-12_Grades_K
Benish, M., Oreg, S., & Berson, Y. (2022). The contribution of peer values to children's values and behavior. *Personality and Social Psychology Bulletin, 48*(6), 844–864.
Berman, M. (1991). *All that is solid melts into air*. Verso.
Binet, A., & Simon, T. (1905). Méthods nouvelles pour le diagnostic du niveau intellectuel des anormaux. *L'année Psychologique, 11*, 191–244.
Bjorklund-Young, A. (2016). *What do we know about developing students non-cognitive skills?* https://jscholarship.library.jhu.edu
Boase, D., et al. (2012). *Global education project*. https://www.researchgate.net
Boix Mansilla, V. (2015). *Project zero*. Harvard Graduate School of Education.
Borghans, L., et al. (2008). *The economics and psychology of personality traits*. https://www.nber.org/papers/w13810
Bourdieu, P. (1986). The forms of capital. In J. G. Richardson (Ed.), *Handbook of theory and research for the sociology of education* (pp. 241–258). Greenwood Press.
Bourdieu, P., & Passeron, J. (1977). *Reproduction in education, society and culture*. Sage.
Bourdieu, P., & Passeron, J. (1990). *Reproduction in education, society and culture* (2nd ed.). Sage Books.
Brame, C. J., & Biel, R. (2015). *Setting up and facilitating group work: Using cooperative learning groups effectively*. Vanderbilt University Center for Teaching. Retrieved December 3, 2021. http://cft.vanderbilt.edu/guides-sub-pages/setting-up-and-facilitating-group-work-using-cooperative-learning-groups-effectively/
Breitweiser. (2019). *Cultural identity in classrooms: Ideas and suggestions for a more inclusive culture*. https://medium.com/teachers-on-fire/cultural-identity-in-classrooms-ea9ca459c480
Bronfenbrenner, U. (1995). *Developmental ecology through space and time: A future perspective*. In: *Examining lives in context: Perspectives on the ecology of human development* (pp. 619–648). American Psychological Association.
Bronfenbrenner, U. (1979). *The ecology of human development: Experiments by nature and design*. Harvard University Press.
Bronfenbrenner, U. (2005). *Making human beings human, bioecological perspectives on human development*. Sage.
Bronfenbrenner, U. (2009). *The ecology of human development: Experiments by nature and design*. Harvard University Press.
Bronfenbrenner, U., & Ceci, S. J. (1994). Nature-nurture reconceptualised: A bio-ecological model. *Psychological Review, 10*(4), 568–586.
Bronfenbrenner, U., & Evans, G. (2000). Developmental science in the 21st century: Emerging questions, theoretical models, research designs and empirical findings. *Review of Social Development, 9*(1), 115–125.
Brophy, J. (1998a). *Motivating students to learn*. McGraw Hill.
Brophy, D. R. (1998b). Understanding, measuring, and enhancing individual creative problem-solving efforts. *Creativity Research Journal, 11*(2), 123–150.
Bruner, J. S. (1960). *The process of education*. Harvard University Press.
Buckle, J. (2022). *6 effective interventions for social emotional learning*. https://www.panoramaed.com/blog/effective-interventions-for-social-emotional-learning
Burris, V. (1988). Reification: A marxist perspective. *Sociologist, 10*(1), 22–43.

Byram, M. (2013). *Foreign language teaching and intercultural citizenship.* https://files.eric.ed.gov/fulltext/EJ1127400.pdf
Carnevale, J. (2023). *Behavioral personality theory: Perspectives and criticism.* https://study.com/learn/lesson/behavioral-personality-theory-perspective-features.html
CASELS' SEL framework. (2020). https://casel.org/casel-sel-framework-11-2020/
Casement, A. (2020). Persona. In *Encyclopedia of psychology and religion.* Springer.
Castells, M. (2006). *Globalisation and identity. A comparative perspective.* https://llull.cat/IMAGES_175/transfer01-foc01.pdf
Castells, M. (2010). *The power of identity* (2nd ed.). Wiley-Blackwell.
Chasteen, S. (2023). *How can I set clear expectations, and motivate students, so that they engage in active learning?* https://www.physport.org/recommendations/Entry.cfm?ID=101200
Cherry, K. (2023). https://www.verywellmind.com/personality-psychology-study-guide-2795699#:~:text=Trait%20Theories%20of%20Personality,to%20behave
Clark, M., & Nance, C. (2000). Teaching values of tolerance and peace through a holistic multicultural curriculum. *Curriculum and Teaching, 15*(1), 5–26.
Comenius. (1649/1907). *The great didactic.* (transl. by M. Keatinge). Adam & Charles Black.
Coombs, P. (1982). Critical world educational issues of the next two decades. *International Review of Education, 28*(1), 143–158.
Copping, L., Campbell, A., & Muncer, S. (2014). Psychometrics and life history strategy: The structure and validity of the high K strategy scale. https://journals.sagepub.com/doi/10.1177/147470491401200115
Corr, P. (2016). *Has history proved Eysenck right about genes and IQ?* http://theconversation.com/has-history-proved-eysenck-right-about-genes-and-iq-54716
Cultural capital. (2022). *Oxford reference.* https://www.oxfordreference.com/view/10.1093/oi/authority.20110803095652799
Dave, R. (1984). Introduction to the thirtieth volume of the IRE. *International Review of Education, 30*(1), 3–5.
Deary, I. (2013). Intelligence. *Current Biology, 23*(16). https://www.sciencedirect.com/science/article/pii/S0960982213008440
Dong, et al. (2022). *Emotional intelligence and personality traits based on academic performance.* https://www.frontiersin
Downloade Eysenck personality test online: http://similarminds.com/cgi-bin/eysenck.pl
Duchesne, S., & McCaughey, A. (2022). *Educational psychology for learning and teaching* (7th ed.). Cengage Learning.
Dunn, K., Dunn, R., & Price, G. E. (1989). *Learning style inventory.* Price Systems.
Dunn, R. (1999–2000). Learning styles: Theory, practice, and research. *National Forum of Applied Educational Research Journal, 13*(1), 3–22.
Durkheim, E. (1984). *The division of labour in society* (transl. by W. D. Halls). The Free Press. (originally published in French in 1893).
Durlak, J. A., Weissberg, R. P., Dymnicki, A. B., Taylor, R. D., & Schellinger, K. B. (2011). The impact of enhancing students social and emotional learning: A meta-analysis of school-based universal interventions. *Child Development, 82*(1), 405–432.
Embarak, O., Zahoor, K., & Binod, G. (2019). *Understanding students personality to detect their learning differences.* https://www.researchgate.net
Erickson, E. (1950). *Childhood and society.* W. W. Norton & Company.
Eysenck, H. (1966). *Check your own IQ.* Harmondsworth. Penguin Books.
Eysenck, H. (Ed.). (1973). *The measurement of intelligence.* Springer.
Eysenck, H. J. (1978). Personality and learning. In S. Murray-Smith (Ed.), *Melbourne studies in education.* Melbourne University Press.
Eysenck, H. (1979). *The structure and measurement of intelligence.* Springer.
Eysenck, H. J. (1981). *A model for personality.* Springer.
Eysenck, H. (1982). Inheritance of intelligence. *New Education, 4*(1), 1–8.
Eysenck, H. (1998). *Intelligence: A new look.* Transaction Publishers.

Farrington, C. A., et al. (2012). *Teaching adolescents to become learners: The role of noncognitive factors in shaping school performance—A critical literature review*. Consortium on Chicago School Research. http://eric.ed.gov/?id=ED542543

Fernig, L., & Bowen, J. (1980). *Twenty-five years of educational practice and theory 1955–1979*. Martinus Nijhoff Publishers.

Finlay, L. (2008). *Reflecting on reflective practice*. Practice-based Professional Learning Paper 52, The Open University.

Fiske, D. W. (1949). Consistency of the factorial structures of personality ratings from different sources. *The Journal of Abnormal and Social Psychology, 44*(3), 329–344. https://doi.org/10.1037/h0057198

Flavell, J. (1993). *The development of children's understanding of false belief and the appearance-reality distinction*. https://onlinelibrary.wiley.com/doi/abs/10.1080/00207599308246944

Flavell, J. H. (1992). Cognitive development: Past, present, and future. *Developmental Psychology, 28*(6), 998–1005. https://doi.org/10.1037/0012-1649.28.6.998

Fontana, D. (1995). *Teaching and personality*. Open Books.

Frydenberg, E., Ainley, M. & Russell, V. (2005). *Schooling issue digest: Student motivation and engagement*. DEST.

Gage, N. L., & Berliner, D. C. (2015). *Educational psychology*. Houghton Mifflin.

Gaither, S. (2019). *Considering your multiple identities: Awareness of various identities has an impact on creativity and social thinking*. https://www.apa.org/science/about/psa/2019/07/multiple-identities

Gardner, H. (2015). *The intelligences, in Howard Gardner's words: A quick overview of the idea of multiple intelligences*. http://teaching.uncc.edu/learning-resources/articles-books/best-practice/education-philosophy/multiple-intelligences

Gardner, H. (1999). *Intelligence reframed*. Basic Books.

Gardner, H. (2003). *Frames of mind. The theory of multiple intelligences*. Basic Books.

Geddes, L. (2018). The truth about intelligence. *New Scientist, 239*, 30.

Ghazvini, S. (2011). *Relationships between academic self-concept and academic performance in high school students*. https://www.sciencedirect.com/science/article/pii/S1877042811004149

Gillies, R. M. (2006). Teachers and students verbal behaviours during cooperative and small group learning. *British Journal of Educational Psychology, 76*, 271–287.

Glossary of Education Reform. (2016). *Student engagement*. https://www.edglossary.org/student-engagement/

Gokkaya, F., & Sutcu, S. T. (2018). Developing a cognitive behavioural intervention program to reduce bully tendencies in primary school children and the program effectiveness. *Education and Science, 42*(193). https://web.b.ebscohost.com/abstract?direct=true&profile=ehost&scope=site&authtype

Gottfredson, L. (2016). Hans Eysenck's theory of intelligence, and what it reveals about him. *Personality and Individual Differences, 103*, 116–127.

Guay, F., Marsh, H. W., & Boivin, M. (2003). Academic self-concept and academic achievement: Developmental perspectives on their causal ordering. *Journal of Educational Psychology, 95*(1), 124–136. https://doi.org/10.1037/0022-0663.95.1.124

Guibernau, M. (2001). Globalization and the nation-state. In M. Guibernau & J. Hutchinson (Eds.), *Understanding nationalism* (pp. 242–268). Polity.

Hagenaars, et al. (2016). Shared genetic aetiology between cognitive functions and physical and mental health in UK. *Molecular Psychiatry, 21*(11), 1624–1632.

Hakimi, S., et al. (2011). The relationships between personality traits and students academic achievement. *Procedia—Social and Behavioral Sciences, 29*, 836–845.

Hattie, J., Biggs, J., & Purdie, N. (1996). Effects of learning skills interventions on student learning: A meta-analysis. *Review of Educational Research, 66*(2), 99–136. https://www.teachertoolkit.co.uk/wp-content/uploads/2014/04/effect-of-learning-skills.pdf

Hay, D. (2005). Early peer relations and their impact on children's development. *Encyclopedia on early childhood development*. The Centre of Excellence for Early Childhood Development (CEECD) and the Strategic Knowledge Cluster on Early Child Development (SKC-ECD).

Hearne, D., & Stone, S. (1995). Multiple intelligences and underachievement: Lessons from individuals with learning disabilities. *Journal of Learning Disabilities, 28*(7), 439–448.

Herrera, L., Al-Lal, M., & Mohamed, L. (2020). Academic achievement, self-concept, personality and emotional intelligence in primary education. *Analysis by Gender and Cultural Group*. https://www.frontiersin.org/articles/10.3389/fpsyg.2019.03075/full

Herrity, J. (2023). 11 Benefits of collaborative learning (Plus tips to use it). In *Indeed*. [Online]. https://www.indeed.com/career-advice/career-development/benefits-of-collaborative-learning

Huber, M. T., & Hutchings, P. (2004). *Integrative learning: Mapping the terrain. The academy in transition*. Association of American Colleges and Universities.

Huitt, W. (2011). Motivation to learn: An overview. *Educational Psychology Interactive*. Valdosta State University. http://www.edpsycinteractive.org/topics/motivation

ICAEW Insights. (2021). *The 5 elements of emotional intelligence*. https://www.icaew.com/insights/student-insights/student-insights-2021-archive/the-5-elements-of-emotional-intelligence

Intelligence, IQ, and g. (2018). https://www.k12academics.com/educational-psychology/intelligence/psychometric-intelligence/intelligence-iq-g

Jackendoff, R. (2002). *Chapter 4 universal grammar*. https://academic.oup.com/book/32834/chapter-abstract/275269828?redirectedFrom=fulltext

Jasper, M. (2003). *Beginning reflective practice*. Nelson Thornes.

Jennings, Z. (2000). Functional literacy of young Guyanese adults. *International Review of Education, 46*(1/2), 93–116.

Jensen, A. R. (1998). *Human evolution, behavior, and intelligence. The g factor: The science of mental ability*. Praeger.

Jensen, A. R. (1983). Factors influencing academic achievement. *Education and Society, 1*(1), 51–62.

John, et al. (2020). The big five personality traits and academic performance. *Journal of Law and Social Studies* (JLSS), *2*(1), 10–19. www.advancelrf.org

Jung, C. G. (1921a). *Psychologische typen*. Rascher Verlag.

Jung, C. G. (1921b, 1971). *Psychological types. Collected works* (vol. 6). Princeton University Press.

Kandel, I. (1957). Equalizing educational opportunities and its problems. *International Review of Education, 3*(1), 1–10.

Kawamoto, T. (2020). *The encyclopedia of child and adolescent development*. Wiley.

Keltner, D. (2009). *Born to be good*. Norton.

Khan, H. (2022). Discipline will take you to places where motivation can't. https://www.linkedin.com/pulse/discipline-take-you-places-where-motivation-cant-hamza-khan/

King, E. (1999). *Looking into the lives of children*. James Nicholas Publishers.

Krause, K., Bochner, S., & Duchesne, S. (2008). *Educational psychology for learning and teaching*. Nelson.

Kulich, C., et al. (2017). *Editorial: Multiple identities management: Effects on (of) identification, attitudes, behavior and well-being*. https://www.frontiersin.org/articles/10.3389/fpsyg.2017.02258/full

Kussrow, P. (2002). In J. Zajda (Ed.), *Learning and teaching*. James Nicholas Publishers.

Laal, M., & Ghodsi, S. M. (2012). Benefits of collaborative learning. https://www.sciencedirect.com/science/article/pii/S1877042811030205

Laryea, J., Saani, A., & Dawson-Brew, E. (2014). *Influence of students self-concept on their academic performance in the Elmina township*. https://www.idpublications.org/wp-content/uploads/2014/09/influence-of-students-self-concept-on-their-academic-performance-in-the-elmina-township.pdf

Lazowski, R. A., & Hulleman, C. S. (2016). Motivation interventions in education: A meta-analytic review. *Review of Educational Research, 86*(2), 602–640. https://doi.org/10.3102/0034654315617832

Lee, B. (2017). *Here are the 27 different human emotions, according to a study*. https://www.forbes.com/sites/brucelee/2017/09/09/here-are-the-27-different-human-emotions-according-to-a-study/?sh=569ca95e1335

Lefrançois, G. R. (2000). *Theories of human learning: What the old man said* (4th ed.). Wadsworth/Thomson Learning.

Lewis, et al. (2019). Standards without standardisation? Assembling standards-based reforms in Australian and US schooling. *Journal of Education Policy, 35*, 1–28.

Ligorio, M. B. (2010). *Dialogical relationship between identity and learning*. https://journals.sagepub.com/doi/abs/10.1177/1354067X09353206

Loes, C. N. (2022). *The effect of collaborative learning on academic motivation*. https://files.eric.ed.gov

Loveless, B. (2023) *Cognitive load theory—the definitive guide*. https://www.educationcorner.com/cognitive-load-theory/#:~:text=There%20are%203%20types

Lyman, F. (1981). The responsive classroom discussion. In A. S. Anderson (Ed.), *Mainstreaming digest*. University of Maryland College of Education.

Mann, M. (2004). Self-esteem in a broad-spectrum approach for mental health promotion. *Health Education Research, 19*, 357–372. https://doi.org/10.1093/her/cyg041

Marinak, B. A., & Gambrell, L. B. (2010). Reading motivation: Exploring the elementary gender gap. *Literacy Research and Instruction, 49*(2), 129–141.

Marsh, H., & Martin, A. (2011). Academic self-concept and academic achievement: Relations and causal ordering. *British Journal of Educational Psychology, 81*(1), 59–77.

Martínez, L. (2021). *Five ways to celebrate your students cultures*. https://greatergood.berkeley.edu/article/item/five_ways_to_celebrate_your_students_cultures

Martschenko, D. (2018). The IQ test wars: Why screening for intelligence is still so controversial.

Maslow, A. H. (1954). *Motivation and personality*. Harper and Row.

Maslow, A. H. (1962). *Toward a psychology of being*. D. Van Nostrand Company.

Maslow, A. H. (1971). *The farther reaches of human nature*. Arkana/Penguin Books.

Maslow, A. H. (1987). *Motivation and personality* (3rd ed.). Pearson Education.

McCarthy, B. (1986). *The hemispheric mode indicator Barrington, 111 excel*.

McCarthy, B. (1990). Using the 4MAT system to bring learning styles to schools. https://www.ascd.org/el/articles/using-the-4mat-system-to-bring-learning-styles-to-schools

McCarthy, B., & McCarthy, D. (2006). *Teaching around the 4MAT cycle: Designing instruction for diverse learners with diverse learning styles*. Sage.

McCrae, R. R., & Costa, P. T. (1985). Updating Norman's adequacy taxonomy: Intelligence and personality dimensions in natural language and in questionnaires. *Journal of Personality and Social Psychology, 49*(3), 710–721.

McDonald, S. (2007). A historical perspective: How a positive cultural identity can increase achievement motivation and self-esteem in young African American students. https://digitalcommons.brockport.edu/cgi/viewcontent

McInerney, D., & McInerney, V. (2010). *Educational psychology: Constructing learning* (5th ed.). Pearson.

Mental health America. (2022). *What is emotional intelligence and how does it apply to the workplace?* https://mhanational.org/what-Metacognitive strategies (2002). https://fcit.usf.edu/mathvids/strategies/tms.html#:~:text=What%20are

Merton, R. K. (1948). The self fulfilling prophecy. *Antioch Review, 8*(2), 193–210. https://doi.org/10.2307/4609267. ISSN 0003-5769.

Mevarech, Z. R., & Kramarski, B. (2003). The effects of metacognitive training versus worked-out examples on students mathematical reasoning. *British Journal of Educational Psychology, 73*(4), 449–471. https://doi.org/10.1348/000709903322591181

Millis, B. J., & Cottell, P. G., Jr. (1998). *Cooperative learning for higher education faculty*. American Council on Education, Series on Higher Education. The Oryx Press.

Mishna, F. (2012). *Bullying: A guide to research, intervention and prevention*. Oxford University Press.

Moreira, P., et al. (2020). Students personality contributes more to academic performance than well-being and learning approach—Implications for sustainable development and education. *European Journal of Investigation in Health Psychology Education, 10*(4), 1132–1149.

Muijs, D. (2017). Can schools reduce bullying? The relation between school characteristics and prevalence of bullying behaviour. *British Journal of Educational Pscyhology, 87*(2), 255–272.

Mullan Harris, K. (2010). An integrative approach to health. *Demography, 47*(1), 1–22.

OECD. (2001a). *Education policy analysis: Education and skills*. OECD.

OECD (2001b). *The wellbeing of nations: The role of human and social capital, education and skills*. OECD Centre for Educational Research and Innovation. OECD.

OECD. (2009). *Creating effective teaching and learning environments*. OECD.

OECD. (2022a). *Students well-being*. OECD.

OECD. (2022b). *Effective learning environments (ELE)*. OECD. https://www.oecd.org/education/effective-learning-environments

OECD. (2023a). *Meeting of the OECD council at ministerial level Paris, 7–8 June 2023*. OECD.

OECD. (2023b). *Student engagement and motivation*. https://gpseducation.oecd.org/revieweducationpolicies/#!node=44131&filter=all

Oei, T. P. S., & Hasking, P. A. (2013). Alcohol use disorders. In P. M. Miller (Ed.), *Principles of addiction: Comprehensive addictive behaviors and disorders* (pp. 647–655). Elsevier.

Padayichie, K. (2023). *Collaborative learning*. https://www.structural-learning.com/post/collaborative-learning

Paraide, et al. (2023). *Revising the reform: Standards-based education*. https://www.researchgate.net/publication/367010478_

Pavlov, I. P. (1927). *Conditioned reflexes: An investigation of the physiological activity of the cerebral cortex* (transl. and edited by G. V. Anrep). Oxford University Press.

Pegalajar-Palomino, M. (2017). *An analysis of self-concept in students with compensatory education needs for developing a mindfulness-based psychoeducational program*. https://doi.org/10.1177/2158244017708818

Pepler, D. J., & Bierman, K. L. (2018). *With a little help from my friends: The importance of peer relationships for social-emotional development*. Pennsylvania State University.

Perera, S. (2020). *What is Maslow's hierarchy of needs, theory of motivation?* https://www.quora.com/What-is-maslow-s-hierarchy-of-needs-theory-of-motivation

Piaget, J. (1950). *The psychology of intelligence*. Harcourt.

PISA. (2018). *PISA 2018c results (volume III). Chapter 2. Bullying*. OECD.

Plank, D., & Sykes, G. (1999). How choice changes the education system: A Michigan case study. *International Review of Education, 45*(5–6), 385–416.

Pritchard, A. (2009). *Ways of learning* (2nd ed.). Routledge.

Practical Psychology. (2024). *Behavioral theory of personality (Definition)*. https://practicalpie.com/behavioral-theory-of-personality/

Raising children network. (2021). *Peer pressure or influence: Pre-teens and teenagers*. https://raisingchildren.net.au/teens/behaviour/peers-friends-trends/peer-influence

Rapoport, A. (2021). Human rights and global citizenship in social studies standards in the United States. *Human Rights Education Review, 4*(1), 111–132. https://doi.org/10.7577/hrer.3997

Ricento, T. (2006). *An introduction to language policy: Theory and method*. https://books.google.com.au/books?hl=en&lr=&id=ADw4TsEoQkAC&oi=fnd&pg=PA10&

Rigby, K. (2007). *Bullying in schools: And what to do about it*. Australian Council for Educational Research.

Rivera-Pérez, S., et al. (2020). *Linking cooperative learning and emotional intelligence in physical education: Transition across school stages*. https://www.ncbi.nlm.nih.gov/pmc/articles/PMC7400461/

Rogers, C. R. (1961). *On becoming a person: A psychotherapists view of psychotherapy*. Houghton Mifflin.

Rogers, C. (1995). *On becoming a person: A therapist's view of psychotherapy* (2nd ed.). Harper One.

Roschelle, J., & Hodkowski, N. M. (2020). *Using research on homework to improve remote and hybrid learning [White Paper]*. Digital Promise. http://hdl.handle.net/20.500.12265/107

Saarni, C. (1999). *The development of emotional competence*. The Guilford Press.

Saha, L. (2021). Cultural and social capital from a global perspective. In J. Zajda (Ed.), *3rd International handbook of globalisation, education and policy research*. Springer. ISBN 978-3-030-66002-4

Sahlberg, P. (2012). *Global educational reform movement is here!* https://pasisahlberg.com/global-educational-reform-movement-is-here/

Scheuringer, B. (2016). *Multiple identities: A theoretical and an empirical approach*. CUP.

Schnotz, W., & Kürschner, C. (2007). A reconsideration of cognitive load theory. *Educational Psychology Review, 19*, 469–508. https://doi.org/10.1007/s10648-007-9053-4

Scholastic Editors. (2024). *6 steps to helping students set strong reading goals*. https://www.scholastic.com/teachers/teaching-tools/articles/6-steps-to-helping-students-set-strong-reading-goals.html

Shapiro, S. (1999). *Strangers in the land: Pedagogy, modernity, and Jewish identity*. Peter Lang.

Shin, et al. (2016). Effects of early childhood peer relationships on adolescent mental health: A 6- to 8-year follow-up study in South Korea. *Psychiatry Investig, 13*(4), 383–8.

Shinohara, H. (2004). Evolution in global identity: The league of nations and the United Nations. In *UNU Global*.

Sieck, W. (2021). *7 ways to improve your motivation to study (Backed by Science)*. https://www.globalcognition.org/improve-your-motivation-to-study/

Sills, J., Rowse, G., & Emerson, L. M. (2016). The role of collaboration in the cognitive development of young children: A systematic review. *Child: Care, Health and Development, 42*(3), 313–324. ISSN 0305-1862.

Skinner, B. F. (1953). *Science and human behaviour*. Macmillan.

Slavin, R. (1990). *Cooperative learning: Theory, research, and practice*. Prentice-Hall.

Slavin, R. (2020). *Education psychology: Theory and practice*. Pearson.

Slavin, R. (2022). *Educational psychology: Theory and practice* (13th ed.). Pearson.

Slee, P. T. (2016). *School bullying: Teachers helping students cope*. Routledge.

Slee, P. (1993). *Child, adolescent and family development*. Harcourt Brace Jovanovich.

Smith, A. (1991). *National identity*. Penguin Books.

Smith, A. (1995). *Nations and nationalism in a global era*. Polity.

Smolicz, G. (2001). Reconciliation and multiculturalism: Towards human rights. In J. Zajda (Ed.), *Education and society*. James Nichalas Publishers.

Snowman, J., Dobozy, E., Scevak, J., Bryer, F., & Barlett, B. (2009). *Psychology applied to teaching*. John Australia.

Snowman, J., & McCown, R. (2015). *Psychology applied to teaching* (14th ed.). Cengage.

Søndergaarda, H., & Mulder, R. (2012). Collaborative learning through formative peer review: Pedagogy, programs and potential. *Computer Science Education*, 1–25.

Souders, B. (2020). *Motivation in education: What it takes to motivate our kids*. https://positivepsychology.com/motivation-education/

Spearman, C. E. (1904). General intelligence, objectively determined and measured. *American Journal of Psychology, 15*(2), 201–293.

Stankov, L., & Lee, J. (2017). Self-beliefs: Strong correlates of mathematics achievement and intelligence. *Intelligence, 61*, 11–16. https://doi.org/10.1016/j.intell.2016.12.001

Steinmayr, R., et al. (2019). *The importance of students motivation for their academic achievement—replicating and extending previous findings*. https://loop.frontiersin.org/people/707921/overview

Strauss, V. (2017). 34 problems with standardized tests. *The Washington Post*, 17 April. https://www.washingtonpost.com/news/answer-sheet/wp/2017/04/19/34-problems-with-standardized-tests/?noredirect=on&utm_term=.2029d93cadfe
Stuart, D. (2023). *The will to learn: Cultivating student motivation without losing your own*. Corwin Press.
Sweller, et al. (2011). Cognitive load theory. In *Cognitive load theory* (pp. 89–98). https://www.researchgate.net/publication/278647688_Cognitive_Load_Theory
TeachThought Staff. (2022). *Learning theories: Albert bandura's principles of social learning*. https://www.teachthought.com/learning/principles-of-social-learning
Terlouw, K. (2017). *Local identities and politics. Negotiating the old and the new*. Routledge.
Thibodeau, T. (2023). *Transforming homework in the UDL classroom: Breaking down barriers*. https://www.novakeducation.com/blog/transforming-homework-in-the-udl-classroom-breaking-down-barriers
Thiel, F., et al. (2018). A moderate dose of alcohol selectively reduces empathic accuracy. *Psychopharmacology (berl), 235*, 1479–1486. https://doi.org/10.1007/s00213-018-4859-y
Thorndike, E. L. (1905). *The elements of psychology*. A G Seiler. https://doi.org/10.1037/10881-000
Timeular. (2023). *6 Reasons why it is important to set realistic goals*. https://timeular.com/blog/why-is-important-set-realistic-goals/
Tlili, A., et al. (2023). *Impact of personality traits on learners navigational behavior patterns in an online course: A lag sequential analysis approach*. https://www.frontiersin.org/articles/10.3389/fpsyg.2023.1071985/full
Tomasik, M., & Silbereisen, R. (2011). In R. Levesque (Ed.), *Encyclopedia of adolescence*. Springer.
Tomasik, M., & Silbereisen, R. (2016). Demands of social change across multiple domains of life and across time at the advent of the global financial crisis. *Research in Human Development, 13*, 312–327. https://doi.org/10.1080/15427609.2016.1234310
Top 11 signs of high emotional intelligence: Explained. (2023). https://maven.com/articles/signs-of-high-emotional-intelligence
Torrego-Seijo, C. J., Caballero-García, P. Á., & Lorenzo-Llamas, E. M. (2021). The effects of cooperative learning on trait emotional intelligence and academic achievement of Spanish primary school students. *British Journal of Educational Psychology, 91*(3), 928–949.
Tran, et al. (2014). The effects of cooperative learning on the academic achievement and knowledge retention. *International Journal of Higher Education, 3*(2), 131–140.
Vygotsky, L. S. (1934). *Thought and language*. Published in 1962 by MIT Press. (It was originally published in Russian in 1934).
Wang, H., et al. (2023). *The influences of the big five personality traits on academic achievements Chain mediating effect based on major identity and self-efficacy*. https://doi.org/10.3389/fpsyg.2023.1065554
Watson, J. B. (1913). Psychology as the behaviorist views it. *Psychological Review, 20*, 158–177.
Wehler, M. (2017). *Students self-fulfilling prophecies: Five ways to break the cycle*. https://www.facultyfocus.com/articles/teaching-and-learning/five-ways-help-students-brek-self-fulfilling-prophecies/
Weichert, J. (2022). *6 tips: The ultimate guide to increase motivation*. https://edyoucated.org/en/blog-posts/increase-learner-motivation
Weiler, K., & Maher, F. (2002). Teacher education and social justice. *Radical Teacher*. http://www.findarticles.com/p/articles/mi_m0JVP/is_2002_Winter/ai_97483138
Wellpoint Care Network. (2023). *101 classroom interventions*. https://wellpointcare.org/media-and-events/blog-stories/101-classroom
Whelan, L. (2019). *Student engagement in the classroom: The best methods to maintain & improve it*. https://engage-education.com/aus/blog/student-engagement-in-the-classroom-the-best-methods-to-maintain-improve-it/
Woolfolk, A., & Margetts, K. (2019). *Educational psychology*. Pearson.
Workman, E. (2012). Teacher expectations of students: A self-fulfilling prophecy? *The Progress of Education Reform, 13*(6). https://eric.ed.gov/?id=ED539026

Wrabel, S., et al. (2017). *Investing in evidence-based social and emotional learning: companion guide to social and emotional learning interventions under every student succeeds act: Evidence review*. https://www.rand.org/pubs/research_reports/RR2739.html
Wylie, J. (2021). *Seven ways to increase student engagement in K-12*. https://www.gwaea.org/2021/11/29/increase-student-engagement-k12-classrooms/
Zajda, R. (1988). The calculable woman. *Discourses of the self and sexuality in the Australian women's magazine Cleo*. Thesis. University of Melbourne.
Zajda, J. (2001). *Curriculum, culture and teaching*. James Nicholas Publishers.
Zajda, J. (Ed.). (2008). *Learning and teaching*. James Nicholas Publishers.
Zajda, J. (2018a). Effective constructivist pedagogy for quality learning in schools. *Educational Practice and Theory, 40*(1), 67–80.
Zajda, J. (2018b). Motivation in the classroom: Creating effective learning environments. *Educational Practice and Theory, 40*(2), 85–103.
Zajda, J. (2019a). Research on discrimination and self-fulfilling prophecy in schools globally. *Education and Society, 37*(1), 59–77. https://auscathuniaus.library.ingentaconnect.com/content/jnp/es/2019/00000037/00000001/art00005
Zajda, J. (2019b). Current research of theories and models of intelligence. *Curriculum and Teaching, 34*(1), 85–105. https://auscathuniaus-library-ingentaconnect-com.ezproxy1.acu.edu.au/content/jnp/ct/2019/00000034/00000001/art00007
Zajda, J. (2021a). *Globalisation and education reforms: Creating effective learning*. Springer Nature Switzerland.
Zajda, J. (2021b). (Ed.). *Second international handbook of globalisation, education and policy research*. Springer. http://www.springer.com/gp/book/9789401794923
Zajda, J. (2022). *Globalisation and education reforms: Overcoming discrimination*. Springer Nature Switzerland.
Zajda, J. (2023a). *Globalisation, and dominant models of motivational theories in education*. Springer Nature Switzerland.
Zajda, J. (2023b). *Globalisation and inclusive schooling: Engaging motivational environments*. Springer Nature Switzerland.
Zajda, J. (2023c). *Discourses of globalisation, cultural diversity, and values education*. Springer Nature Switzerland.
Zajda, J., & Daun, H. (Eds.). (2009). *Global values education: Teaching democracy and peace*. Springer. http://www.springer.com/education/comparative+education/book/978-90-481-2509-8
Zajda, J., & Freeman, K. (Eds.). (2009). *Race, ethnicity and gender in education: Cross-cultural understandings*. Springer.
Zajda, J., & Majhanovich, S. (Eds.). (2021). *Globalisation, cultural identity and nation-building: The changing paradigms*. Springer.
Zajda, J., & Rapoport, A. (Eds.). (2024). *Globalisation, active citizenship education globally*. Springer Nature Switzerland.
Zajda, J., & Zajda, R. (2013). Aptitude. In G. McCulloch & D. Crook (Eds.), *The international encyclopedia of education*. Routledge.
Zhuojun, W., & Hualing, H. (2014). *National identity in the era of globalization: Crisis and reconstruction*. https://www.tandfonline.com/doi/abs/10.1080/02529203.2014.900889
Zajda, J., Biraimah, B., & Gaudelli, W. (Eds.). (2008a). *Education and social inequality in the global culture*. Springer. https://www.springer.com/gp/book/9781402069260
Zajda, J., Davies, L., & Majhanovich, S. (Eds.). (2008b). *Comparative and global pedagogies: Equity, access and democracy in education*. Springer.

Index

J. Zajda, *Engagement, Motivation, and Students' Achievement*, Globalisation, Comparative Education and Policy Research 48,
https://doi.org/10.1007/978-3-031-61613-6

P

Q

R

S

Printed by Printforce, the Netherlands